METAPSYCHOLOGY AND THE FOUNDATIONS OF PSYCHOANALYSIS

Metapsychology and the Foundations of Psychoanalysis redresses faults in Freud's original conception to develop a coherent theoretical basis for psychodynamic theory. Simon Boag demonstrates that Freud's much maligned 'metapsychology', once revised, can provide a foundation for evaluating and integrating the plethora of psychodynamic perspectives, by developing a philosophically informed position that addresses the embodied, interconnected relationship between motivation, cognition and affects.

The book centres upon the major concepts in psychoanalysis, including the notion of unconscious mental processes, wish-fulfilment, fantasy and repression. Both philosophical considerations and empirical evidence are brought to bear upon these topics, and used to extract the valuable insights from major approaches. As a result, Boag's revised general psychology, which stays true to Freud's intention, addresses psychoanalytic pluralism and shows it is possible to develop a unified account, integrating the insights from attachment theory and object relational approaches and acknowledging the rightful role for neuropsychoanalysis.

Metapsychology and the Foundations of Psychoanalysis will be of interest to psychoanalysts, psychiatrists, philosophers of mind and psychologists, as well as anyone concerned with neuropsychoanalysis or psychoanalysis and attachment theory.

Simon Boag is an Associate Professor in the Department of Psychology, Macquarie University. He has published extensively on the topics of psychoanalytic and psychological theory, personality and unconscious processes, and is the author of *Freudian Repression, the Unconscious, and the Dynamics of Inhibition*. He has also co-edited two volumes on the philosophy of psychoanalysis (*Philosophy, Science & Psychoanalysis*, and *Psychoanalysis & Philosophy of Mind*).

METAPSYCHOLOGY AND THE FOUNDATIONS OF PSYCHOANALYSIS

Attachment, Neuropsychoanalysis and Integration

Simon Boag

LONDON AND NEW YORK

First published 2017
by Routledge
2 Park Square, Milton Park, Abingdon, Oxon OX14 4RN

and by Routledge
711 Third Avenue, New York, NY 10017

Routledge is an imprint of the Taylor & Francis Group, an informa business

© 2017 Simon Boag

The right of Simon Boag to be identified as author of this work has been asserted by him in accordance with sections 77 and 78 of the Copyright, Designs and Patents Act 1988.

All rights reserved. No part of this book may be reprinted or reproduced or utilised in any form or by any electronic, mechanical, or other means, now known or hereafter invented, including photocopying and recording, or in any information storage or retrieval system, without permission in writing from the publishers.

Trademark notice: Product or corporate names may be trademarks or registered trademarks, and are used only for identification and explanation without intent to infringe.

British Library Cataloguing-in-Publication Data
A catalogue record for this book is available from the British Library

Library of Congress Cataloging-in-Publication Data
Names: Boag, Simon, author.
Title: Metapsychology and the foundations of psychoanalysis: attachment, neuropsychoanalysis and integration / Simon Boag.
Description: 1 Edition. | New York: Routledge, [2017]
Identifiers: LCCN 2016012309 | ISBN 9781138926752 (hardback) |
ISBN 9781138926769 (pbk.) | ISBN 9781315683034 (ebook)
Subjects: LCSH: Psychoanalysis.
Classification: LCC BF173 .B63412 2017 | DDC 150.19/5—dc23
LC record available at https://lccn.loc.gov/2016012309

ISBN: 978-1-138-92675-2 (hbk)
ISBN: 978-1-138-92676-9 (pbk)
ISBN: 978-1-315-68303-4 (ebk)

Typeset in Bembo
by codeMantra

For Annika and Matthias

CONTENTS

Acknowledgements		ix
	Introduction	1
1	The metaphysics of metapsychology	17
2	The biological foundations of personality	38
3	Repression and the metapsychology of defence	65
4	The metapsychology of the unconscious	87
5	The metapsychology of the self	107
6	The metapsychology of object relations	122
	Conclusion	135
References		139
Index		159

ACKNOWLEDGEMENTS

This book was written while on sabbatical at the University of Sydney. I would like to extend my gratitude to the Head of School of Psychology there, Professor Frans Vertstraten, who warmly welcomed me. It was also at Sydney University that I was first introduced to the work of Professor John Maze, and if anyone's thinking has shaped my writing in this book, it is his. I would also like to thank Professor Julie Fitness, Head of Department at Macquarie University, for her ongoing support of my research and for encouraging a rigorous and cohesive intellectual environment in our Department. Special thanks also go to Linda A. W. Brakel and Vesa Talvitie, both of whom continue to make important contributions to the philosophy of psychoanalysis, and both of whom I have had the pleasure of collaborating with. Lastly, thanks go also to Claudio Colace, Nigel Mackay, Terry McMullen, Joel Michell, Tamas Pataki and Agnes Petocz, who have all influenced the ideas set out in this book.

Thank you to Karnac books for kindly granting permission to reprint some material in this book, which was originally published in *Philosophy, Science, and Psychoanalysis: A Critical Meeting*, edited by Simon Boag, Linda A. W. Brakel, and Vesa Talvitie (published by Karnac Books in 2015), and *Psychoanalysis and Philosophy of Mind: Unconscious Mentality in the Twenty-first Century*, edited by Simon Boag, Linda A. W. Brakel, and Vesa Talvitie (published by Karnac Books in 2015).

INTRODUCTION

Pluralism and metapsychology in psychoanalysis

The current state of psychoanalysis

At first blush current day psychoanalysis presents itself to the outsider as a fertile and vibrant mix of approaches. The once seemingly authoritarian Freudian monolith has since given way to a pluralistic "spirit of non-denominational openness" (Fonagy & Campbell, 2015, p. 237), where one can choose from any number and manner of psychoanalytic schools. This pluralism, it is said, not only frees us from the tyranny of a single-minded approach, but is even necessary for the discipline to grow: conformity provides a formula for stagnation, whereas pluralism and the resulting conflict act as constructive strife, stimulating development (Schafer, 1990).

Nevertheless, not all is well in the current state of psychoanalysis, and pluralism is increasingly being viewed as a problem for the discipline(s). Rather than stimulating growth, pluralism, for many, has meant that psychoanalysis has disintegrated into a confusing plethora of conflicting approaches. There may be anywhere between twelve to twenty psychoanalytic schools (Frank, 2000; Novick & Novick, 2002), and rather than benefitting from constructive dialogue, each school generally remains insulated and prevented from development that would otherwise occur in a more interactive and rigorous discipline (Frank, 2000; Green, 2005; Rangell, 1988). Furthermore, rather than building upon a common foundation, psychoanalysis has become weakened as a result of this fragmentation. Rangell (2000) even writes that "such splintering and its confusing and divisive effects are more responsible for the modern decline in the status and popularity of psychoanalysis than ecological or external etiologies" (p. 453). Fonagy and Target (2000) go even further, viewing the "increasing fragmentation of theory" as potentially fatal for the future of psychoanalysis: "This fragmentation, euphemistically discussed as pluralism, could on its own spell the demise of psychoanalysis" (p. 408).

2 Introduction

There are various sources of pluralism, including longstanding disagreements concerning the very nature of the psychoanalytic enterprise itself (see Holt, 1981; Wallerstein, 2006, 2009). For example, while Freud saw psychoanalysis standing within the natural science framework (Freud, 1925d, 1933a), others see the discipline as some sort of special human science (e.g. Gill, 1976; Green, 2005) or not even a science at all, and instead primarily a hermeneutical exercise (e.g. Ricoeur, 1977). Similarly, while Freud (1950[1895]) saw neuroscience as a necessary foundation for the mind, for others, the rightful place of neuroscience in psychoanalysis is uncertain. Whereas some believe that engaging with neuroscience is necessary for the field's development (e.g. Panksepp & Solms, 2012; Solms & Turnbull, 2002, 2011; Yovell, Solms, & Fotopoulou, 2015), others feel that neuroscience, at best provides an unnecessary compliment to psychoanalysis and, at worst, a reductionist approach which threatens to rob psychoanalysis of subjectivity and meaning (e.g. Barratt, 2015a; Blass & Carmeli, 2007). On the other hand, in the area of therapy, fundamental disagreements also exist concerning the factors necessary for therapeutic success and even what constitutes psychoanalytic therapy (Rangell, 1988; for instance, see Blum, 2003a, 2003b; Fonagy, 1999b; Fonagy & Target, 2000). All of this points to an identity crisis within the psychoanalytic discipline.

A common ground for psychoanalysis

Symptomatic of the above is the ongoing discussion concerning the need for a common psychoanalytic ground and a unified theory (e.g. Frank, 2000; Rangell, 2000; Wallerstein, 2005a, 2005b, 2009). Rangell (2000), for instance, calls for the various perspectives to be integrated into a unified theory of psychoanalysis, which "will contain all elements considered necessary and sufficient in the combined alternative theories" (p. 452; cf. Frank, 2000, p. 177). Such a theory is considered important for clinical practice since, as Wallerstein (2002) notes, if we want to know which theory best accounts for human experience to inform clinical practice, then presumably that best theory would be the sought-after common ground.

In many ways, the current pluralistic state of psychoanalysis is, however, an instance of the broader issue of disunification in psychology more generally (see Goertzen, 2008, 2010; Green, 2015; Marsh & Boag, 2013; Sternberg & Grigorenko, 2001). As in psychoanalysis, not everyone sees disunification in psychology as necessarily problematic, or unification even desirable (whatever form that may be taken to be) (e.g. Kirschner, 2006). Furthermore, even if a unified theory in psychoanalysis is desirable, some question whether unification is even attainable. Bohleber et al. (2015), for instance, write that "integration is an ideal to which we must adhere without thereby falling prey to the illusion that it can ever actually be attained" (p. 706), while on the other hand, Fonagy and Campbell (2015) see pluralism as inevitable given the 'Dodo-bird' verdict (*viz.* the finding that psychodynamic therapies are generally each as effective as one another): "pluralism is to be applauded, but it is also a symptom of the fact that when it comes to psychoanalysis, no one theory or school of thought can, with any authority, claim to know what works, or why" (p. 237).

Whether this is or is not the case is difficult to determine, but Wallerstein (2002, 2005a, 2005b) believes that there is an emerging trend towards unity in psychoanalysis, although this is still primarily at a clinical level rather than a theoretical one. However, what Fonagy and Campbell's (2015) position above indicates is that a major hurdle for any attempt at unification is determining which approach is better than others, and on this point, Bohleber et al. (2015) recently write that "to date, there is no consensus on how to decide in favour of one or the other competing, at times mutually contradictory theories, and how to integrate divergent concepts and theories" (p. 705).

At first glance a reasonable response to the state of psychoanalytic pluralism would be to appeal to the evidence. After all, evidence should provide us with the necessary tools for evaluating which theories are correct, and clearly Freud saw empirical evidence as the ultimate arbiter of truth, trumping speculative philosophy (e.g. Freud, 1914c, 1933a). However, the situation is not so simple since what constitutes sufficient evidence is determined by various philosophical considerations, especially with respect to causal explanation and inference. 'Evidence' is always 'evidence for something', and this 'something', by and large, is typically a general claim that extends beyond what is observed in any specific instance. Furthermore, the same empirical evidence may be interpreted and 'explained' by any number of theoretical positions, making determining which theory is correct problematic (cf. Popper, 1959). As Frank (2000) observes with respect to psychoanalytic pluralism,

> these different frames of reference or schools of thought do not base their positions on new data, but have been seen to look at the same kind of clinical data we all have, but through the lens of their own belief systems.
>
> *(p. 176)*

Accordingly, we need other methods for ascertaining which theories are better than others.

One step towards a solution here is to develop a core foundation that accommodates genuine new theoretical insights, while helping determine which theoretical innovations are problematic since they conflict with the foundational theoretical superstructure. In fact, there is some indication that it is precisely such a lack of theoretical foundation that allows the proliferations of psychoanalytic positions, since any new theoretical innovation re-writes the foundations. As Rangell (2000) writes concerning psychoanalytic pluralism, "[i]n each alternative theory, it is not what is new that is the divisive element, but what is omitted or underplayed in the alternative theoretical system" (p. 460), whereas what is needed, in his view, is a 'total'

4 Introduction

psychoanalytic theory, which "does not discard elements that are indispensable, continually adds new advances that are valid, and retains all new insights and discoveries that are enduring" (p. 459; cf. Rangell, 1988). That is, any such unified (total) theory will be able to embrace the genuine insights found in the various positions and consolidate these into a coherent and comprehensive theory (Frank, 2000; Rangell, 1988, 2000). However, here a stumbling point emerges, since what makes any element indispensable requires elaboration. It is not simply good enough, for instance, to assert that 'drive' is a fundamental concept if there are serious problems with the concept. Instead a coherent position needs to be developed for including any given concept, and it is only once we have a sound theoretical basis that we can begin to really propose a coherent psychoanalytic position.

Metapsychology and the foundations of psychoanalysis

The general objective of this book is to demonstrate that Freud's 'metapsychology', once revised and divested of its problematic elements, provides a common ground and foundation for a total theory, which can integrate the plethora of psychodynamic perspectives and accommodate their genuine insights. However, 'metapsychology' is a loaded term, and while Zepf (2001), for instance, describes metapsychology as "[t]he core of the theoretical common ground" (p. 463), and Novick and Novick (2002) believe that metapsychology defines psychoanalysis and differentiates it from other psychology approaches, as will be shown, it was problems with Freud's specific metapsychology that provided a major impetus for psychoanalytic pluralism (Holt, 1981). The wave of criticism that arose during the 1970s towards Freudian metapsychology (see Holzman & Gill, 1976) viewed Freud's approach as clinically irrelevant pseudo-biology masquerading as psychology (e.g. Gill, 1976). Furthermore, as will be discussed, if anything, major distinct schools of psychoanalysis, including object relational approaches (Fairbairn, 1952) and attachment theory (Bowlby, 1969), defined their positions in contrast to Freud's metapsychology perspective. At the same time, metapsychology now equates generally with 'theoretical perspective', so that each of the various psychodynamic schools have their own 'metapsychologies' (e.g. Wallerstein, 2005a, 2005b). T[hus] psychoanalytic pluralism can be seen, in fact, as a "pluralism of metapsychologies" (Wallerstein, 2005b, p. 635).

The divergent views about the nature of metapsychology make critically assessing its value difficult, and as Brenner (1980) writes, "[t]hose who attack metapsychology and those who defend it are by no means in agreement about what it is that is being attacked or defended" (p. 202; cf. Holt, 1982). As will be developed, however, there are genuine problems with Freud's specific metapsychological points of view. Nevertheless, since the divisions leading to pluralism are primarily metapsychological in nature, the solution must itself be metapsychological, and without a common foundation, new psychoanalytic discoveries will continue to be taken as constituting new theories, rather than reflecting new dimensions (or 'parts') within a general theory (cf. Frank, 2000; Novick & Novick, 2002; Rangell, 2000). Since such a common theory would provide a foundation accommodating the genuine insights of any psychoanalytic development (Rangell, 2000; Wallerstein, 2002), in this manner a metapsychology is thus the solution to pluralism: "It is the richness, complexity, and integrative power of the metapsychological theory that remains the solid ground on which all other ideas can build" (Novick & Novick, 2002, p. 349). As will be demonstrated, by redressing faults in Freud's *specific* metapsychological account, Freud's *general* metapsychological position provides a coherent theoretical foundation for psychodynamic theory that is both grounded philosophically and scientifically.

What do we mean by 'metapsychology'?

Freud appears to first use the term metapsychology (*Metapsychologie*) in a letter to Wilhelm Fliess dated 13 February 1896 (in Masson, 1985): "I am continually occupied with psychology—really *meta*psychology ... I hope something will come of it" (p. 172, his italics). What Freud specifically means here is unclear and his subsequent usage of the term is inconsistent (see Brenner, 1980). The prefix *meta-*, however, suggests an approach 'beyond', 'behind', or 'transcending' psychology, and, in fact, Freud's first published reference to the term 'metapsychology' indicates a psychology of what is behind 'conscious' appearances—that is, a scientific approach penetrating behind the ordinary psychology of the 'person'. In this respect, Freud equates metapsychology with the 'psychology of the unconscious', which sheds light on the processes underlying mythical and supernatural experiences. Freud here writes that the mythological worldview "*is nothing but psychology projected into the external world*" (1901b, his italics). Metapsychology, as the science of the unconscious, transforms this projection "back ... into the *psychology of the unconscious*" (1901b, p. 258, his italics), such that supernatural phenomena are explicable with respect to understanding the underlying psychodynamics (cf. Brenner, 1980). Freud concludes that "[o]ne could venture to explain in this way the myths of paradise and the fall of man, of God, of good and evil, of immortality, and so on, and to transform *metaphysics* into *metapsychology*" (Freud, 1901b, p. 259, his italics).

Laplanche and Pontalis (1973) believe that Freud thus uses the term metapsychology "to define the originality of his own attempt to construct a psychology 'that leads behind consciousness' ..., as compared to the classical psychologies of consciousness" (p. 249), and, as such, metapsychology lays claim to being the essence of psychoanalysis as a depth psychology. Brenner (1980) agrees, writing that as a depth psychology, going beyond conscious experience to the unconscious sources of our mental lives, metapsychology "was intended as no more than a synonym for psychoanalytic psychology or psychoanalytic theory" (p. 196).

6 Introduction

In some sense, such a general metapsychology involves the biological foundations of motivation—drives and affects—as well as unconscious processes, conflict and repression. However, the picture is not so clear cut, since while metapsychology might be a synonym for psychoanalysis generally, Macmillan (1991) points out that Freud was neither clear nor consistent on what he means by the term, and in fact, the term 'metapsychology' only appeared in nine of Freud's publications. Nevertheless, it would be a mistake to underestimate its importance for Freud, since "metapsychological concepts and ways of thinking dominated his theorizing during most of his career" (Holt, 2002, p. 338; cf. Holt, 1982), from Freud's earliest writings including his *Project for a Scientific Psychology* (Freud, 1950[1895]), Chapter VII of *The Interpretation of Dreams* (Freud, 1900a), and *Formulations on the Two Principles of Mental Functioning* (Freud, 1911b), to his later ones including *Beyond the Pleasure Principle* (Freud, 1920g), *The Ego and the Id* (Freud, 1923b), and *An Outline of Psycho-analysis* (Freud, 1940a[1938]).

Freud's specific metapsychology

In contradistinction to metapsychology as the psychology of the unconscious, Freud also provides a more specific understanding of metapsychology with respect to what he describes as three co-ordinates: "I propose that when we have succeeded in describing a psychical process in its dynamic, topographical and economic aspects, we should speak of it as a *metapsychological* presentation" (Freud, 1915e, p. 181, his italics; cf. Freud, 1925d, pp. 58–59). Metapsychology here addresses personality *dynamics* (motivation and conflict), *topographics* (domains and structures), and mental *economics* (entailing a system of psychical energy). In describing this approach, Freud (1925d) writes that this metapsychological perspective "seemed to me to represent the furthest goal that psychology could attain" (pp. 58–59), even if he there also states that his attempt "remained no more than a torso" and that he broke it off "since the time for theoretical predications of this kind had not yet come" (p. 59). The significance of this metapsychological breakdown, for Freud, was that these components provide the foundations for informing any specific psychodynamic explanation, whether it is for dreams, neurotic symptoms or normal behaviour.

This specific view of metapsychology became the entrenched view, in large part due to Rapaport and Gill (1959) who provide the first formal systematic exposition of psychoanalytic metapsychology, while also supplementing Freud's dynamic, economic and topographic co-ordinates with genetic (developmental) and adaptive ones.[1] The five metapsychological points of view, write Rapaport and Gill, constitute the framework of psychoanalytic metapsychology, and "*all* psychoanalytic propositions involve *all* metapsychological points of view" (Rapaport & Gill, 1959, p. 154, their italics), and so. In this specific sense, Freud's metapsychology provides "a multidimensional approach" (Novick and Novick, 2002, p. 350; cf. Frank, 2000, p. 177).

Freud's specific metapsychology and pluralism: the case of attachment theory

However, it is precisely problems with Freud's specific metapsychology that appear to provide instigation for several post-Freudian developments, including object relations approaches (e.g. Fairbairn, 1952) and attachment theory (Bowlby, 1969, 1982). In particular, it is Freud's metapsychological components that are considered especially problematic, and give rise to various schools arising based on rejecting what were considered necessary theoretical commitments to Freudian theory. This is particularly the case with Freud's 'economic' co-ordinate, whereby Freud postulates that mental activity involves drives discharging energy ('drive-discharge' theory), and the psychical apparatus functioning to regulate this. The economic account was singled out as a major failing of Freud's metapsychology, prompting some to move away from the foundations provided by Freud for understanding human behaviour, including the concept of drive, and to develop alternative theories in response to it. For example, Bowlby (1969, 1982) believes that while many of his own ideas "are to be found plainly stated by Freud" (1969, p. xvi) and that "attachment theory was developed as a variant of object-relations theory" (1982, p. 670; cf. Bowlby, 1969, p. 17), he believes that the principal area of divergence is with Freud's metapsychology and specifically Freud's drive-discharge theory. Bowlby (1982) thus sought "to offer an alternative to the traditional metapsychology of psychoanalysis …" (p. 668), and hence Freud's metapsychology clearly provided a stimulus for developing an alternative theory to the Freudian one.

Of course, metapsychology was not the only source of division between Freud and Bowlby—Bowlby, for instance, also singles out Freud's Lamarkian rather than Darwinian stance (see Bowlby, 1973, p. 81), as well as focusing on observation of actual real-life events instead of phantasy and private thought (Bowlby, 1982, pp. 666–668), but these differences are not foundational disputes, whereas rejecting Freud's metapsychology, at least in Bowlby's view, necessarily delineates attachment theory from psychoanalysis. Rather than focusing upon similarities, differences take priority, and in response, psychoanalysis tends to view attachment theory as over-simplifying motivation, affects, personality structure, and the unconscious, and it is only relatively recently that the two approaches have become at all reconciled with one another (Blatt & Levy, 2003; Fonagy & Campbell, 2015; Fonagy & Target, 2007; Gullestad, 2003; Holmes, 2000; Hopkins, 2015; Shane & Shane, 2001; Yovell, 2008a). Nevertheless, Fonagy and Campbell (2015) also write that attachment theory's view that there is an "innate need for relationship" has come "to be accepted by the majority" of psychoanalysts (p. 231), which indicates that contemporary psychoanalysis and attachment converge precisely on the point where they diverge from Freud's metapsychology, and as will be developed, a revised metapsychological approach is required for addressing the coherency of such motivational claims and to provide a theoretical foundation for integrating both attachment and psychoanalysis. However, such integration necessarily requires philosophical considerations,

8 Introduction

and for Freud and psychoanalysis generally, such considerations are a source of fracture within the discipline itself, and considered by many best left untouched.

Metapsychology and philosophy

Despite stressing the importance of his metapsychological theorising, Freud appears quite ambivalent towards his 'metapsychology', describing it as both his "ideal and woebegone child" (in Masson, 1985, letter to Fliess, 17 December 1896, p. 216; see also Holt, 1982, pp. 245–246; 2002, p. 337). Freud had initially planned to publish a collection of metapsychological papers in book form under the title *Zur Vorbereitung einer Metapsychologie—Preliminaries to a Metapsychology* with the intention "to clarify and carry deeper the theoretical assumptions on which a psycho-analytic system could be founded" (Freud, 1917d, p. 222n; see also Gay 1988, pp. 361–374; Jones, 1955, pp. 184–186). However, only five of the original twelve papers within the series made it to publication while the seven others were apparently written but then destroyed.

Freud's ambivalence towards his metapsychology may have been facilitated by his apparent distaste for philosophy and his desire for a science reliant primarily on observation. Laplanche and Pontalis (1973), in fact, believe that it "is impossible to overlook the similarity of the terms 'metapsychology' and 'metaphysics', and indeed Freud very likely intended to draw this analogy ..." (p. 249). Gay (1988) similarly believes that Freud's metapsychology was, if anything, a rival to "that grandiose and futile philosophical daydream, metaphysics" (p. 363), but this comparison somewhat misses the mark because Freud's metapsychological theorising was not 'idle philosophy' but rather a theoretical superstructure informing scientific enquiry. Holt (2002), in fact, observes that "in metapsychology he [Freud] came as close as he ever did to building a comprehensive, deductive system" (p. 338). This deductive system, if anything, was based on *a priori* theorising providing foundations for the theoretical superstructure within which psychoanalytic explanation operated, which Freud explains is thus most open to revision: "Psycho-analysis is founded securely upon the observation of the facts of mental life; and for that very reason its theoretical superstructure is still incomplete and subject to constant alteration" (Freud, 1926f, p. 266; cf. Freud, 1914c, p. 77; 1915c, p. 117; 1926f, p. 266).[2]

Nevertheless, such *a priori* theorising, in Freud's mind, meant metaphysical speculation, which Freud saw as the hallmark of philosophy, and so, when describing his theoretical and metapsychological writings, Freud writes:

> I should not like to create an impression that during this last period of my work I have turned my back upon patient observation and have abandoned myself entirely to speculation. ... Even when I have moved away from observation, I have carefully avoided any contact with philosophy proper. This avoidance has been greatly facilitated by constitutional incapacity.
>
> *(Freud, 1925d, p. 59)*

Hence Freud typically uses metapsychology and 'speculative' in the same breath, describing his metapsychology as "speculative theory" (Freud, 1914c, p. 77; cf. Freud, 1915c, p. 117; 1925d, p. 59), and even "the Witch Metapsychology" (Freud, 1937c, p. 225), 'speculative' to the point of phantasy: "Without metapsychological speculation and theorizing—I had almost said 'phantasising'—we shall not get another step forward. Unfortunately, here as elsewhere, what our Witch reveals is neither very clear nor very detailed" (Freud, 1937c, p. 225).

While Zepf (2001) believes that Freud's reference to 'speculation' is "meant ironically" (p. 472)—and it is not difficult to imagine that Freud employed a self-deprecatory writing style when discussing his metapsychology as a defence against being accused of over-reaching its significance—this association between metapsychology and speculative philosophy has led many to view metapsychology as abstract theory, remote from actual experience (e.g. Mitchell, 1988). In some respects, metapsychology is no longer seen as psychoanalytic theory *per se* but rather its theoretical assumptions. For instance Arlow (1975) defines metapsychology as the "a priori assumptions beyond hypotheses derivable within the clinical setting" (p. 517). Rapaport and Gill (1959) similarly write that metapsychology refers to the "minimal set of assumptions on which the psycho-analytic theory rests" (p. 153), while metapsychological enquiry entails "the study of the assumptions upon which the system of psycho-analytic theory is based" (p. 153). As such, for many, Freud's metapsychology does appear as speculative philosophy, far removed from experience, a viewpoint epitomised by Fulgencio (2005). Metapsychology, writes Fulgencio, refers "to a set of speculative concepts with no defined empirical content—such as those of drive [*Trieb*], libido, psychic apparatus" (p. 99, cf. Fulgencio, 2007), which he contrasts with Freud's descriptive "psychology of clinical facts" and subjective experience. In this manner, Fulgencio's position reflects the long-standing perceived division between metapsychology and psychoanalytic clinical theory (Barratt, 2015a, 2015b; Gill & Holzman, 1976; Holt, 1976, 1982; Klein, 1976; Mitchell, 1988; Pulver, 2003; Rosenblatt & Thickstun, 1977; Stolorow & Atwood, 2013; Talvitie & Ihanus, 2006; Wallerstein, 2005a). Wallerstein (2005a), for instance, distinguishes between "experience-near clinical theory" and "experience-distant diverse metapsychologies, or general theories …" (p. 623), the former dealing with persons, Intentionality, subjectivity and meaning, while the latter is viewed as impersonal, materialistic, objectivistic and remote from experience (Wallerstein, 2002, 2005a). For many, rather than Freud's problematic metapsychology, "[i]t is the clinical theory that was Freud's revolutionary contribution" (Klein, 1976, p. 16), and, for some, the two approaches are totally different in aims:

> Clinical psychoanalysis asks 'why' questions and seeks answers in terms of personal reasons, purposes, and individual meanings. Metapsychology asks 'how' questions and seeks answers in terms of the nonexperiential realm of impersonal mechanisms and causes.
>
> *(Stolorow & Atwood, 2013, p. 412)*

10 Introduction

Holt (1982), in fact, theorises that Freud was attracted towards developing a meta-psychology because it was consistent with the reductionistic, physicalist, mechanistic program that was seen as constituting the nineteenth-century natural science approach at the time (under the influence of Helmholtz, Brücke, Meynert, etc.), which simultaneously acted as an intellectualising defence "replacing the data-close terms of the clinical theory with the more abstract, impersonal, and austere language of natural science and mathematics" (p. 250; cf. Stolorow & Atwood, 2013, p. 413).

However, drawing a distinction between clinical theory and metapsychology depends in part upon what precisely metapsychology refers to, and if metapsychology means general psychoanalytic theory, as some propose (e.g. Brenner, 1980; Rangell, 2000), then there need be no antithesis between the supposed 'two theories'. After all, clinical terms are drawn from the general theory and general theory, assuming that it is correct, is itself instantiated in clinical experience (Mackay, 2002; Rangell, 2000). In fact, it is difficult to imagine how one could ever understand clinical phenomena if not in terms of the meanings provided by general theory. As Dreher (2005) points out, "meanings are embedded into the theoretical presuppositions of the analytic *Weltbild*—namely, the ideas about structure and function of the human psyche" (p. 365). The clinical phenomenon of 'resistance', for instance, necessarily draws upon a dynamic, metapsychological conception of the mind (i.e. the mind being capable of conflict, which, in turn, implies affective and motivational concepts). Thus, as Macmillan (1991) points out, attempting to create a hierarchy that places metapsychology as the highest level of abstraction compared to a more immediate clinical theory cannot be maintained since clinical theory necessarily involves metapsychological generalisations. Accordingly, any discussion of clinical findings, unless they are to be discussed in a conceptual vacuum, necessarily entails concepts from a general psychoanalytic theory. In this respect, general theory subsumes clinical theories, and so, as Mackay (2002) notes, if the clinical theory and the general theory are incompatible, then serious questions can be asked about the coherency of the position(s) proposed. Consequently, Freud's metapsychological approach is not simply idle philosophy but rather practical in clinical terms. Just as "psychoanalytic theories are also 'tools' guiding the clinician's work" (Talvitie & Ihanus, 2011, p. 1588), then the general account of the metapsychological model mind provides the explanatory tools for understanding clinical phenomena, as well as of informing what practice should affect therapeutic success (cf. Mackay, 1996, 2002). As Bowlby (1982) writes concerning the practical benefits of theory more generally, "[w]ithout a reasonably valid theory of psychopathology, therapeutic techniques tend to be blunt and of uncertain benefit" (p. 676), and so any attempt to alienate general theory from clinical practice is misguided.

Metapsychology and the brain

The distinction between an impersonal metapsychology and personal experience does, however, mirror views concerning the relation between neuroscience, psychoanalysis and subjective experience. Indeed, many take psychoanalytic meta-psychology to be an extension of Freud's apparent attempt found in his aborted *Project* to reduce psychology to biology, and thereby reduce human experience to the neuronal level (Barratt, 2015a; Gill, 1976; Klein, 1976). It is true that in his *Project*, Freud states that his "intention is to furnish a psychology that shall be a nat-ural science: that is, to represent psychical processes as quantitatively determinate states of specifiable material particles" (1950[1895], p. 295), and many since Freud have viewed metapsychology as primarily an account of the biological founda-tions for psychoanalysis. For instance, Waelder (1960) appears to have this in mind when he writes that Freud's "metapsychology is an attempt to build a physicalist foundation or superstructure, for his theory of motivation" (p. 173). It is, however, easy enough to find instances in Freud's writing that dispel any consistent reduc-tionistic stance in Freud's metapsychological writings (see Zepf, 2001, p. 468; see also Macmillan, 1991, p. 512), although metapsychological theorising does appear to nevertheless retain an intimate relation to Freud's biological premises. For instance, acquaintance with Freud's *Project* (1950[1895]) helps with understanding Freud's psychological approach in the later theoretical chapters in *The Interpretation of Dreams* (Freud, 1900a), although a precise account of Freud's meaning is open to interpretation.

However, the relation between neuroscience and psychoanalysis provides another source of division and pluralism in psychoanalysis, especially concerning the proper place of neuropsychoanalysis. For many, psychoanalysis, both in theory and therapy, is concerned with human experience and meaning, and as later discussion will clarify, psychological experience and meaning cannot be reduced to neuroscientific dis-course, in a similar fashion to the way that appreciation of a work of art cannot be reduced to a chemical analysis (Blass & Carmeli, 2007, p. 36). For this reason, Talvitie and Ihanus (2011) propose that psychoanalysis and neuropsychoanalysis have nothing in common, writing that "neuroscience has nothing to say about meanings. Thus, psy-chological and neurophysiological explanations are different in kind ..." (Talvitie & Ihanus, 2011, p. 1587; cf. Barratt, 2015a, p. 200; Karlsson, 2010, pp. 52–53). Blass and Carmeli (2007), go even further, writing that neuropsychoanalysis is inherently problematic since it draws attention away from experience and towards neural levels of explanation. Based on this, Talvitie and Ihanus (2011) dispute whether neuropsy-choanalysis has anything to offer psychoanalysis, partly because of the incongruity between psychoanalytic and neuroscientific levels of explanations:

> Only the psychological reasons enable us to *make sense* of phenomenal expe-riences and behaviour, and only the neurosciences can present the *causes* (in the strict sense of the term) *of behaviour*. Thus, just as we cannot determine the meanings of van Gogh's paintings through chemical analysis, neuroscientific models will not replace psychological explanations.
>
> *(Talvitie & Ihanus, 2011, p. 1587, their italics; cf. Karlsson, 2010; Talvitie & Ihanus, 2010)*

12 Introduction

For similar reasons, many authors see neuroscience as having little clinical value or even detracting from psychoanalytic therapy (e.g. Arlow, 1975)—Talvitie and Ihanus (2011) go so far as to say neuropsychoanalysis "has not produced a single contribution that clinicians admit have made a difference to their work" (p. 1588)—even if relevant to developing general psychoanalytic theory (e.g. Barratt, 2015a, 2015b; Pulver, 2003). While ascertaining whether there are genuine problems with neuropsychoanalysis requires further consideration (and will be addressed later), it does appear nevertheless that many clinicians find neuropsychoanalysis relevant, even if only for providing a greater understanding of what underpins the human mind. This alone suggests that any general theory must address the relationship between mind and brain and the role of neuroscience for psychoanalytic investigations.

For their part, Solms and Turnbull (2011) do not see neuropsychoanalysis as a separate 'school' or a source of division in psychoanalysis. Instead, for them, neuropsychoanalysis "is far better conceptualised as a link between *all* of psychoanalysis and the neurosciences" (p. 141). Similarly, according to Panksepp and Solms (2012),

> [n]europsychoanalysis seeks to understand the human mind, especially as it relates to first-person experience. It recognizes the essential role of neuroscience in such quests. However, unlike most branches of neuroscience, it positions mind and brain on an equal footing.
>
> *(p. 6)*

One might suppose, then, that any unified, general theory of human behaviour will embrace findings from neuroscience, simply because humans are embodied. Nevertheless, any substantive discussion of the relation of neuroscience to psychoanalysis requires addressing the nature of mind and body, which necessarily requires philosophical inquiry and thus conceptual and theoretical work is essential for developing a unified theory.

Conceptual and theoretical research

Conceptual research has a long history in both science generally (see Machado & Silva, 2007) and within psychoanalysis specifically (e.g. Dreher, 2005; Laplanche & Pontalis, 1973; Richfield, 1954; Sandler, Dreher, & Drews, 1991). Dreher (2005) defines psychoanalytic conceptual research as "concerned with the systematic and methodological investigation of the explicit and implicit meanings of psychoanalytic concepts and conceptual fields in their clinical and extraclinical use" (p. 362), and such investigation can be used for assessing the logical coherency of concepts, propositions and theories. As Machado and Silva (2007) write, "[s]cience has always included the screening of concepts and arguments for clarity and coherence" (p. 680), and this screening for clarity is essential for empirical research since theory must be clarified *prior* to empirical assessment (Boag, 2007c, 2012; Mackay, 2006; Michell, 2000; Petocz & Newbery, 2010). If a theory fails the logical test, then it could never refer to any actual state of affairs and thus can be rejected *a priori* (Petocz & Newbery, 2010), and so, accordingly, we cannot compare psychoanalytic theory with empirical evidence until we have first clarified what we are talking about in terms of both concepts and theories.

Conceptual and theoretical research further contributes to the interpretation of empirical findings, as well as shaping meaningful and valid avenues for future research directions (Bell, Staines, & Michell, 2001; Boag, 2011a, 2011b; Machado & Silva, 2007; Petocz & Newbery, 2010). Thus, Bowlby (1982) aptly acknowledges that "[w]ithout good theory as a guide, research is likely to be difficult to plan and to be unproductive, and findings are difficult to interpret" (p. 676), while Wright and Panksepp (2012) similarly observe that "the way in which something is conceptualized is not arbitrary or merely a manner of semantics, but is essential in guiding future research and the interpretation of past data" (Wright & Panksepp, 2012, p. 8). Conceptual and theoretical research is thus a potential tool for addressing pluralism in psychoanalysis specifically.

Despite this, it is well known that vague and ambiguous terms permeate psychoanalytic theory (Erdelyi, 1985; Fonagy & Target, 2000; Sandler et al., 1991), and this lack of clarity leads to various practical problems, including understanding the nature of pluralism itself. For instance, if there is a lack of shared meaning between rival theories, then genuine communication between various proponents and schools is stifled, and discerning whether genuine or only apparent differences between theories exist becomes difficult to determine. As Blum (2003b) writes, "[p]art of the problem of current analytic discourse resides in analysts using the same term with different meanings" (p. 510; cf. Bohleber et al., 2015; Oppenheim, 2012), and thus, as Fonagy and Target (2000) recognise, clarification of terms "is … essential if we are to find out where theoretical differences are real and where they may only be imagined" (p. 410).

Furthermore, despite advances in technology, conceptual and theoretical research is essential for evaluating the increasing integration of psychoanalysis and neuroscientific research (e.g. Epstein, 1998; Kandel, 1999; Kaplan-Solms & Solms, 2000; Schore, 2002, 2009; Solms, 2014; Solms & Turnbull, 2002, 2011). As Wright and Panksepp (2012) write,

> [a] problem that continues to impede productive psychoneurological research is the lack of generally accepted conceptual frameworks through which both psychological and modern neuroscientific perspectives can be integrated, studied, and understood in a common language.
>
> *(Wright & Panksepp, 2012, p. 5)*

The problem is especially acute for neuropsychoanalytic research since such a venture presents conceptual and theoretical challenges with respect to understanding physical and psychological interactions. In this respect, Bennett and Hacker (2003) have recently drawn attention to the myriad conceptual issues and confusions

14 Introduction

involved in neuroscientific theorising, while Talvitie and Ihanus (2006) note that "a need exists for a 'philosophy of neuropsychoanalysis'" (p. 96). Consequently, addressing the rightful role of neuropsychoanalysis within a psychoanalytic general theory requires a theoretical framework for understanding the relationship between mind and body.

Metapsychology and the foundations of psychoanalysis

The Australian psychoanalytic theorist John Maze writes, "Freud's metapsychology, though unfinished, was the one great systematic attempt in modern psychology to outline a deterministic, physiologically based theory of motivation and extend it to embrace all of human behaviour, bodily and mental" (1983, pp. 142–143). In this respect, writes Maze, Freud's metapsychology was a bold attempt to develop an integrative position addressing motivation, cognition and affective processes. This metapsychology acknowledges the rightful role of biological processes, but without reducing the mind to brain processes, while also situating the study of human experience within a natural science framework. Rather than a piecemeal approach to psychology where each psychological phenomenon is studied in relative isolation, Freud's general metapsychological approach provides a view of the organism as a whole, which allows assessing how the parts fit within the whole and the logical coherency of the human system.

At the same time, there are many unresolved tensions within Freud's writings which, in turn, have provided foundations for the emergence of divergent schools, and thus an assessment of the coherency of Freudian metapsychology is required to extricate the logically sound features of his theory and reject any incoherent aspect. Furthermore, since pluralism, in some respects, reflects a pluralism of metapsychologies (Wallerstein, 2005b, p. 635), a case is then apparent for assessing the foundations provided by Freud and the rival metapsychological positions, including object relations and attachment theory. By assessing these foundations, the aim here is to provide a coherent, twenty-first-century metapsychological foundation for both unifying and critically evaluating psychoanalytic theories. Any such metapsychological perspective must provide a coherent philosophy of mind that can be reconciled with neuroscientific research, and such a metapsychology must also further be able to account for the strengths of various psychoanalytic schools while not succumbing to their problems. To achieve this, an interdisciplinary focus is required, straddling both philosophy and (neuro)psychology, as recognised by a long-standing critic of metapsychology, who writes:

> There is still an important place for a new metapsychology. A much revised and improved clinical theory of psychoanalysis will need to have explicit links to the biological sciences, on the one hand, and the social sciences, on the other. Moreover, it must be grounded in a consistent world hypothesis or metaphysical system. It will need to make explicit its assumptions about the

mind-body problem and the problem of free will, for example, ideally taking a position that is compatible with contemporary sciences of the organism and the human person as a social, cultural, political, spiritual being.

(Holt, 2002, p. 341; cf. Holt, 1981)

The aim of the present book

The aim of this book is to take a bottom-up, foundational approach towards developing a unified psychoanalytic theory. To achieve this, it is first necessary to address the metaphysical foundations of psychoanalysis, since any theoretical position entails metaphysical assumptions that provide a foundation for what is theoretically permissible and guide further discussion of core theoretical concepts in psychoanalysis, including unconscious processes, drive and affects, and repression. Any approach to both empirical and theoretical research is necessarily embedded within a philosophical framework, and this is especially important for considering the rightful place of neuropsychoanalysis in modern psychoanalysis. To address this, a philosophical approach is put forward that is consistent with a materialist position but which does not necessarily reduce psychological relations to brain processes.

After setting the philosophical foundations, Freud's general and specific metapsychological positions are addressed and evaluated. If any theory deserves to provide a foundation for psychoanalysis it is Freud's. As noted earlier, Freud's metapsychology was an attempt to provide such a foundation by addressing the core elements for understanding personality, as well as co-ordinating how those parts contribute to the whole. Freud's specific metapsychology—the economic, topographic, and dynamic frames of reference—attempted to achieve this, and while problematic as will be shown, when recast in general terms of motivations (including drives and affects), personality structures and their cognitive acts, as well as psychological conflict (accounting for motivational dynamics), then Freud's general metapsychology provides a suitable general foundation that is well placed to address the issue of unification by drawing together the distinct schools and their varying contributions. Here, the book further aims to demonstrate that a revised metapsychological approach provides a common foundation for the various strands of psychoanalysis, including object relations and attachment theory, allowing the genuine insights from each approach to be appreciated, while jettisoning the components that do not withstand critical scrutiny. As stated before, the major splits that occurred in psychoanalysis—including both object relational and attachment perspectives—essentially constitute metapsychological differences since these schools arose due to perceived problems with Freud's metapsychology. As such, while Freud's specific metapsychology contributed to division and pluralism, the solution to pluralism is necessarily metapsychological in nature, which a revised metapsychology provides.

16 Introduction

Notes

1 Rapaport and Gill (1959) write concerning the genetic (developmental) and adaptive points of view: "The *genetic* point of view demands that the psycho-analytic explanation of any psychological phenomenon include propositions concerning its psychological origin and development" (Rapaport & Gill, 1959, p. 161, their italics). On the other hand, the adaptive point of view at its broadest refers to 'environmental relations' and requires that "psycho-analytic explanation of any psychological phenomenon include propositions concerning its relationship to the environment" (Rapaport & Gill, 1959, p. 159). However, while any comprehensive theory should account for both the origins and relations of the phenomena of interest, Macmillan (1991) notes that the genetic and adaptive viewpoints are different in kind to Freud's dynamic, topographic and economic co-ordinates since the former views are not actually assumptions from which explanations can be derived.

2 Such a *priori* theorising is, itself, empirically informed, however.

1
THE METAPHYSICS OF METAPSYCHOLOGY

Introduction

A reasonable place to begin addressing the foundations of psychoanalysis might be with a discussion of the 'basic concepts' of the theory, as did Freud (1915b), and to then assess whether psychoanalytic theory is logically coherent and consonant with empirical findings. However, these are not, in fact, the true foundations, since Freud embedded psychoanalytic theory within a particular worldview (see Freud, 1933a). If anything, this worldview is the logically prior foundation since the development of psychoanalytic theory is informed by these assumptions, any of which may be more or less implicit or explicit. Thus, while Rapaport and Gill (1959) rightly note that "[a]t some point in the development of every science, the assumptions on which it is built must be clarified" (p. 153), rather than assessing the theory prior to assessing the assumptions, an alternative position is to question one's assumptions first. In fact, and as hinted at previously, many of the divisions underlying psychoanalytic pluralism are metaphysical in nature, and the logical starting point, then, for clarifying the foundations of psychoanalysis, is not with psychoanalytic theory *per se* but instead with addressing the metaphysical foundations of psychoanalysis.

However, addressing the metaphysics of psychoanalysis is no small undertaking, and even the term 'metaphysics' is open to diverse interpretation (see van Inwagen & Zimmerman, 2008). Most commonly, however, at least in recent writings, Freud's theory is typically seen as adopting Immanuelle Kant's philosophical stance (see especially Tauber, 2010). Fulgencio (2005), for instance, writes that "Freudian psychoanalysis was built on the firm ground of the metaphysics of nature of the Kantian kind" (p. 110; cf. Fulgencio, 2007), and from this perspective, "[m]etaphysics concerns ultimate reality" (Talvitie & Ihanus, 2011, p. 1588). For Kant,

18 The metaphysics of metapsychology

we do not know the world as it is, but instead via mind-imposed categories, such as space and time, and thus we can never directly access an unknowable, 'ultimate' reality lying beyond experience. On the other hand, mind and body are seen as phenomenal aspects of this underlying unknowable reality (*das-Ding-an-sich*—the thing in itself) and proponents of neuropsychoanalysis explicitly subscribe to this position (e.g. Solms & Turnbull, 2011, p. 137). This viewpoint has major implications for interpreting Freudian theory. For instance, interpreted through a Kantian lens, unconscious processes are viewed in terms of this underlying unknowable reality, rather than referring to ordinary 'phenomenal' mental acts (e.g. Solms, 2003). However, viewed as such, it is difficult to see how anyone can have knowledge of an unknowable reality (see Karlsson, 2010), or what clinical relevance such unknowable states might have, and critics of philosophy rightly seize upon this necessarily speculative approach.[1]

Instead, an alternative approach to metaphysics, and one more in line with a natural science framework, simply entails enquiry concerning the nature of reality. In contradistinction, then, to the Kantian position, metaphysics here "is not about an unknowable reality behind experience; it is about the reality that is already in and required by experience" (Petocz & Mackay, 2013, p. 217; cf. Hibberd, 2014). On this view, insofar as Freud or anyone else is claiming to be talking about anything that exists, metaphysical considerations are implicated and consequently, any scientific discussion necessarily entails metaphysical considerations concerning the nature of reality. Furthermore, no matter which metaphysical position is adopted, such philosophical considerations are especially critical for psychology generally and psychoanalysis specifically because the relation between mind and body requires critical attention. As Talvitie and Ihanus (2011) observe:

> The study of metaphysical issues is often seen as useless speculation … Metaphysics is the key issue when the relevance of neuroscience to psychoanalysis is considered. In this situation it is very important that neuropsychoanalytic studies are explicit in their metaphysical commitments.
>
> *(p. 1597)*

Holt (1981, 2002) thus recognises that any comprehensive psychoanalytic theory must address metaphysical issues, and the foundational divisions in psychoanalysis, to some degree, reflect different metaphysical stances:

> The underlying difficulty, I believe, is metaphysical: the more one tends, consciously or not, toward a dualistic position on the mind-body problem, the more one will feel that there is an unbridgeable gulf between the subjective and objective world, between the realm of external physicochemical fact and that of inner meaning, and thus between science and the humanities.
>
> *(Holt, 1981, p. 131)*

The metaphysics of metapsychology **19**

Accordingly, addressing pluralism in psychoanalysis requires evaluating the supposed metaphysical divisions and whether they hold up to scrutiny or not. By way of example, the supposed tension between general metapsychology and clinical theory (e.g. Fulgencio, 2005, 2007) involves proposing a dualism between the metaphysical categories of *universality* and *particularity*. Fulgencio (2007), for instance, attempts to create a dualism between facts and theory: "facts are invariably singular and contingent, while theories and concepts are always universals" (p. 445). However, particular facts cannot be divorced from general theory or concepts, since any so-called singular, particular fact will also refer to types of events of a general (universal) kind—to say otherwise would require that every description be necessarily a novel utterance. Instead, since any situation involves both universals (types of things) and specific instances of those types of things, then any particular clinical description of persons ('facts') entails describing universal features of those persons (or what can be described as 'general theory'). Thus, while clinical descriptions may pertain to a particular individual, these descriptions are not in isolation but necessarily embedded within a broader general 'metaphysical' theory, and thus there is not a dualism between clinical theory and descriptions on the one hand and metapsychology on the other.

Consequently, metaphysical enquiry concerns itself with issues such as the relation between mind and brain, causality and freedom, issues which must all be explicitly addressed since they are essential to the whole scientific psychology enterprise. Ignoring such issues simply provides a recipe for confusion and a foundation for apparent but false divisions between theories. As Holt (1981) again observes, metaphysics "takes its revenge on those who ignore it":

> It is of the very nature of the questions metaphysicians tackle that everyone must take some implicit stand on them, and it is dangerous to remain unaware of that fact … Psychoanalysts—of all people—should respond positively to the idea that what you don't know *can* hurt you, and that there is a clear gain in expanding our consciousness of matters we aren't usually aware of.
>
> *(Holt, 1981, p. 132, his italics)*

Consequently, clarifying the metaphysical foundations of psychoanalysis is directly relevant to addressing Freudian metapsychology since many of the criticisms of metapsychology entail philosophical considerations concerning the nature of mind and brain, and the nature of causality, and thus evaluating whether a metapsychological position is coherent necessitates addressing its metaphysical commitments. Whether such claims are consistently and coherently put forward requires philosophical assessment, and thus, a critical philosophical analytic approach is necessary for both developing a coherent metaphysical position for situating psychoanalytic theory within, as well as providing a critical evaluation tool for assessing the coherency of any proposed psychoanalytic position.

20 The metaphysics of metapsychology

Evaluating metaphysical standpoints

Evaluating the coherency of any given metaphysical standpoint is not, however, a simple matter since it is commonly supposed that such *a priori* philosophical considerations are not open to empirical evaluation. Talvitie and Ihanus (2011), for instance, while arguing for the critical role of metaphysics in psychoanalysis, nevertheless write, "we cannot avoid asking on what grounds we might know which metaphysical position is more accurate than another … every branch of study must rest on some metaphysical propositions, which cannot be verified empirically" (p. 1598). Similarly, Solms and Turnbull (2002) believe that metaphysical positions are not assessable empirically, and instead one must simply accept the worldview *a priori*:

> Loath as we may be to admit it, the testable hypotheses that scientists can work with are embedded in sets of broader propositions that are themselves untestable. These broader propositions define the world view (*Weltanschauung*) within which a scientist operates; and world views are not subject to proof.
> *(Solms & Turnbull, 2002, p. 54)*

Nevertheless, it cannot simply be the case that 'anything goes', such that any and all world views are on equal footing and one is simply left free to choose whatever metaphysical position that one fancies (cf. Barratt, 2015b). After all, there appear to be empirical facts and achievements that give a scientific *Weltanschauung* greater credence compared to, say, religious ones, since there appears to be more compelling evidence for the metaphysical thesis of determinism (taken here to be that events arise out of causes) compared to the claim of miraculous intervention.

On the other hand, Talvitie and Ihanus (2011) propose resolving the choice of metaphysical stance by employing Occam's razor: "we should avoid non-necessary presuppositions and, if there are two models that explain a phenomenon equally well, then we should favour the one that makes fewer metaphysical postulates" (p. 1598). In this context, 'metaphysical postulates' refer to assumed-but-unobservable entities, such as 'the unconscious' in psychoanalytic theory, which presupposes that theoretical entities are necessarily speculative:

> Because the existence of the unconscious part of the mind (or the unconscious) has not been empirically proven (and many think that it is not even worth trying to do so), it should be taken as a metaphysical assumption. The mental unconscious is an *unobservable*—or we might say that the Freudian unconscious contains several kinds of unobservables: the psychic apparatus, drives, unconscious fantasies, repressed desires and memories.
> *(Talvitie & Ihanus, 2011, p. 1589, their italics)*

The metaphysics of metapsychology **21**

Talvitie and Ihanus's application of Occam's razor would thus mean accepting a theory postulating fewer theoretical entities compared to other theories (cf. Morgan, 1894, p. 53). Nevertheless, while there might be some heuristic merit to this strategy, this stance is nevertheless problematic because the razor ignores the *logical coherency* of any given metaphysical supposition. Would we really accept a theory with, say, two incoherent metaphysical suppositions (or theoretical entities) but reject a theory with three coherent ones? Obviously, the issue of logical coherency needs to be the paramount consideration, and while a metaphysical thesis such as determinism might not be empirically demonstrable—no one could ever demonstrate that causality occurs everywhere, and for all time—such theses are nevertheless open to logical scrutiny, and while logic itself might be accused of entailing various metaphysical presuppositions, it is nevertheless the best resource open to us in resolving such matters.

A realist metaphysics

Despite Freud's apparent deference to Kant, Freud also adopts a realist philosophy underlying his general scientific approach (e.g. Freud, 1933a). Realism here simply means that there is a mind-independent reality, which Freud believes provides a basis for scientific knowledge, since we can both come to know this mind-independent reality and make objective claims about it. A realist philosophical framework thus fits with Freud's broad commitment to the natural scientific approach involving both empiricism (knowledge through experience) and a commitment to determinism (all events arise out of antecedent conditions and go on to cause other events) (see Freud, 1933a, pp. 170, 182; 1940a[1938], pp. 158–159; 1940b[1938], p. 282). Such a realist metaphysics implicates universally present, mind independent 'categories' that are logically necessary for anything to occur, which has practical value since these categories "provide the logical constraints which any theory, model, or general account must meet" (Hibberd, 2014, p. 167), and thus provide a approach for evaluating the logical coherency of theories. Based on the realist philosophy of the Scottish-born Australian philosopher John Anderson (see Anderson, 1962), Hibberd (2014) identifies thirteen "pervasive, logically necessary conditions or features (categories)" (p. 165), which include the *spatio-temporal context, identity, difference, existence, relation, generality* (or universality), *particularity, number, order, quantity,* and *causality*. It is not the place here to enter into whether Hibberd's list of categories is satisfactory or exhaustive (Anderson, for instance, views space and time as the context for the categories—Anderson, 1962; Baker, 1986; see also Michell, 2011), but for present purposes, the category of relation is particularly pertinent for addressing Freudian theory since it is implicated in evaluating theories, both with respect to description and explanation, as well as logical errors commonly attributed to Freud's metapsychology, such as reification and circular explanation (as described below).

22 The metaphysics of metapsychology

The world we live in can be seen as consisting of various *qualities* (or properties) that stand in a variety of *relations* to one another. Any individual, for example, consists of various properties constituting the individual, and the individual also stands in any infinite amount of relations, whether they be spatial, temporal, familial, or legal (etc.). What relations have in common is that they involve at least two or more distinct *terms* standing with respect to one another, and any terms standing in relation must have their own intrinsic properties to constitute what stands in the relation. As Mackie (in Anderson, 1962) writes, "a quality is an intrinsic feature of a thing, it belongs to the thing itself, whereas a relation holds between two or more things" (p. 266), and while the terms of the relation must have their own intrinsic properties, they must nevertheless be logically independent from one another, in order to be related. If it were otherwise, we would not be able to speak of *what* is in relationship. As Maze (1983) writes:

> Anything that can stand ... in any relation at all, must have at least some intrinsic properties. If that were not the case ... then we could not understand what it was that was said to have those relationships. A relation can only hold between two or more terms, and a part of what is involved in seeing those terms as related is being able to see them as distinct, that is, as each having its own intrinsic properties, so that we can say what the terms *are* that are related. This means that each term of the relation must be able in principle to be described without the need to include any reference to its relation to the other.
>
> *(p. 24, his italics; cf. Maze, 1954, p. 231; Michell, 1988, p. 234)*

So, for instance, to borrow an example from Bell, Staines and Michell (2001), in the situation where John is different from Mike, both John and Mike must exist and have properties that they differ on. The relation of 'difference', however, cannot be reduced to either of the terms (i.e. 'difference' cannot be reduced to either John or Mike) since difference is not a property of either term. So, while John and Mike must have their own characteristics that they differ from one another on, the relation of difference is *between* those properties of John and Mike rather than being a property of either. Taken as such, the relation itself is not some type of third entity, since, as Michell (1988) writes, a relation "is not a kind of *stuff* that binds the terms. It is just how the terms are with respect to each other" (p. 234, his italics; see also Hibberd, 2014, pp. 168ff). Furthermore, relations need not be simply between *two* terms and some concepts, such as 'meaning' can be viewed as a ternary relation between the signifier, the signified, and a cognising subject (Petocz, 1999; cf. Hibberd, 2014, pp. 173f), and as will be developed later, affective processes can be understood as particular ternary relations as well (see Chapter 2).

The logic of relations and conceptual analysis

Appreciating the logic of relations provides a means of conducting conceptual analysis in two important ways. First, any concept or theoretical term can be assessed for

The metaphysics of metapsychology **23**

whether it refers to a property or quality of something (including whether it refers to an entity that consists of its own intrinsic properties), or to specific relations between qualities or entities. One means of achieving this is through dissecting what a concept is said to *be*, and what it is said to *do*. If a theorist is proposing, for instance, that a certain quality or entity exists, then it should have intrinsic features that can be identified independently of any relation entered into, which would mean describing the property independently of any particular performance or activity (Maze, 1983). On the other hand, certain concepts are relational, although not always clearly so. Concepts such as 'impulse-control', 'risk-taking', 'sociability', 'adaptability', 'cautiousness' and 'conformity' all suggest activities—controll*ing* impulses, tak*ing* risks, adapt*ing* to circumstances, be*ing* cautious, or conform*ing* to the group, and thus given the logic of relations, the concepts can be further dissected into the terms standing in the relation. For instance, we might say that a 'person' controls impulses, or a person conforms to the group, (i.e. *S* controls *x*, or *S* conforms to *y*, where *S* is the subject and *x* and *y* are the object terms of the relation). Accordingly, one advantage of recognising concepts such as impulse-control or conformity as relations is that further questions can be asked concerning exactly *what* stands in the relation. What, for instance, is doing the controlling, or taking risks, or conforming, etc.? If the answer is the 'ego' or 'self', then we can further enquire into the specific nature of this 'ego', its intrinsic features and so forth (see also Boag, 2010b, 2011b).

A second advantage involves clarifying the distinction between description and explanation, a distinction that can give rise to the conceptual fallacies of reification and circularity when not properly understood (Boag, 2010b, 2011a, 2011b, 2015a; Kubie, 1947; Maze, 1954; Rosenblatt & Thickstun, 1977). This issue is particularly pertinent to assessing psychoanalytic metapsychology because a number of criticisms implicate precisely such errors. For instance, Beres (1965) writes that "we have become accustomed in psycho-analytic theorizing to use certain words and phrases which on closer examination prove to be tautological, analogical or pseudo-explanatory" (p. 53), while Macmillan (1991) writes that "metaphorical description ... confused with explanation" appears especially pronounced in metapsychological theorising (p. 599). In fact, a common charge against Freudian metapsychology here is that it simply restates clinical descriptive phenomena as technical sounding explanatory terminology, and thus, such 'explanations' of clinical problems informed by metapsychology are in fact tautological, stemming from "restating observation in terms of another level of discourse ..." (Arlow, 1975, p. 518). For this reason, Holt (2002) is led to conclude:

> despite its appearance of being a serious intellectual achievement, Freud's metapsychology is scientifically trivial and useless. It merely supplies a jargon in which observations may be restated in impressive-sounding terms that actually add nothing to the original clinical formulations.

(p. 341)

24 The metaphysics of metapsychology

Now, addressing Holt's conclusion requires appreciating the logic of relations and especially the logical errors of reification and circularity. As stated earlier, while any set of terms may indeed be related, they must nevertheless be logically distinct from one another to be able to say what stands in the relation (Maze, 1983, p. 24; cf. Hibberd, 2014, p. 168). Reification, or the 'fallacy of misplaced concreteness' (Beres, 1965, p. 56), involves mistaking relations with properties (Bell, Staines, & Michell, 2001, 2011a, 2011b; Boag, 2010b, 2011a, 2011b, 2015a; Passmore, 1935; see also Breuer & Freud, 1895d, pp. 227–228), and Freud's metapsychology and related concepts such as drive and energy, for instance, are seen as especially prone to this error (Beres, 1965; Bowlby, 1969, 1973; Holt, 1976; Kubie, 1947). The problem of reification generally arises from failing to recognise the logical independence of terms and mistakenly taking relationships between things to be either properties (or qualities) of things, or taken to be the entities themselves. For instance, to use the earlier example, to say that John is taller than Mike is to note a relationship between John and Mike and, as such, 'being taller' cannot be reduced solely to a property of either term. However, to misconceptualise 'being taller' as an intrinsic feature of (in this case) John, would be to reify the relationship (i.e. to mistake a relationship for a property).

A related error is the fallacy of constitutive relations, which is to "treat relations as if they were terms, entities possessing independent natures of their own" (McMullen, 1996, p. 61) and thus constitute an entity or thing solely in terms of its relatedness rather than in terms of intrinsic properties (Maze, 1983). An example of this fallacy is apparent in accounts postulating the 'self' as an agent (i.e. the subject term standing in the doing relation). As a term in the relation performing activities, the 'self' should have intrinsic features that are logically independent from that which it is said to do. However, some accounts propose that this agentic self is, in fact, constituted in relationship. For example, in Macmurray's (1961, 1969) account, the self is said to be a cognising agent that performs various activities (1969, p. 87), and so given the logic of relations discussed above, such a self should stand as the subject term in the doing and knowing relations (i.e. the agent S that does x/the agent S that knows p). However, Macmurray (1961) also claims that the self is constituted by relatedness: "[T]he Self exists only in dynamic relation with the Other [the world] ... the Self is constituted by its relation to the Other" (p. 17). However, if the 'self' is constituted by relatedness, then this leaves unanswered what the 'it' is (i.e. the subject term) that has those same relations (cf. Maze, 1983), and if the self or knower is only defined in relation to other things (i.e. without intrinsic qualities of its own), as Macmurray suggests, then it succumbs to the fallacy of constitutive relations and cannot be said to be capable of standing as an independent subject term. Consequently the 'self as agent', as proposed by Macmurray, cannot stand as the subject having those same relations (see Boag, 2005 for further discussion).

The fallacy of constitutive relations is particularly relevant to assessing functional and process accounts of mind, which are similarly pertinent to understanding and evaluating psychoanalytic metapsychology. Beres (1965), for instance, believes that

The metaphysics of metapsychology **25**

metapsychology is best understood as a 'process theory of mind' and, as a process theory, Beres proposes that we should avoid analysing and identifying 'things' (or structures) and instead focus upon identifying processes (or functions). However, as Hibberd (2014) writes, "that which changes is *in process*" (p. 165, her italics), and consequently some discussion of *what* is in process is required, since otherwise, the 'process' simply becomes another reified entity. Similarly, any discussion of functions requires some account of what is functioning (some kind of structure), independent of the act of functioning itself, and as discussed in Chapter 5, such concerns are directly relevant to evaluating Freud's theory of personality developed in his 'structural theory'.

The fallacy of constitutive relations also lends itself to the fallacy of circular explanation. Circular explanation occurs when the explanation of some effect (the *explanans*) is equivalent to the effect that it is said to explain (the *explanandum*), such that the explanation for some occurrence is the occurrence itself (Bell et al., 2001; Boag, 2011a, 2011b, 2015a). Circular explanation can easily occur when a *description* of behaviour becomes mistakenly treated as a property and then used to explain that same behaviour (a problem raised at various times in the history of modern psychology—Bandura, 1999; Cervone, 1999; Howe, 1990; Kroger & Wood, 1993; Maze, 1954; Skinner, 1953). Such 'verbal-magic' essentially involves "giving a name to a certain kind of event and then using the name as if it accounted for the *occurrence* of that kind of event" (Maze, 1954, p. 226; his italics), and provides the illusion of knowing the relevant causes when in fact we have no clear idea of what the actual causes are (cf. Boag, 2011a, 2011b, 2015a; Cervone, 1999).

However, a further major source of confusion with assessing the logical coherency of Freud's account is his use of metaphor. While all fields of science make use of metaphors and analogy for illustrative purposes (Cheshire & Thomä, 1991; Petocz, 2006), the scientific value of metaphors is determined by understanding precisely how far such metaphors extend. This, according to Cheshire and Thomä (1991), is possible by 'marking off the area of negative analogy', which requires knowing the necessary points of contrast and spelling out the relevant characteristics of both the phenomenon and metaphor. Without knowing this distinction, then the possibility of conceptual errors arises, especially with respect to the logical errors, such as reification, described earlier. As Beres (1965) writes,

> [m]etaphor is a basic element in language and serves as illustration and as emphasis in scientific discourse as well as in ordinary discourse. It is when metaphor is treated concretely and used as an explanatory tool that it leads to a false sense of understanding.
>
> *(p. 561; cf. Rosenblatt & Thickstun, 1977, p. 538)*

Conceptual clarification is thus also required for 'cashing out' the metaphors in psychoanalytic theory (Petocz, 2015), and unfortunately, Freud's writings typically do not provide clear enough indications for marking off the area of negative analogy

26 The metaphysics of metapsychology

(see Cheshire & Thomä, 1991, p. 448). On top of this, Freud's metaphors are often conflated with anthropomorphism, leading Freud to seemingly hold two contrary pictures of mind, one explicable in terms of causal, mechanistic operations, the other in terms of agency and 'persons' (Gouws, 2000; Grossman & Simon, 1969; Sartre, 1956; Thalberg, 1982), leading Nagel (1959), to observe:

> though psychoanalysis explicitly proclaims the view that human behavior has its roots in the biophysical and biochemical organization of the body, it actually postulates a veritable 'ghost in the machine' that does work which a biologically oriented psychology might be expected to assign to the body.
>
> *(p. 47)*

As will be later discussed (especially in Chapter 6), anthropomorphic descriptions of the psyche might be appropriate when taking into account the influence of object relations in the development of the psyche (e.g. the development of 'imagos' or proto-types of the parents, for example; see Beres, 1965; Gardner, 1993; Hopkins, 1995), and Gillett (1990) further observes that anthropomorphic language "can be useful and acceptable as long as it is clear how it can be translated into causal terms" (p. 560). Nevertheless, *explaining* behaviour and cognition with respect to an internal person or agent invokes the problematic homunculus, and Freud's model of personality has been criticised for postulating multiple homunculi (e.g. id, ego, and superego) (Grossman & Simon, 1969; Laplanche & Pontalis, 1973; Wiedeman, 1972). Plainly put, the problem with such homunculi, as Grossman and Simon (1969) note, is that any 'person-within-the-person' model simply defers explanation since any explanation in terms of agents or persons requires further explanation (ultimately in terms of causal antecedents and mechanisms), if a vicious regress of explanations to (sub) persons is to be avoided (Boag, 2012; Gardner, 1993; Grossman & Simon, 1969; Maze, 1983, 1987; Wegner, 2005). Alternatively, should the homunculus have 'free will' then "the homunculus causes things merely by deciding, without any prior causes leading to these decisions" (Wegner, 2005, p. 20), which, as Wegner correctly notes makes behaviour literally inexplicable.

The metaphysics of neuropsychoanalysis

Another metaphysical issue directly relevant for assessing Freudian theory, and particularly relevant to neuropsychoanalytic theorising, involves the mind–body problem. Talvitie and Ihanus (2006, 2011) recently write that neuropsychoanalytic theorising has yet to satisfactorily address such critical metaphysical issues for addressing the relevance of neuroscience for psychoanalysis, while Brakel (2013) comments that, if anything, neuroscientific findings are obscuring rather than clarifying our understanding of mind-brain relations, since advances in neuroscientific research have not addressed the necessary metaphysical questions concerning the

The metaphysics of metapsychology **27**

ontology of mind/brain. Instead, claim Talvitie and Ihanus, neuropsychoanalysis has rushed into empirical research at the expense of thinking through its metaphysical position, with the result being that "[d]iscussions on the subject of neuropsychoanalysis often wander aimlessly, devoid of clear points and arguments" (Talvitie & Ihanus, 2011, p. 1598; cf. Karlsson, 2010). To rectify this, Talvitie and Ihanus (2011) propose that the proponents need to squarely address their metaphysical foundations: "What should be done in order to proceed with neuropsychoanalysis is to divert for a moment from exclusively gathering neurophysiological data and to consider whether, and if so how, metaphysical controversies can be resolved" (Talvitie & Ihanus, 2011, p. 1598; cf. Talvitie & Ihanus, 2006, p. 96).

However, Solms (2015) views matters differently, writing with respect to the mind-body problem, that "it is generally recognized that there is no 'correct' solution to this philosophical conundrum. The mind/body problem is generally considered insoluble by empirical means" (p. 216), and consequently, on the various positions to the problem, Solms concludes that these "are matters of belief, not of fact" (p. 216). However, it is, of course, not good enough to simply pass the situation off as an insoluble philosophical problem, and Barratt (2015b) quite rightly replies that this "does not imply that anything goes, or that how we think about the issue is unimportant" (p. 223).

On the other hand, there are, of course, many approaches to the mind-body problem (see, for instance, Brakel, 2013 and Meissner, 2003 for reviews), and turning to Freud here for solutions is of little help. Freud's theory straddles a number of ontological positions on the mind/brain relation, allowing various commentators to seize upon comments either promoting or denying the importance of organic processes for psychoanalysis (for instance, compare and contrast, interpretations from Zepf, 2001 and Solms, 2013). For its part, neuropsychoanalysis generally subscribes to *dual-aspect monism* (Panksepp & Biven, 2012; Solms, 2014; Solms & Turnbull, 2002, 2011), whereby mind and body are said to be one and the same, simply seen from either subjective or objective points of view respectively. Solms and Turnbull (2002) comment, for instance, that "we are made of only one type of stuff" but "this stuff is *perceived* in two different ways" (p. 56, their italics), while Panksepp and Biven (2012) similarly write:

> Although it may appear that the mind and brain are different entities, the mind being incorporeal and the brain being physical, they are really one and the same thing. The MindBrain (or BrainMind) is a unified entity lacking any boundary with the body—it is integral to the physical system as a whole.
>
> *(p. xiii)*

Accepting dual-aspect monism "implies that *in our essence* we are *neither* mental nor physical beings" (Solms & Turnbull, 2002, p. 56, their emphasis), and in its Kantian vein proposes that "we can never perceive the *underlying* mind-body stuff *directly*" (p. 57, their italics). Again:

28 The metaphysics of metapsychology

> Our picture of the mental apparatus *itself* will ... always be a figurative one—a model. We possess concrete perceptual images of its two observable manifestations (the brain and subjective awareness), but the underlying entity that *lies behind* those perceptual images will never be directly observable.
>
> *(Solms & Turnbull, 2002, p. 57, their italics;*
> *cf. Solms & Turnbull, 2011, p. 136)*

However, there are several problems with dual-aspect monism, which indicate that it cannot provide a defensible foundation for (neuro)psychoanalytic theorising. The first problem concerns the supposed relation between mind and brain. While mind and brain are purportedly one and the same, Karlsson (2010) points out that Solms (2014) nevertheless treats them as distinct by claiming that brain processes generate consciousness. As Karlsson (2010) notes, however, for brain processes to *generate* consciousness would mean that mind and brain are separate terms, where one exists prior to the other, and as he points out, the very nature of any supposed monism means that there cannot be any such causal relation between body and mind:

> dual-aspect monism can be described as if the mental, subjective and bodily states are two sides of the same thing. Such a formulation excludes seeing the relationship in causal terms, since the dual-aspect monism presupposes that each bodily state is indissolubly correlated with a specific subjective state.
>
> *(Karlsson, 2010, p. 44)*

On top of this, however, a fatal flaw for dual-aspect monism is that it actually fails to account for the psychological *activities* (such as perceiving, introspecting and awareness) involved in *coming to know* the supposed mind/body. Consider the following two examples provided by Solms and Turnbull:

> When I perceive myself externally (in the mirror, for example) and internally (through introspection), I am perceiving the *same thing* in two different ways (as a *body* and a *mind*, respectively).
>
> *(Solms & Turnbull, 2002, p. 56, italics in original)*

> our mental experience arises out of introspection; we perceive the mind (as opposed to matter) by looking inwards.
>
> *(Solms & Turnbull, 2002, p. 67)*

From the above we can see that there is something *known* (i.e. mind/body) and also *coming to know* that same 'thing' (i.e. the perceiving, introspecting and awareness of that same mind/body). Such 'coming to know' activities are obviously psychological in nature and yet must be distinct from the mind/body monad that is known. So, while dual-aspect monism accounts might account for what is *known*

The metaphysics of metapsychology **29**

(*viz*. the mind/body) it does not address the ontological status of the *knowing* of that same mind/body.[2] Consequently, since dual-aspect monism does not account for all psychological processes, it cannot be accepted as a coherent solution to the mind/body problem or provide a tenable foundation for (neuro)psychoanalysis.

A different approach: the body, brain, and psychological activities

If dual-aspect monism is not a justifiable foundation then an alternative mind/body position that does not succumb to the intractable problems of dualism (*viz*. accounting for how mind and brain interact given their supposed antithetical relation—McMullen, 1996, p. 66; see also Hibberd, 2014, p. 176) is required. There are, however, non-reductionist, realist, materialist approaches to mind such as a real-ist relational approach to the mind/body issue, which situate both mind and body within the one and the same spatio-temporal universe and yet treat them as distinct (see Anderson, 1962; Hibberd, 2014; Mackay & Petocz, 2010; Maze, 1983; Michell, 1988; Petocz, 1999, 2015; Petocz & Mackay, 2013). The concept of relations dis-cussed above is, however, necessary for making sense of this, and without then attempting to trivialise what is necessarily a complicated matter, the thesis here is that it is possible to advance a non-dualist materialist approach to mind that does not reduce the mental to materiality. This is achievable by viewing psychological processes as specific relational acts occurring between the brain/perceptual system and various states of affairs in the world, where the psychological act cannot be reduced to the body (or synapses, etc.) even if bodily states are necessary condi-tions for psychological ones to occur.[3] In some respects, this position is implicated in viewing the 'mind as the brain's activities'. Brenner (1980), for instance, writes that "[m]ind is but an aspect of brain functioning, quite as much as respiration is of pulmonary and diaphragmatic functioning or circulation is of cardiac functioning" (Brenner, 1980, p. 206). That is, mind, if anything, is an *activity* of the brain, and even if the brain is a necessary condition for psychological acts, that activity is logically distinct. Thus, while Brenner makes it clear that there are limits with his analogy, he nevertheless can rightly say that "what we *do* know is that mind has no 'exist-ence,' no meaning, apart from brain" (p. 206, his italics), without necessarily being reductionistic.

Zepf (2010), however, interprets Brenner's view here as a crude reductionism (a "vulgar-materialistic view", which ignores any role of the environment, says Zepf—p. 4), and insists that Brenner "mistakenly identifies the material substra-tum of mental activities, the neuronal processes, as the source of these activities" (p. 4; cf. Zepf, 2001). However, there is nothing remiss about proposing that the brain (including the nervous system, etc.) acts as the source (or foundation) of the mind, performing various *psychological* activities (thinking, perceiving, etc.) and that these same activities are reliant on those same structures but not reducible to them.

30 The metaphysics of metapsychology

The ontological distinction is, however, between an *entity* (brain, etc.) and its *activities*, both existing in the same spatio-temporal universe but nevertheless logically distinct from one another.

The brain, of course, performs many activities, not all of which would be described as 'psychological' acts. Some aspects of brain functioning are instead describable as simply physical activities rather than psychological ones, even if those same activities constitute necessary conditions for whatever we take to mean a psychological act (e.g. neuronal activity and changes in brain oxygenation). As will be developed later (Chapter 3), a 'psychological act' is typically taken to be an *Intentional* activity, whereby psychological activities such as believing, thinking, remembering, wishing, and desiring intend objects (e.g. a person, for instance, believes that x, or desires that y obtains—Brentano, 1874). Psychological acts then are directed towards states of affairs and thus are particular types of relations between a cognising subject and some known state of affairs, and it is this 'knowing about' or 'knowing that' that distinguishes psychological acts from physical ones. As Maze (1983) writes, "psychological processes are … typified by a kind of relation not to be found in merely physical interactions, and that is the relation of *knowing about* or *referring to*" (p. 83, his italics; cf. Maze & Henry, 1996, p. 1089).

Tamas Pataki (2015) recently takes issue with this account, however, arguing that the position above neither helps elucidate what distinguishes *varieties* of mental acts, nor addresses false beliefs since, "if belief were a species of knowing you could know what was false" (*n*3, p. 38). However, concerning differences between, say, knowing, believing, fearing and wishing (etc.), this is, of course, a sensible matter of enquiry, but like the genus/species distinction, the specific issue being addressed concerns the nature of 'psychological processes' *generally* (i.e. their genus), which identifies their common Intentional character: S believes x; S fears y; S wishes for z, etc., rather than identifying species-level distinctions, even if these are pertinent to any comprehensive position. However, if we take fearing and wishing as examples, the difference appears at least in part to involve a distinct motivational attitude (dislike/like), but in common, all such cases of 'believing', 'fearing', or 'wishing for' (etc.) require knowing *something*, and thus psychological acts can be described as a knowing subject psychologically related to some known object term. On the other hand, in response to Pataki's latter point, it is fair to say that in falsely believing some state of affairs, a 'something' is nevertheless mistakenly believed (i.e. the object of the false belief), such as when a person mistakes a fallen branch for a snake.[4] Thus, falsely believing nevertheless entails falsely believing *something*, and thus an intended object obtains, even if this referring is misdirected.

Determinism and agency

The last essential metaphysical consideration for (neuro)psychoanalytic theorising concerns the nature of causality and specifically the contrast between deterministic

The metaphysics of metapsychology **31**

and teleological approaches. Here metaphysical divisions again underlie criticisms of metapsychology since the distinction of metapsychology and clinical theory is, at times, cast in terms of 'reasons' versus 'causes' (e.g. Stolorow & Atwood, 2013). The topic of causality itself, is of course, complex (see Mackie, 1974; White, 1990) and the position advanced here proposes that rather than simply a cause–effect chain, causality is best understood as a network involving causes and effects occurring within a *causal field* in which both causes and effects operate ("a background against which the causing goes on"—Mackie, 1974, p. 63).[5] Acknowledging the causal field within which both causes and effects operate is important since "different factors can produce the same changes on different fields, and the same factors can produce different changes if interacting with different fields" (Hibberd, 2014, p. 180). A spark, for instance, will cause a particular gas to combust in one causal field (where, say, oxygen is present) and not in another (where, for instance, oxygen is absent). Closer to the psychoanalytic situation, the causal field is directly relevant to whether therapy will be efficacious or not. Insofar as therapy aims to be influential (i.e. causes therapeutic change), any ensuing effects of therapy will be shaped by any individual causal field. Since each person entering therapy constitutes his or her own causal field, psychotherapy might be causally efficacious for one person but not for another, and so, to use a very simple example, while psychotherapy might be effective for people with intact brains, it may be ineffective for someone with pre-existing brain lesions.

For his part, Freud recognises that determinism is necessary for understanding human behaviour (e.g. Freud, 1933a, p. 182; 1940a[1938], pp. 158–159), which entails addressing the necessary and sufficient antedating conditions for any event. A central tenet of Freud's thinking (even if not always consistently espoused), is that "there is, of course, no such thing as arbitrary determination in the mind" (Freud, 1901a, p. 680; cf. 1898b, p. 294; 1906c, pp. 104–105; 1933a, p. 182; 1940a[1938], pp. 158–159), and since every event in the mind is caused, it is such determinism that makes human activity explicable in the natural world. Simply put, without a deterministic outlook, the scientific study of any phenomenon would be impossible, since random, non-causal fluctuations could pervade any field of research (see Maze, 1983, 1987).

While there are various approaches to understandings of determinism (e.g. 'Hard'/'Soft' varieties—James, 1884; Sappington, 1990), it is taken here to simply mean that all events arise out of causal antecedents and go on to cause other events (Hibberd, 2014; McMullen, 1996), and in this respect, causality is a necessary condition for anything to exist. As McMullen (1996) writes:

> Any situation in the world is continuous with certain other situations in that it flows out of some and helps give rise to others. New qualities of things come into being, other qualities cease to be. To perceive this continuity between spatio-temporal complexes is to appreciate that whatever occurs,

32 The metaphysics of metapsychology

> occurs under conditions and is itself a condition for the occurrence of other things. This is the core of determinism. Nothing occurs without conditions, without prior events which give rise to it ... The actions of human beings then, like anything else, are subject to conditions of occurrence and are themselves conditions of other occurrences.
>
> *(p. 65)*

Arguments for or against determinism have a long history, of course (e.g. see, for instance, Stoic philosophy—Bobzien, 1998) and the intention here is not to reiterate this debate (see, however, Berofsky, 1966). It is, however, noteworthy that the view that all behaviour is *caused* clashes with the apparently universal naïve viewpoint that behaviour is a matter not only of choice, but also that this choice is more or less *free* (Sarkissian et al., 2010), a position bound up with our sense of 'agency' and our experience of self-determining our actions. For such reasons, Immergluck (1964) writes that "it is important to realize that psychology, in its broadest sense, represents a very natural last outpost for vitalistic and antideterministic viewpoints" (p. 274), and this antideterminism is seen in the recent resurgence of the so-called psychology of the 'person' which posits a central role for 'agency'. Martin, Sugarman and Thompson (2003), for instance, write that

> *agency* ... refers to the deliberative, reflecting activity of a human being in selecting, framing, choosing, and executing his or her actions in a way that is not fully determined by factors and conditions other than his or her own understanding and reasoning.
>
> *(p. 112, their italics)*

However, their reference to 'not fully determined', indicating that free will and determinism can be somehow compatible (a position sometimes described as 'soft determinism'—Sappington, 1990) is logically flawed since it creates an untenable dualism between the free and caused realms (Hibberd, 2014; McMullen, 1982, 1996; Passmore, 1961). How, for instance, does an unconditioned free act interact with a determined world without annulling the notion of causality itself? Immergluck (1964) recognises the logical implications here:

> Would, for example, the adherents to this view be willing to specify the precise point at which determinism ends and indeterminism, in form of some kind of spontaneous free will, begins? ... Indeed, were we to pursue this point to its logical sequitur, we should be forced to conclude that some areas of behaviour are simply not open to research exploration in the ordinary meaning of that term, namely the uncovering of systematic relationships.
>
> *(p. 276)*

On the other hand for choice to be literally 'free' would mean that under identical causal circumstances different choices and courses of behaviour are possible

The metaphysics of metapsychology **33**

(Immergluck, 1964; Maze, 1983, 1987; McMullen, 1996), as in William James's (1884) example of the decision to either walk down Divinity Avenue or Oxford Street, "everything else being the same" (p. 30). While much attention is still devoted to the possibility of such strict free will (see Kane, 2002), with determinism, if identical causal antecedents obtain then identical effects do so, as well. If this were not the case—so that instead humans could act independently of (or in violation to) those causes—then it would mean that human decisions could somehow violate the fabric of the universe itself: it would be "in principle possible for an organism to cut across, to suspend, whatever mechanical forces might be operating (inside or outside it) to bring about its behaviour" (McMullen, 1982, pp. 226–227). This notwithstanding, how any act of will could literally arise from nothing is impossible to comprehend: such free will would have to be "literally independent of material causes, arising *de novo* from some unconditional source such as a spontaneous act of will" (McMullen, 1982, p. 227; 1996, p. 65). A literal account of free will thus subsequently belongs to the realm of miracles rather than serious scientific enquiry.

Humans, of course, do *appear* to choose between courses of actions (cf. Maze, 1983) but that such choice is illusory is backed up by studies indicating that it is possible to manipulate the illusion of free will (Aarts & van den Bos, 2011; Wegner & Wheatley, 1999). In this respect, one task then for psychology is to explain any apparent choice in terms of causal antecedents (Wise, 2004), some of which include unconscious sources of motivation and cognition, and this is where Freud's metapsychology, as a psychology of what lies beyond naïve consciousness, can make a contribution. However, while the possibility of strict free will can be easily rejected, many psychoanalytic theorists still feel uneasy accepting determinism. Determinism is explicitly rejected in some psychoanalytic writings (e.g. Erdelyi, 1985; Mitchell, 1988; Weinberger & Westen, 2001; Yovell, 2008a), even if these same writers attempt to otherwise *explain* behaviour (whether it be symptoms or the effects of manipulations, etc.) with respect to causal antecedents, which raises the question as to what they take 'determinism' to mean. In this regard some criticisms of Freudian metapsychology indicate that determinism is, at times, taken to be a reductive materialist account of causality, devoid of subjectivity, meaning and 'teleology' (e.g. Gill, 1976), leading to the supposed opposition between 'causes' and 'reasons', sub-intentional versus intentional explanations, or personal versus sub-personal explanations. In some respects here, the apparent tension between metapsychology and clinical theory reflects, on the one hand, the tension between a reductionistic and non-psychological determinism, and on the other, the role of teleology in human activity (goal-directedness, Intentionality and purpose) (e.g. Holt, 1976), and thus an important consideration for psychoanalytic theorising.

Teleology and determinism

Teleological explanations entail a *telos* ('end' or 'purpose'), which acts as a final cause constituting an explanation or partial explanation (for instance, as discussed by Aristotle—see Audi, 1995). For Aristotle, at least, teleology extends to explaining

34 The metaphysics of metapsychology

both animate and inanimate nature (e.g. the apple falls in order to reach its natural resting place) and, taken as such, teleological explanations of behaviour rest upon the premise that an end-state (an effect) is somehow causally efficacious, where, for example, an agent does *A in order to bring about B* (where *B* is some future state of affairs) (see Rychlak, 2000). Humans, of course, do desire states of affairs and such desires appear to be at least partly relevant to explaining what we as humans do when acting purposefully. Nevertheless, it cannot literally be the case that future events—events that have not as yet occurred and may never occur—can actually provide explanations of events. As Mackay (1996) notes, "[t]eleological explanations breach the conditions for explanations; they treat the causes of current actions as goals, states which have not yet come about and indeed may never come about" (p. 10). If anything, the *telos* is an effect to be explained, which would seem explicable via identifying efficient causal antecedents. As Maze (1983) illustrates using an example of the release of adrenaline in response to threat:

> it might be said in describing the 'emergency pattern' of physiological discharges that the adrenal glands secrete adrenalin *in order to* procure the release of red blood cells from the spleen, and that the spleen releases these red blood cells *in order to* provide for the more rapid distribution of oxygen (in case this should be required for the energetic use of the muscles in fighting or fleeing) ... [However] [i]f the adrenaline *causes* the release of the red blood cells, then on any particular occasion (leaving aside the matter of the survival value of such a mechanism making it genetically more common over many generations) the consequences of the spleen's behaviour would be perfectly irrelevant to its occurrence.
>
> *(p. 19, my italics)*

In this example, the 'emergency pattern', while appearing purposive, can be explained sufficiently in terms of causal antecedents, and the supposed 'purpose' does not contribute to the explanation, even if one can understand such responses as resulting from antedating (distal) evolutionary selection pressures. In this respect, Bowlby (1969) similarly realises that while observed behaviour appears teleological, explanation nevertheless requires being made consistent with determinism (Chapter 8 and p. 124). As he says, "[t]he puzzle has always been to understand how an action which has such predictable and useful results can be the effect of causes conceived in terms that are compatible with hard-headed science" (Bowlby, 1969, p. 125). So, while evolutionary accounts might suggest evidence of teleological explanations (for instance, males purportedly prefer to have many sexual partners *in order to* maximise their chances of gene transfer, etc.), such findings can nevertheless be explained in terms of past consequences (acting as *distal* causal antecedents) rather than causally efficacious future consequences (see Wise, 2004, p. 159; Mackie, 1974, pp. 273ff). In fact, White (1990, p. 4) suggests that Aristotle's *telos* can be taken to

The metaphysics of metapsychology **35**

simply refer to a natural outcome rather than an aim or goal *per se*. Consequently, the *telos* is simply an effect to be explained and irrelevant to any causal explanation, and, if anything, teleological 'explanations' simply confuse effects with causes. As Wise (2004) recognises, "[t]he apparent goal direction of motivated behaviour explains nothing; it is the mystery that remains to be explained" (p. 160), and so teleology thus provides another instance of circular explanation, whereby a description of what occurs masquerades as the supposed explanation, under the guise of serving a 'purpose'. Thus, as Waelder (1960) writes, "[w]ithout such explanations of 'how it works,' teleological explanations explain nothing; they merely add to a description of a process the information that it is useful for a purpose, implying that its existence is due to its usefulness" (Waelder, 1960, p. 171).

It is, however, possible to read teleology into Freud's theory, as does Zepf (2001), and this has major consequences for psychoanalytic understanding. For instance, because Freud writes in the *Project* (1950[1895]) that "we have certain knowledge of a trend in psychical life towards *avoiding unpleasure*" (p. 312, Freud's italics; cf. 1916–1917, p. 356), Zepf takes Freud here to mean that we act *in order to* avoid unpleasure, rather than being motivated by unpleasure itself as a causal antecedent, and this leads Zepf (2001) to subsequently conclude that "Freud considers the engine of mental life to be not an efficient but a final cause" (p. 469). Based on this evaluation, if we act in order to avoid unpleasure, Zepf then believes that "the basis of the repression is seen to be not causal but a matter of Intentionality" (p. 468), so, rather than triggered by anxiety, repression is, if anything, done for a reason and is the result of forethought and planning, which would appear antithetical to the outcome of repression itself.

Waelder (1960), however, notes that Freud's use of teleological concepts is generally descriptive: "[t]he teleological concepts of psychoanalysis are used only descriptively and are not meant to be explanations. Freud tried to study their mechanism" (Waelder, 1960, pp, 172–173; cf. Beres, 1965, p. 61), and even the most committed determinist will speak loosely in terms that construe teleological meaning when none is intended. Brierley (1942), in fact, notes that it is unfortunate that Freud shortened what he initially referred to as the 'unpleasure-pleasure principle' to simply the 'pleasure principle' (p. 111), given the shift in theoretical implication discussed above. A non-teleological reading of the unpleasure-pleasure principle would be that, rather than aiming for pleasure (or acting to avoid unpleasure), repression is efficiently instigated by unpleasure, as indicated when Freud writes that "[t]he id, guided by the pleasure principle—that is, by the perception of unpleasure—fends off these tensions in various ways" (Freud, 1923b, p. 47; see, also, Boag, 2012).

Nevertheless, any coherent theory must account for teleology, and here Talvitie and Ihanus (2010) believe that a challenge for (neuro)psychoanalysis is accounting for the interface between these two classes of explanation (pp. 134–135). Macmillan (1991), however, writes that "[a] rigid opposition between cause and reason is no more necessary than one between mind and body" (p. 598), and the apparent

36 The metaphysics of metapsychology

teleology associated with 'reasons' can be accommodated within a deterministic account of causal antecedents. While the thoroughgoing determinism adopted here recognises that nothing occurs without conditions, human factors are just as much part of the causal fabric as anything else (Hibberd, 2014, p. 178), and cognitive acts themselves may stand as causal antecedents influencing behaviour (Maze, 1983; McMullen, 1996; Michell, 1988), even if such human factors must also be explicable in terms of causal antecedents, rather than simply the person determining him- or herself (Hibberd, 2014; Maze, 1983; McMullen, 1996). Cognitive acts, including believing and planning, are not incommensurable with determinism then since there is no logical objection to postulating such processes as causal antecedents involved in apparent goal-directed activity (Maze, 1983; Michell, 1988). The only difference is that these cognitive acts are themselves caused and constitute part of the wider causal circumstances leading to effects. Consequently, denying teleology is not to deny a role for human consciousness, fore-thought, planning, and so on, in behaviour, but how these fit together requires careful consideration.

The metaphysics of psychoanalysis

What this all indicates is that metaphysical issues must be a fundamental concern for psychoanalytic theorists since such considerations are centrally relevant to the development of theory and various associated logical errors. Moreover, many of the underlying divisions in psychoanalysis appear metaphysical in nature, and thus metaphysical enquiry is necessary for providing a tenable foundation for psychoanalytic theory. While Kantian metaphysics are generally ascribed to Freud, a realist position that recognises the important distinction between relations and their terms helps account for distinguishing various essential theoretical issues, including that of structure and function, body and mind, as well as causality and teleology, all of which are directly addressed in critical discussions of Freudian metapsychology. While critics of metapsychology believe that Freudian metapsychology fails to adequately address the teleology of human actions, apparent teleology can be addressed deterministically and non-reductively with respect to psychological processes acting as causal antecedents. However, whether Freud's theory does so successfully is another matter, and here we must turn to his account of drives as the biological foundations of human action.

Notes

1 Metaphysics is even seen by some as a defence that helps avoid contact with actual experience by postulating general abstract claims, which is further attributed to Freud's metapsychological approach. Stolorow and Atwood (2013), for instance, see metapsychology as a form of "metaphysical illusion through which he [Freud] sought to evade the experience of finitude and existential vulnerability" (p. 413). Nevertheless, Stolorow and Atwood (2013), of course, cannot themselves avoid making general

The metaphysics of metapsychology **37**

abstract claims about the nature of reality, and so appropriately realise that they themselves "have not escaped the metaphysical impulse" (p. 418).

2 Michell (1988) employs a similar argument in his criticism of cognitive representationism. While the object of cognition (the mental representation) is in some sense accounted for in representationalist accounts, the actual *knowing* of that representation is not.

3 Brakel's (2013) diachronic conjunctive token physicalism (DiCoToP) provides a sophisticated account for addressing the relationship between brain states and psychological events. The strength of this position is that it takes into account both synchronic (specific time) and diachronic (across time) views. At any point in time (i.e. synchronically) there will be a specific neuronal assembly of neurons causally relevant to specific mental states. Across time, however (i.e. diachronically), for multiple instances of any given mental state, a conjunctive group of neuronal assemblies must be considered rather than postulating a single synchronic neural assembly. As Brakel recognises, this position provides a platform for understanding neural and psychological changes associated with therapy, and one could add for also understanding neural changes associated with the lifting of repression.

4 There are, of course, various complexities with accounting for such 'errors' but since the objective here is to distinguish psychological activities from physical brain processes the interested reader is referred to Ranzten (1993), Galloway (2000), and Tonneau (2004).

5 Further discussion of causal fields can be found in Baker (1986, Chapter 8), Hibberd (2014, p. 180) and White's (1990) discussion of 'causal frames' (p. 14).

2

THE BIOLOGICAL FOUNDATIONS OF PERSONALITY

Drives and affects

Introduction

Addressing the metaphysical ground prior to theory development provides a foundation for understanding persons and explaining human activity, and given the metaphysical position developed in the previous chapter, a ground-up approach to psychoanalytic theory means assessing whether psychoanalytic accounts satisfy the requirements of a realist, determinist psychology. Freud was also clearly cognisant of such assumptions, and grounded his theory of personality in *Triebe*, translated by Strachey as 'instincts' but now commonly referred to as 'drives' (e.g. McIntosh, 1986; Solms & Turnbull, 2002; Zepf, 2001). These drives are wedded to the economic component of Freud's specific metapsychology, giving rise to the 'drive-discharge' model that became a focal point for criticisms of Freudian metapsychology, and instigating dissent (Bowlby, 1969; Holt, 1976; Klein, 1976). As will be argued, the drive-discharge model is fatally flawed, but whether the concept of drive is necessarily problematic depends upon what is specifically meant by 'drive'. On the position to be developed here, drives anchor mind and personality within the body, which, in conjunction with cognition and the environment, provide a physiological–motivational basis for understanding both rational and irrational actions (cf. Maze, 1983).

The economic viewpoint

The 'economic' viewpoint entails hypothetical nervous energies which can increase, decrease, accumulate, etc., and so can loosely be termed 'quantitative', and are products of the drives. Drives ('instincts') and their mental representatives (which are prototypically 'wishes') accumulate energy and operate within a mental

The biological foundations of personality **39**

apparatus that functions according to laws similar to the theory of thermodynamics (see Laplanche & Pontalis, 1973). The mental apparatus, according to this line of thinking, is set up in such a way that allows (when functioning efficiently) mental energies to 'flow', as well as keeping the amount of energy as low as possible (the so-called Nirvana principle—Freud, 1920g). Freud (1926f) writes:

> From the *economic* standpoint psycho-analysis supposes that the mental representatives of the instincts have a charge (*cathexis*) of definite quantities of energy, and that it is the purpose of the mental apparatus to hinder any damming-up of these mental energies and to keep as low as possible the total amount of the excitations with which it is loaded.
>
> *(pp. 265–266, his italics; cf. Freud, 1914c, pp. 85–86)*

Psychical energy is specifically compared to a substance that accumulates and requires 'discharge', leading to an economic view of affective processes where "affects and emotions correspond to processes of discharge" (Freud, 1915d, p. 178), and constitute the experienced dimension of psychical energy. Freud (1894) writes:

> in mental functions something is to be distinguished—a quota of affect or sum of excitation—which possesses all the characteristics of a quantity (though we have no means of measuring it), which is capable of increase, diminution, displacement and discharge, and which is spread over the memory-traces of ideas somewhat as an electric charge is spread over the surface of a body … This hypothesis … can be applied in the same sense as physicists apply the hypothesis of a flow of electric fluid.
>
> *(pp. 60–61)*

The economic position plays a particularly significant role in Freud's thinking since it is tied up with primary and secondary processes, and free and bound energies respectively (Freud, 1915e, 1940a[1938]). Furthermore, economic factors determine whether conflict becomes psychopathological or not (Freud, 1910a, p. 50; Freud, 1915d, p. 152; 1916–1917, p. 374), as well as also explaining psychoneurotic symptom formation with respect to the re-channelling of blocked excitation. That is, since "repressions behave like dams against the pressure of water" (Freud, 1937c, p. 226), the blocked excitation is diverted into a substitute outlet, so, for instance, blocked psychical energy could be transformed into bodily symptoms and other afflictions, as seen in conversion hysteria.

Problems with the economic viewpoint

Freud's economic line of thinking has been extensively criticised (see Rosenblatt & Thickstun, 1977 for an extensive discussion) and taken literally, the thesis is simply

40 The biological foundations of personality

false given that there is no indication that the nervous system accumulates or discharges 'psychic energy' (Linke, 1998; Mackay, 1996; Maze, 1983, 1993; McCarley, 1998; Rosenblatt & Thickstun, 1977). However, there are various interpretations of what Freud actually means by his economic position. Some believe that the economic point of view, if anything, re-describes psychological processes as quasi-physical ones (e.g. Applegarth, 1971; Klein, 1976; Zepf, 2010), whereas others view Freud's economics as metaphors for motivational states. For instance, as McIntosh (1986) writes, "urges are more or less strong, desires more or less intense. The term 'psychic energy' means simply 'magnitude of urge or desire'" (p. 431; cf. Horowitz, 1977; Lewin & Kubie, in Kubie, 1947; Rosenblatt & Thickstun, 1977; Schwartz, 1987; Wallerstein, 1977; Zepf, 2001). On the other hand, several recent attempts equate Freud's concept of mental energy with brain states and arousal (e.g. Pfaff, 1999; Pfaff & Fisher, 2012; Yovell, 2008a), as found in, for instance, Solms and Zellner (2012a):

> When activity increases in the brainstem nuclei of this system ... the metabolism and activity levels of cortical areas are changed, and organisms become more or less active and more or less responsive to external stimuli. We think that it is therefore fair to make a broad brushstroke correlation between the concept of *psychical energy* in the Freudian model, which is the amount of energy available for performing mental acts, and the functioning of core brain arousal mechanisms in neuropsychological models.
>
> *(p. 54, their italics)*

Alternatively, Freud's economic position has also recently been discussed in relation to free energy and hierarchical cortical systems (Carhart-Harris & Friston, 2010, 2012; Fotopoulou, 2013; Hopkins, 2012, 2015; Solms, 2013). On this viewpoint, the brain is seen as essentially an adaptive inference machine employing Bayesian probability to minimise 'free energy' (otherwise described as prediction error or 'surprise') (Carhart-Harris & Friston, 2010; Friston, 2009, 2010; Friston, Kilner & Harrison, 2006). The brain is able to minimise free energy by employing top-down expectations (internal hierarchical models) to predict sensory input and thus minimise prediction error. Carhart-Harris and Friston (2010, 2012) believe that their model parallels Freud's economic position with respect to the secondary process ego minimising (inhibiting/binding) 'free energy': "In both accounts, higher cortical areas are trying to organize (and thereby explain) activity in lower levels through suppression of their energy" (2012, p. 221; cf. Friston, 2013, p. 39). The adequacy of this specific account will be discussed shortly, but it is noteworthy that neither 'arousal' nor 'free energy' resemble Freud's view whereby amounts of energy require discharge, explain symptom formation, and so on. Instead, given that Freud situates his economic position in relation to motivational states, some discussion of motivation is necessary, to examine whether Freudian theory can provide a foundation for understanding human activity.

What do we mean by motivation?

Any substantive explanation of human behaviour requires an account of motivation to explain why we do what we do. Motivation is historically associated with *conation* (sometimes equated with striving, volition or will), alongside cognition and affection, within the classical trilogy of the mind (Hilgard, 1980). Striving and volition themselves are often coupled with concepts such as goal-directedness, purposive behaviour and teleology—concepts that are commonly taken to mean that human behaviour occurs *for a purpose* and may even be 'free' (see Sappington, 1990). As discussed in the previous chapter, such concepts are problematic, and while some such concepts may be potentially rehabilitated, this needs to be in terms of non-teleological causal antecedents. Deterministic motivational accounts, on the other hand, look to what *moves* or drives behaviour, both in the sense of the causal factors underlying driven behaviour and in the determinants of the direction of those behaviours (Mackay, 1996; Maze, 1983, 1993; Watt, 2012). Accordingly, having rejected teleology in the previous chapter, any coherent account of motivation entails a deterministic account of the antecedent conditions that drive and shape both our behaviour and our psychological relationships with the environment.

Explaining behaviour: desires and beliefs

Wollheim's (1991) observation that Freud extended and deepened the common-sense desire-belief account is a useful starting point for approaching motivational explanations of behaviour. The common-sense (or folk-psychological) model explains behaviour in terms of desires and beliefs, where the 'desire' component provides the motivation for behaviour while the 'belief' component (which includes believing, planning, etc.) plays an instrumental role with respect to guiding the desire. Accordingly, when explaining person P's doing A, for instance, we posit that (i) P desires B; and (ii) P believes that doing A leads to B, and so, to use one of Wollheim's examples, an act of drinking is explicable with respect to both a desire to drink and a belief that water will satisfy that desire.

Beliefs, although necessary, are not sufficient for explaining behaviour since they are *policy neutral* and cannot explain why one person acts upon the belief and why another person does not (e.g. Boag, 2012; Mackay, 1996; Maze, 1973, 1983, 1987; Michell, 1988). Maze (1987) writes:

> Any information which can be put into the form X *leads to* Y can be used either in promoting Y or in avoiding it … The belief, for example, that a certain diet will increase body weight may lead one either to adopt that diet or to avoid it, depending on one's already existing motives or drive state; it may

42 The biological foundations of personality

> produce opposing behaviours in the same person at different times. Thus, as it is identically the same belief operating in each case, it cannot be said to imply either policy. Factual information in itself is policy-neutral; it can initiate behaviour only if it is perceived as relevant to one of the person's existing policies—that is, as relevant to the success of some action pattern specific to a currently active drive state.
>
> *(p. 191, his italics)*

For this reason, attempts to replace Freud's metapsychology with cognitive concepts alone, whether it be with 'schemas' (e.g. Slap & Slap-Shelton, 1994) or 'beliefs' (Frank, 1996), are necessarily incomplete since the belief needs to be supplemented with a desire to explain whether an individual acts upon the belief or not. The same holds, too, for cognitive-perceptual accounts of motivation, as found in the previously discussed position proposing that the brain is essentially an inference machine employing Bayesian probability to minimise free energy (prediction error) (Carhart-Harris & Friston, 2010, 2012; Fotopoulou, 2013; Friston, 2009, 2010; Friston, Kilner & Harrison, 2006). As described earlier, on this view, the brain minimises prediction error (or free-energy) by employing top-down expectations (internal hierarchical models) to predict sensory input, and the better these models are, the better the predictions, and thus less 'surprise'. According to this theory, minimising 'surprise' is the brain's *raison d'etre*, and this position can be described as a cognitive-perceptual account of motivation since it proposes that we primarily act so as to minimise free energy. As Friston et al. (2006) write, "the system will expose itself selectively to causes in the environment that it expects to encounter" (Friston et al., 2006, p. 74), and thus, according to proponents of this view, "a free energy principle for the brain can explain the intimate relationship between perception and action" (Friston et al., 2006, p. 71; cf. Friston, Daunizeau, Kilner, & Kiebel, 2010).

As it stands, however, the free-energy principle is *prima facie* problematic since it is expressed teleologically—"[t]he free energy principle states that systems change to decrease their free energy" (Friston et al., 2006, p. 71; cf. Friston, 2010)—and so we act primarily in order to maintain expectations. In terms of motivation, according to this position, we are essentially predicting creatures and correct prediction is the determining factor of action: "in short; goal-directed behaviour might not be the 'selection' of responses but an emergent property of 'prediction'; in which high-precision predictions seem to have greater motivational salience and control over action" (Friston, 2010, p. 300; cf. Friston et al., 2006, p. 77). Fotopoulou (2013) similarly writes that we act upon the world "to ensure that we satisfy our predictions about the sensory input we expect to receive" (p. 34), and so it follows, then, that "we may not interact with the world to maximise our reward but simply to ensure it behaves as we think it should" (Friston et al., 2006, p. 78).

The biological foundations of personality **43**

However, this account is necessarily incomplete because it provides no specific account of what we are likely to expect in the first place. Consider, for instance, a free energy account of explaining an insect's 'preference' for darkness. Rather than appealing to efficient causes (for example, where light acts as an irritating stimulus), or some kind of motivational system, the insect is said to act *in order to* maintain expectations:

> A simple example might be an insect that 'prefers' the dark; imagine an insect that has evolved to expect the world is dark. It will therefore move into shadows to ensure it always samples a dark environment. From the point of view of an observer, this adaptive behaviour may be [mis]construed as light-avoiding behaviour that has been reinforced by the value of 'shadows'.
>
> *(Friston et al., 2006, p. 78)*

The problem with such an account, however, is that even if the teleology can be made consistent with a deterministic psychology, this proposal of preferences and 'satisfying expectations' leaves motivational policy unspecified and simply 'explains' after the fact. For instance, not all insects avoid sources of light—some, like moths, apparently seek it—and thus some source of the preference (motivational policy) needs to be accounted for. Instead, and as with teleological accounts generally, such cognitive-perceptual accounts of motivation look to effects to explain causes, confuse the two, and are necessarily incomplete and provide no predictions of behaviour.

The nature of desire

However, appealing to 'desires' as efficient causes is not so straightforward either. Desires can be understood as particular psychological relations whereby a subject S desires some state of affairs *p* (e.g. a person desires to eat food or to be free from influenza). Desiring some state of affairs implicates knowing that same state of affairs (although possibly unconsciously, as will be developed) and thus desires, as such, are cognitive acts. While psychological acts themselves may be causally efficacious, there are several problems with using 'desires' as explanations for behaviour. Essentially, the problem with using desires as explanations is that cause and effects are conflated since there is no clear distinction between the desire (as *explanans*) and the behaviour (as *explanandum*). More specifically, if we try to explain S doing *p* by postulating a 'desire for *p*' then the effect is logically connected to the cause and thus cause and effect are conflated with one another, and thus no real explanation is provided (Maze, 1983, pp. 24–25). To avoid circularity (i.e. to avoid explaining the effect in terms of itself), requires that causes and effects be logically distinct (see Boag, 2011a, 2015a; Maze, 1983), and since a 'desire for *x*' describes a relationship

44 The biological foundations of personality

(what the person is doing, *viz.* desiring), we essentially need to know about the internal causes of the person giving rise to desire in the first place, independently of the effect (i.e. the structures and interactions giving rise to that desiring relationship—Maze, 1983).[1] As Mackay (1996) points out,

> any theory must, if it is to be coherent and a serious account of motivation, specify the states of the person that motivate action independently of the motivated action, and be able to show in principle how such states become linked to objects.
>
> *(pp. 10–11)*

Bowlby (1969), agrees, writing that 'wishes' and 'desires' are unsatisfactory causal explanations since such acts similarly require further explanation: "The terms 'wish' and 'desire' refer to a human subject's awareness of the set-goal of some behavioural system or integrate of systems that is *already* in action, or at least alerted for action" (p. 138, his italics). Consequently, attempting to explain what someone is doing in terms of desires and wishes leaves us knowing what a person is doing without knowing what actual causal antecedents are involved, and this consequently rules out some proposed alternatives for Freudian metapsychology. For instance, in his pronouncement that "drive is dead; long live wish!" (Holt, 1976, p. 194), Holt writes that we could "rehabilitate the clinical theory of motivation by clearing away the deadwood of metapsychology, which has buried it to a great extent" (p. 161). This, says Holt, essentially entails replacing the concept of drive with wish. However, since a wish is always for some state of affairs, Holt's proposal can never be satisfactory since it suffers from the same deficiency as appealing to desires as explanations.

Instead, what we need to know is why certain situations are desired in the first place and the relevant causal antecedents and internal states underlying such desires. This is where the concept of drive potentially has something to contribute. As Maze (1983) writes,

> the concept of desire must be turned around from 'striving towards' something to 'being driven' by something else, and the nature and the number of these driving engines be discovered, if we are to avoid that instantly available and completely trivial form of pseudo-explanation, 'Because he wanted to'.
>
> *(Maze, 1983, p. 7)*

The concept of drive

For Freud (1915c), 'drive' (*Trieb*) was a basic concept that was necessary for explaining human behaviour and motivation, as well as providing a bodily foundation for

The biological foundations of personality **45**

the mind's activities. Freud places investigation of drives as the most important consideration for psychology:

> There is no more urgent need in psychology than for a securely founded theory of the instincts on which it might then be possible to build further. Nothing of the sort exists, however, and psycho-analysis is driven to making tentative efforts towards some such theory.
>
> *(Freud, 1925d, pp. 56–57; cf. Freud, 1905d, p. 168, n2 [added 1924])*

Nevertheless, he was painfully aware of the limitations associated with the *psychological* investigation of drives. Drives were "at once the most important and the most obscure element of psychological research" (Freud, 1920g, p. 34; cf. Freud, 1905d, p. 168; 1915c, p. 118) and Freud even describes drives as "mythical entities magnificent in their indefiniteness. In our work we cannot for a moment disregard them, yet we are never sure that we are seeing them clearly" (Freud, 1933a, p. 95).

The place of drives in modern psychoanalysis is, however, much less certain, and many subsequent developments in psychoanalysis have either rejected the drive concept outright (e.g. Holt, 1976; Stolorow & Atwood, 2013), or, if not dispensing with drives altogether, viewing them as add-ons rather than essential foundations for understanding the mind (e.g. Mitchell, 1988). Neuropsychoanalysis, on the other hand, has embraced the drive concept as providing a biological foundation for understanding the mind and behaviour (e.g. Solms & Zellner, 2012a, pp. 50–51), and as Solms and Turnbull (2002) note, without some kind of the drive concept, psychoanalytic explanation becomes divorced from the body, and thus also biology and the natural world:

> The concept of drive seems to be unfashionable in psychoanalysis nowadays. It is unclear why this happened, but it has had the unfortunate result of divorcing psychoanalytic understanding of the human mind from knowledge derived from all other animals. We humans are not exempt from the evolutionary biological forces that shaped other creatures. It is therefore difficult to form an accurate picture of how the human mental apparatus really works without using a concept at least something like Freud's definition of 'drive'.
>
> *(p. 117)*

Nevertheless, it is not difficult to see why there are difficulties with the drive concept in Freudian theory because Freud paints an ontologically obscure picture of them. As Pataki (2014a) notes, "drives are inconsistently characterised throughout Freud's work: sometimes as somatic entities, sometimes as psychological entities and sometimes, rather unhelpfully, as borderline entities" (p. 32). Freud (1913j), for example, writes that "[w]e cannot help regarding the term 'instinct' [drive]

46 The biological foundations of personality

as a concept on the frontier between the spheres of psychology and biology" (p. 182). Again:

> an 'instinct' [drive] appears to us as a concept on the frontier between the mental and the somatic, as the psychical representative of the stimuli originating from within the organism and reaching the mind, as a measure of the demand made upon the mind for work in consequence of its connection with the body.
>
> *(Freud, 1915b, pp. 121–122; cf. Freud, 1905d, p. 168)*

As a frontier concept, drives appear then to somehow either straddle, or exist somewhere in between, mind and body, which has, in turn, led to a variety of interpretations of what Freud actually means here. For instance, Solms (2015) proposes that Freud can be taken to mean that "drives transcend the mind/body split" (p. 216), whereas Barratt (2015a) believes that Freud's drives are "both psyche and soma, yet neither purely psychic … nor purely somatic" (Barratt, 2015a, p. 196). Where interpretations of the frontier concept tend to converge, however, is upon the view that drives are 'forces'. For example, Yovell (2008a) writes that drive "is neither a mental concept nor a biological concept": "like gravity, drive is an inference, an inferred force. It is never something you feel or see, but, rather, something that explains and predicts what you feel and see" (p. 119). Barratt (2015a) similarly writes that drive "is a subtle energy force that *conjoins* psyche and bios" (pp. 197, his italics), while Solms and Zellner (2012a) state that "a drive is something prior to all such mental things— it is the force that gets the mind going. As such, from the mental point of view, drives are inferred entities, unconscious states of 'mind'" (Solms & Zellner, 2012a, p. 52).

This view of drives as forces, somewhere between mind and matter, has been pounced upon by critics of drive theory as speculative metaphysics, devoid of empirical content. Fulgencio (2005), for example, believes that drives are necessarily disembodied forces simply abstracted from observations of behaviour (p. 106; 2007, p. 449), whereas Holt (1976), views drives as reified abstraction giving rise to a "pseudoexplanatory mythology" (p. 180; cf. Stolorow & Atwood, 2013). Freud's life and death drive account (Freud, 1920g) whereby drives appear to simply reflect general trends such as life and death, would appear to support such interpretations, and it is also this conceptualisation of drives as disembodied forces which appears to provide the primary impetus for the development of attachment theory as an alternative approach.

An alternative to the Freudian drives: behavioural systems and attachment

While Bowlby says that attachment theory derived from Freud's, the fundamental difference between Bowlby's and Freud's approaches centres on the adequacy

The biological foundations of personality **47**

of Freud's drive-discharge metapsychological approach. In fact, in comparing his theory to Freud's, Bowlby writes that "[i]t is only at a more abstract metapsychological level [i.e. with respect to psychical energy] that substantial differences exist between the two conceptual systems" (1969, p. 172). In this respect, Bowlby was specifically critical of the economic position entailing "psychical energy that flows and can be discharged through different channels", as well as Freud's proposal of "extremely generalised forces, the life and death instincts" (1969, p. 173). Drive-discharge theory is simply wrong, believes Bowlby, and he cites both empirical and theoretical problems discounting Freud's position. Empirically, says Bowlby, Freud's drive-discharge model simply does not account for the facts. For instance, nest-building behaviour does not stop when any such 'nest-building' drive is exhausted, but rather stops when the nest is built and begins again if the nest is destroyed, neither of which indicate an accumulation or discharge of energy. By the same token, a baby cries when the caregiver is out of sight but stops when the caregiver returns, and such activation and termination of behaviour is similarly not readily explicable in terms of supplies and discharge of energies: "In each case ... the change of behaviour is readily understood as due to signals arising from a change in the environment" (Bowlby, 1969, p. 19; cf. Rosenblatt & Thickstun, 1977).

Aside from failing to address the empirical evidence, Bowlby points to theoretical problems with the Freudian drive approach, including verbal-magic invoked in drive explanations of behaviour. In a similar vein to proposing a 'pulsific faculty' to explain the beating of the heart, Bowlby (1969) sees 'drives' as place-holders for the actual causes of behaviour:

> The truth is that the better we come to understand the causal factors influencing instinctive behaviour the less useful the concept of drive becomes. So long as the springs of action are unknown it is easy and perhaps inevitable to suppose that some special force drives the behaviour forward, perhaps not only initiating it but also directing it in a mysterious yet beneficent way ... Engineers have no need to postulate a special 'aircraft-shooting drive' to account for the behaviour of a predictor-controlled gun, nor physiologists a 'blood-supply drive' to account for the action of the cardio-vascular system.
>
> *(Bowlby, 1969, p. 135)*

Bowlby's criticism here is essentially proposing that, if anything, 'drive' is fundamentally a description of a set of behaviours, and thus no real explanation of the behaviour is provided.

In contrast to Freud's approach, Bowlby (1969) initially avoids 'drive' or 'motivation theory', altogether, and instead focuses on 'instinctive behaviour' (p. 17*n*). Instinctive behaviour, of which attachment is a prime example, follows a recognisably similar pattern amongst all members of a species (or of a sex within a species), and rather than being a simple response, such behaviour reflects a sequence

48 The biological foundations of personality

that has survival value consequences for the individual and/or species, often occurring in the absence of learning opportunities. Nevertheless, in later writings Bowlby shifts his position, and proposes that underlying attachment behaviour is a specific motivational system. Attachment, he says, is "a fundamental form of behaviour with its own internal motivation distinct from feeding and sex, and of no less importance for survival" (Bowlby, 1982, p. 669). Furthermore, this attachment system is "conceived on the analogy of a physiological system organized homeostatically to ensure that a certain physiological measure, such as body temperature or blood pressure, is held between appropriate limits" (Bowlby, 1982, p. 670).

While Bowlby's proposal of attachment system approximates what might be considered a homeostatic drive approach, in place of the drive-discharge model, Bowlby proposes an activation–deactivation mechanism whereby both internal and external environmental cues turn particular behavioural systems on and off. Instinctive behaviour results from the operation of behavioural 'control systems' acting within certain environments, in concert with cognition for prediction and adaptation: "In the place of psychical energy and its discharge, the central concepts are those of behavioural systems and their control, of information, negative feedback, and a behavioural form of homeostasis" (Bowlby, 1969, p. 18; see also Mikulincer & Shaver, 2008).

Bowlby (1969) posits multiple such 'behavioural systems' involved in attachment, including some involved in simple non-goal-corrected Fixed Action Patterns, to other, more complex goal-corrected systems (p. 251). Such behavioural systems, according to Bowlby, are organised via a hierarchy of systems and require knowledge of both the world and one's capabilities, and thus, in contrast to Freud's essentially blind mechanical forces involved in his drive-discharge model, Bowlby's motivational account necessarily embraces cognition. The role of cognition here includes the development of working models of self and others (see Shaver & Mikulincer, 2002, 2008), as well as the critical concept of 'feedback', where the effects of performance are compared with some initial instruction which, in turn, modifies the action to closer approximate reaching the final target. Bowlby thus compares control systems to regulating devices such as a room thermostat, where, in the context of action "the machine is constantly checking the effects of its own performance and basing its further action on the extent to which these effects conform with instruction" (Bowlby, 1969, p. 42). The advantage of such feedback, says Bowlby, allows one to attribute goal-directedness to a machine (such as a guided missile), which addresses apparent teleology teleonomically,[2] and thus makes apparent goal-directedness consistent with a deterministic psychology.

Information also takes on further significance in terms of both the initiation and termination of behaviour. Rather than activity requiring an accumulation of energy, behavioural acts are initiated by information from external and/or bodily sources and terminated via further information concerning the results of the action

The biological foundations of personality **49**

taken. In this respect, behavioural systems are guided by *orienting* stimuli (stimuli that guide behaviour towards a set goal) and *terminating* stimuli (stimuli that bring a sequence of behaviour to an end).[3] Bowlby nevertheless acknowledges a variety of causal antecedents underlying behaviour, including neural processes: "Causal factors … include hormonal levels, actions of the central nervous system, environmental stimuli of special sorts, and proprioceptive feedback from within the organism" (Bowlby, 1973, p. 82). But, in contrast to the drive-discharge model, there is no accumulation of drive energy: "As regards the energy necessary to make the whole work, none is postulated, except, of course, the energy of physics: that is what differentiates the model from the traditional theory" (Bowlby, 1969, p. 18; cf. Mikulincer & Shaver, 2008).[4]

However, while Bowlby's inclusion of cognition and performance feedback is an advance on the drive-discharge model, there is nevertheless a practical problem with identifying behavioural systems in his account. For Bowlby (1969), any number of behavioural systems might be implicated in one and the same behaviour, and thus to avoid the 'placeholder' criticism which he attributes to Freud's drive-discharge model, Bowlby needs to provide a means of objectively identifying such behavioural systems, by, for instance, locating the necessary neural substructures for various behavioural systems. However, while apparently aware of the complexity of deducing systems from behaviour alone, Bowlby and others after him (e.g. Mikulincer & Shaver, 2008), nevertheless maintain a top-down approach by attempting to deduce such systems from behavioural sequences alone. However, as we will see, such a top-down approach leads to the problem of arbitrary assignment of behavioural systems, and simply provides an instance of *ad hoc* theorising (see Boag, 2011a, 2015a; Maze, 1983).[5]

An alternative to the drive-discharge-force account

Freud (1915b), in fact, provides a strategy for avoiding the problems of *ad hoc* theorising about the nature of drives, and despite the problems surrounding his drive-discharge model, Freud proposes a much more sophisticated position whereby drives are not blind bodily forces but instead *psychobiological* systems acting as endogenous stimuli. In this account, drives are complex and a number of components need to be taken into consideration to appreciate what drives actually are. The components include a somatic *source*—drives are embodied—and they operate according to an *aim*, that being obtaining satisfaction, this latter component also related to changes in the somatic source. Instrumental to achieving this aim are *objects*, which involve a variety of environmental situations including oneself, others, various substances, and so forth, which are necessary for achieving the aim. Finally, drives exert a *pressure* by engaging both motor systems and impelling certain psychological activities (such as wishing for, and desiring, certain states of affairs). While this pressure can be metaphorically referred to as a 'force', this is none

50 The biological foundations of personality

other than a reference to either the initiating and stimulating conditions underlying action, or a reference to the activity itself:

> a universal and indispensable attribute of *all* instincts—their instinctual [*trieb-haft*] and 'pressing' character, what might be described as their capacity for initiating movement.
>
> *(Freud, 1909b, p. 141)*

> by the pressure [*Drang*] of an instinct we understand its motor factor, the amount of force or the measure of the demand for which it represents. The characteristic of exercising pressure is common to all instincts: it is in fact their very essence. Every instinct is a piece of activity.
>
> *(Freud, 1915c, p. 122; cf. Freud, 1933a, p. 96)*

In this account of drives, taking all of these aspects of drives into account (source, aim, objects and pressure) substantiates what Freud means by drives as 'frontier' concepts: drives are somatic systems acting as endogenous stimuli that actively impel the organism, both psychologically and behaviourally, into certain relations with the environment, where, and unlike external stimuli, their activity persists until an activity or action is performed leading to a state of 'satisfaction' (i.e. the removal of the endogenous exciting condition) (Freud, 1950[1895], pp. 296–297; 1905d, p. 168; 1915c, pp. 118–119; 1926e, p. 200; 1933a, p. 96). Thus, for Freud, drive sources provide the somatic foundations of personality necessary for understanding the motivational states that drive cognitive activity and all behaviour. In this respect one might view the drive sources as the "metabolic and endocrinological impera-tives of the body" (Solms & Zellner, 2012a, p. 49) and this fact alone about Freud's theory refutes any claim that drives are *disembodied* forces, as some claim (e.g. Fulgencio, 2005, 2007). Fulgencio (2007) even makes the extraordinary claim that Freud *excludes* the body from his theory, writing that

> in Freudian psychoanalysis, the body is as it were excluded, remaining only the representation of the body, or rather the affect, which is a representative of the corresponding bodily excitation. To Freud, the body is a medical or biological, but not a psychoanalytical, issue.
>
> *(p. 450)*

However, to claim that Freud's theory is not interested in somatic processes utterly fails to recognise the *source* of drives, and while the frontier-force concept is enig-matic, 'force', if anything, points to the distinction between what something is (in this case, the somatic drive source) and what it does (the drive's activities). Drives are embodied, but their activities cannot be reduced to the body alone since the drives engage in cognitive/behavioural activities with the environment. Thus,

The biological foundations of personality **51**

Freud is proposing that drives are clearly psychobiological systems since they both stimulate behaviour and engage in cognition, the latter especially evident in the wishful character of the mind and the phenomenon of *wish-fulfilment*.[6] As Hopkins (1995) notes, the phenomenon of wish-fulfilment indicates a distinction between drive *satiation* and *pacification*: with the latter, a drive system may be more or less temporarily *pacified,* if the wished-for situation is believed to obtain (through illusory gratification), whereas *satiation* occurs when the actual satisfying conditions necessary for terminating a drive's operations obtain. The fact that drives may be pacified through illusory gratifying beliefs demonstrates both an essential role for cognition in drive activity, as well as (and contra Bowlby, 1969), a critical role for feedback as an important influence upon drive activity. Furthermore, contra drive critics such as Westen (1997), Freud's drive account does accommodate learnt experience, since learnt sources of satisfaction are clearly influenced by experience (as in the case of shifting love objects), and Freud (1915b) makes clear that it is precisely the influence of experience that creates *vicissitudes* in the expression of drives.

Consequently, while Freud's frontier-force account of drive is opaque, taking into account Freud's complex drive account (which necessarily takes into account the drive's source, aim, object and pressure) means that drives are not ontologically obscure, blind, disembodied forces. Even Fulgencio (2005, 2007), who dismisses drives as speculative disembodied forces, readily accepts that drives (or what he prefers to call 'instincts', to distance his position from Freud's) can be substantiated as "bodily excitations that acquire a meaning and that demand a course of action to achieve satisfaction" (2007, p. 450). On the present analysis, Fulgencio's 'instincts' are not so radically different from Freud's complex accounts of drive, and so Fulgencio might rightly reject the drive-discharge model without necessarily rejecting Freud's sophisticated position on drives *per se*. Insofar as drives are physical sources engaging in psychological activities, drives are not ontologically awkward frontier concepts since they are the embodied foundations underlying psychological and behavioural acts. In this respect, writes Mackay (2002), "drives are the engines of action, and cognitions are the servants of the passions" (p. 6).

Maze's elaboration of drives as 'biological engines'

As just developed, Freud's recognition of the relationship between drives, objects and aims means that the drives are psychobiological systems. However, to further substantiate Freud's position and address the somatic sources underlying the motivational component of the desire-belief model, Maze (1983) proposes that drives exist as neurophysical 'biological engines'. Maze's position is broadly consistent with what is currently known concerning (homeostatic) drives (Berridge, 2004; Sewards & Sewards, 2002, 2003; Watt, 2012; see also Bazan & Detandt, 2013 for a comparison of contemporary neuroscience and Freudian drive theory), and his concern is to provide an account of such drives that satisfies the requirements of

52 The biological foundations of personality

a deterministic psychology. As biological 'engines', Maze's position dispenses with Freud's problematic drive-discharge model since "drives neither store nor create energy" (Maze, 1983, p. 153):

> Instead of an accumulation of energy, one would think … of a continuing input of some specific type of nervous impulse, together in the case of some drives with specific biochemical factors, to the brainstem structure of which the instinctual drive mechanism basically consists. Rather than the consummatory action using up an accumulated store of tension, it would (through some feedback loop) terminate the input to the drive mechanism. In order that the consummatory action should not run off abortively in the absence of the necessary object, the output of the brainstem structure into the motor nerve system would have to be modified by those ongoing processes in the cerebral cortex that mediate the organism's cognitions about the environmental situation; that is, its perceptions of what is present and its beliefs about the effects of possible actions. In these ways the model incorporates the motivational and cognitive aspects of the 'desire plus belief' account of so-called teleological behaviour.
>
> *(Maze, 1983, p. 151)*

It should be immediately apparent from comparing Maze's position above with Bowlby's (1969) proposal earlier that this account of drives does not suffer from the failings of Freud's drive-discharge model, while accommodating the essential role of feedback that Bowlby proposes. Maze's proposal is also consistent with a deterministic psychology, since the drives do not instigate their own behaviour but instead are set in motion by excitatory sensory and biochemical input, such as deprivation or noxious stimulation, whereas drive operation similarly ceases when specific conditions obtain. However, in contradistinction to Bowlby's account, Maze proposes neural drive excitation and satiation centres, even if such centres may be complex and anatomically diffuse (Maze, 1983), and these centres, in principle, provide an objective approach for identifying primary drives. Furthermore, these drives are not immune to experience, and while they initially operate according to inbuilt action programs (*consummatory actions*), such action programs are highly plastic and modifiable, becoming elaborated through learning experiences and motor development, and distorted due to conflict (see Boag, 2012; Maze, 1983; Petocz, 1999).

Consequently, Maze's account of the drives provides a platform for integrating the strengths of both Freud's and Bowlby's respective accounts of motivation, while eliminating the problematic aspects of either account, such as the awkward economics of drive-discharge theory. Furthermore, Maze's account is consistent with both Freud's and Bowlby's deterministic stance, accommodating apparent teleology in goal-directed activity, whereby Maze highlights the essential roles of cognitive states and feedback as causal antecedents, which thus addresses a major criticism of the Freudian drive account (Bowlby, 1969). Additionally, since drives are biological

The biological foundations of personality **53**

(neural) structures they stand logically distinct from the behaviours that emanate from them, and thus such drives provide potential candidates for substantiating the desire-belief model, insofar as drives are logically independent of the behaviours that they are said to cause (see Boag, 2005, 2012; Maze, 1983; Michell, 1988). Furthermore, in terms of motivational policy, drives explain why any event is 'naturally' reinforcing or punishing, and why one and the same event may be gratifying at some times and not at others, given differences in drive activation.

Which drives exist?

Maze (1983) recognises that Freud, in fact, provides an in-principle solution to the problem of arbitrarily deducing which drives exist. If located anywhere, drives exist as *physiological systems* embodied within the individual and Freud appreciated that *psycho*analytic observations of behaviour are limited with respect to what can be inferred about the *source* of any drive (Freud, 1915b). As Freud recognises (contra Schmidt-Hellerau, 2012, p. 116), attempting to identify the precise nature of drives through psychological (or psychoanalytic) enquiry alone is problematic since any behavioural aim may reflect any number of basic drives, where, for instance, consuming food might in fact be satisfying 'hunger', or it might be serving as a substitutive response to sexual frustration. For Freud, then, to circumvent postulating instinctual drives *ad hoc* and *ad libitum,* drives must be identified through investigating the internal workings of the body in terms of their 'source'. As Bibring (1969) recognises, since the behaviours and cognitions emanating from the drives are variable, "the source is relatively constant and is therefore the best qualified to serve as a basis for a classification of the instincts" (p. 295; cf. Freud, 1915c, pp. 123–124; 1933a, p. 97), and as will be later discussed, this strategy allows Panksepp (2008) to identify primary *affective* systems via source criteria, rather than inference from behaviour alone (p. 167).

As discussed elsewhere (e.g. Boag, 2012; Maze, 1983), this is, in fact, a major insight of Freud's since it allows him to avoid the problems associated with the instinct theories of his contemporaries such as McDougall (1923), as well as motivational theories after his, such as Maslow's (1943). For McDougall, for instance, instincts were defined by their *goals* or *aims*: "We must … define any instinct by the nature of the goal, the type of situation, that it seeks to bring about, as well as by the type of situation or object that brings it into activity" (McDougall, 1923, pp. 118–119). However, the early realist writer Holt, commenting on McDougall's instinct theory in the 1930s, recognised that this is a specious explanatory strategy. As Holt writes:

> man is impelled to action, it is said, by his instincts. If he goes with his fellows, it is 'herd instinct' which activates him; if he walks alone, it is the 'anti-social instinct'; if he fights, it is the 'pugnacity instinct'; if he defers to

54 The biological foundations of personality

> another it is the instinct of 'self-abasement'; if he twiddles his thumbs, it is the thumb-twiddling instinct; if he does not twiddle his thumbs, it is the thumb-not-twiddling instinct. Thus, everything is explained with the facility of magic—word magic.
>
> (Holt in Yankelovich, 1973, p. 413)

In other words, attempting to explain any given behaviour by attributing a drive responsible for it is vacuous since the 'evidence' for the drive is always available (Maze, 1983, 1993), and as Freud further recognises, any attempt at specifying drives based on behaviour alone remains only more or less arbitrary:

> What instincts should we suppose there are, and how many? There is obviously a wide opportunity here for arbitrary choice. No objection can be made to anyone's employing the concept of an instinct of play or of destruction or of gregariousness, when the subject-matter demands it and the limitations of psychological analysis allow of it. Nevertheless, we should not neglect to ask ourselves whether instinctual motives like these, which are so highly special-ised on the one hand, do not admit of further dissection in accordance with the *sources* of the instinct, so that only primal instincts—those which cannot be further dissected—can lay claim to importance.
>
> (Freud, 1915c, pp. 123–124, his italics; cf. Freud, 1933a,
p. 95; 1940a[1938], p. 148)

Freud thus recognises that given that several drives may contribute to any behavioural act, or that a drive may find substitutive aims, the goal of any given behaviour is not transparent. Similarly, Yovell (2008b) points out that apparent 'proximity seeking' in adults may be due to any variety of motives (security, sexuality, to provide comfort, reaction to aggressive impulses, or any combination of these), and thus identifying the 'true' goal of any activity thus requires some intuitive interpretation of what someone is really doing, and so does not pro-vide an objective basis for identifying drives (Freud, 1915b; Maze, 1983, 1993). Given this, it is not at all obvious, for instance, that a parent's self-sacrifice for an offspring necessarily means that "social bonding and attachment underpin our most deepest and powerful motivational drivers, at least in those with 'good-enough' socialization" as Watt (2012) believes (p. 104). While there might be merit to Watt's position, outward displays of 'love' may also conceal any number of self-rewarding behaviours, including narcissistic identification (Freud, 1914c; Maze, 1993), and accordingly, when theorists attempt to identify behavioural systems via top-down approaches alone (i.e. examining what an organism or species does) (e.g. Bowlby, 1969; Mikulincer & Shaver, 2008; Rosenblatt, 1985; Rosenblatt & Thickstun, 1977), such approaches are problematic since they fail to provide an objective manner of identifying drives.

Is aggression a primary drive?

An example of the problem of the arbitrary specification of drives is seen when addressing whether aggression is a primary drive requiring satisfaction, or a secondary response to frustration (as in what might be termed 'reactive aggression'). Although some authors consider Freud's (1920g) concept of a death drive (or elaboration thereof) clinically useful (e.g. Feldman, 2000; Segal, 1993), or useful in conjunction with a notion of a primary aggressive drive (e.g. Kernberg, 2009), the specific problem is that one and the same aggressive act can be 'explained' in terms of it being an expression of either a primary aggressive drive or reactive aggression. While obviously context and other factors might provide some evidence for one over the other, a more satisfactory approach would be to examine bio-neurological evidence of a primary death/aggressive drive (i.e. the source) to determine the satisfying basis of such behaviour. It is not enough, however, to simply point to any biological process such as catabolism or apoptosis (e.g. Freud, 1920g; Hoffman, 2004) since what occurs at the cell-level will not necessarily translate into a primary aggressive aim requiring satisfaction. Consequently, it is still possible to agree with Kernberg (2009) that aggression is a "major motivational system" (p. 1018), but whether we have primary aggressive aims that require satisfaction remains to be seen (see also Boag, 2014).

Neuropsychoanalysis and drive theory

Given that somatic sources are best placed to determine which primary drives exist, neuropsychoanalysis has much to potentially offer by way of addressing this question. While there is still no precise list of primary drives (Wright & Panksepp, 2012), at first glance, the accumulating evidence of neural structures underlying drive behaviour is impressive. Solms and Zellner (2012a) go so far as to locate the *source* of drives within hypothalamic need detection mechanisms, involving homeostatic regulatory functions, while associating the *aim* with activation of the mesolimbic dopamine system. On the other hand, the *objects* of the drives, they say, are mediated by the amygdala, orbitofrontal cortex and medial temporal areas.

Nevertheless, there are some thorny theoretical issues that further complicate matters. For instance, it is commonly believed, including by neuropsychoanalysts, that human behaviour requires more than simply primary drives, since both learning and memory ('secondary drives') and higher cognitive processes ('tertiary drives') also need to be taken into account (e.g. Wright & Panksepp, 2012). Such secondary and tertiary drives are believed to reflect an evolutionary hierarchical development of the mind, and the implication and adequacy of this viewpoint will be addressed in Chapter 5. In the meantime, however, there is a question of how affective processes fit into the picture, and while Freud's homeostatic drives may be important (especially within an evolutionary guided account of human

56 The biological foundations of personality

motivation), Watt (2008) believes that Freud failed to satisfactorily link homeostatic drives with primary emotional systems:

> The problem for psychoanalytic drive theory was how to square such simple drive concepts (where one could readily conceptualize how a primary regulatory imbalance generated corrective behaviors) with the far greater complexity of primary emotional systems, especially the vast complexities of adult humans interacting in a complex social and cognitive space.
>
> *(Watt, 2008, p. 174)*

The primary emotional systems are typically interpreted in light of Panksepp's (1999) taxonomy of basic emotions referred to briefly earlier (e.g. Hopkins, 2015; Solms, 2013; Solms & Zellner, 2012b). Panksepp and colleagues (e.g. Panksepp, 1999, 2001, 2005; Panksepp & Biven, 2012; Panksepp & Moskal, 2008) identify seven sub-cortical emotional systems or 'basic emotional command systems', which include SEEKING (appetitive foraging), LUST, FEAR (freezing and flight), RAGE, CARE, PANIC/GRIEF (separation distress), and PLAY, and are distinguished from 'homeostatic affects' (the latter giving expression to the Freudian drives such as hunger and thirst), and also 'sensory affects' such as surprise and disgust (Solms, 2013, 2014; Solms & Zellner, 2012b). However, while the basic emotions are distinguished from 'homeostatic affects' (or Freudian drives), the basic emotions appear to subserve the more basic drives of hunger, thirst and sexuality (etc.), given that these basic emotions appear to be 'action tools' of the primary drives. As Solms and Panksepp (2012) write:

> subcortical affective processes come in at least three major categorical forms; (a) the homeostatic internal bodily drives (such as hunger and thermoregulation); (b) the sensory affects, which help regulate those drives (such as the affective aspects of taste and feelings of coldness and warmth); and (c) the instinctual-emotional networks of the brain, which embody the action tools that ambulant organisms need to satisfy their affective drives in the outside world (such as searching for food and warmth). These instinctual 'survival tools' include: foraging for resources (SEEKING), reproductive eroticism (LUST), protection of the body (FEAR and RAGE), maternal devotion (CARE), separation distress (PANIC/GRIEF), and vigorous positive engagement with conspecifics (PLAY).
>
> *(p. 157)*

From this it appears that the basic emotions are responsive to drive states, and is especially apparent with the SEEKING system, which acts as a general purpose Expecting/Wanting system involved in: (i) goal-directed activities; (ii) generating anticipation and excitement; (iii) 'coupling' (linking drives to objects), and;

The biological foundations of personality **57**

(iv) 'enacting' via consummatory actions (Wright & Panksepp, 2012). Panksepp (1999) similarly writes that "[t]he SEEKING system, under the guidance of various regulatory imbalances, external incentive cues, and past learning, helps take thirsty animals to water, cold animals to warmth, hungry animals to food, and sexually aroused animals towards opportunities for orgasmic gratification" (Panksepp, 1999, p. 167). So, when basic drives are in an excitatory phase, SEEKING instigates "an insistent urge to act in certain ways" which "increases an organic pressure to action" (Liotti & Panksepp, 2004, p. 53).

However, given that the basic emotions are the drives' action tools, it would thus appear incorrect to diminish the importance of the Freudian drives, then, which Solms and Zellner (2012b) nevertheless appear to advocate when they write:

> We should integrate Panksepp's perspective and revise Freud's basic affect theory by diminishing the importance of homeostasis and drive in affective life, giving more emphasis to the 'phylogenetic memory' level of the basic emotions, and adopting Panksepp's taxonomy of drives and emotions as a fresh starting point for collecting human clinical data.
>
> *(p. 142)*

The problem with Solms and Zellner's position above, however, is that they are essentially recommending paying attention to some elements rather than others, to the detriment of understanding how the elements work together as a whole, and thus undoing the integrative metapsychological position that Freud worked so hard to develop. While it is, of course, true that pleasure/unpleasure related to homeostatic gratification/frustration provides only a very basic account of affective experience (Solms, 2014; Solms & Zellner, 2012b), there is no necessary tension between homeostatic drives on the one hand (and their pleasure and unpleasure associated with satiation and frustration respectively), and more complex emotional responses such as anxiety, love, anger etc., on the other. On the contrary, the drives are the policymakers of affective responses generally, which includes accounting for responses such as grief to loss of attachment figures, as well as fear and anger responses (cf. Solms, 2014). Accordingly, when Panksepp and Biven (2012) write that "[a]ll of us get angry at times, especially when our interests are ignored or thwarted" (p. ix), such interests, should one take an embodied account of motivation seriously, will be determined by the drives, and Maze (1987) observes that it is precisely the drive state that is an underlying factor here. To provide a simple example:

> A particular kind of happening might sometimes make a person angry and sometimes not, depending on what pursuit he was engaged in. If I were hungry and wanted to eat, and somebody came and laid out dishes of food

58 The biological foundations of personality

> on my table, I should be quite pleased, but if I were not hungry and wanted to work on that table, and someone came and insisted on covering it with things to eat, I should probably be angry.
>
> *(p. 57)*

Maze's example here indicates that affective responses such as anger are *brought into being* through drive/environment interactions, and it is the drive state that provides the foundation for explaining for both how objects are 'selected', as well as for the intensity and perseveration of any response. Obviously, any integrated psychoanalytic position thus needs to provide a working account of the relationship between embodied drives, affective responses, and their relationship with cognition.

A comment on the relation between motivation, affect and cognition

Taking both motivational and affective systems into account provides a foundation for understanding the role of cognitive processes, including learning and memory, and so-called 'higher' cognitive functions associated with the neocortex. What does not appear to be in contention is the view that our motivational/emotional systems are intimately connected with complex cognitive states such as anticipation. Wright and Panksepp (2012), for instance, claim that "all basic affects have some kind of intrinsic anticipatory function (e.g. FEAR anticipates and protects against destruction)" (p. 9), and, if anything, cognition is in the service of the motivational/affective systems:

> The underlying forces of the mind, which were intrinsically motivational, now provide the future orientation needed for planning and the coherence for more explicit ideas in the mind, and a much more focused experience of motivation emerges, which still has intrinsic and often compelling urges to be enacted but also allows for the experience and analysis of other competing or alternative motivations.
>
> *(Wright & Panksepp, 2012, p. 24)*

In this regard, Watt (2008) suggests that the primary emotional systems might be relevant to predicting homeostatic threat (e.g. potential pain), where, for instance, basic emotional states

> may emerge from forward-looking predictions of pending homeostatic threat (fear anticipates tissue damage and pain, even though these things have not yet been manifested; analogously, separation distress presumably anticipates multiple imminent biological dangers, including compromised thermoregulation and nutrition and exposure to predation).
>
> *(Watt, 2012, p. 100)*

It has also long been recognised that the anticipation of both pleasurable and unpleasurable events gives rise to affective experiences (Freud, 1950[1895], 1926d; Jacobson, 1953), and as Brenner (1974) writes,

> human beings react powerfully, not only to intense unpleasure but even to the expectation or prospect of it. The mere prospect of the repetition of what was painful in the past is enough to cause unpleasure in the present, just as the prospect of what was pleasurable before is enough to cause pleasure now.
>
> *(p. 542)*[7]

However, while affects appear to involve cognition, greater consideration of what affects are is required for determining their precise relation to motivational states.

What are affects?

Freud writes that "psycho-analysis unhesitatingly, ascribes the primacy in mental life to affective processes" (Freud, 1913j, p. 175), and that, emotions correspond to "transformations and end-products arising from these instinctual forces" (p. 179). The problems associated with Freud's drive-discharge theory have, however, led some to propose an antithesis between the supposedly impersonal and non-experiential drives on the one hand, and the clinically relevant, subjectively experienced affects on the other (reflecting the distinction between metapsychology and clinical theory, more generally). For instance, Symington (1993) eschews drive theory because it "obscures our understanding of the mind's emotional activity" (p. 4) and various authors reject drives altogether and favour affects as the primary motivational factor (e.g. Sandler, 1985; Westen, 1997). However, as the preceding discussion indicates, there is no necessary tension between drives and affects, even if some clarification is required concerning their precise relationship.

It is generally accepted that a *sine qua non* of affective states is that they are subjectively experienced. Solms and Zellner (2012b), for example, write that "it is absolutely intrinsic to emotion that it is subjectively felt" (p. 135; cf. Solms, 2013, 2015), and Freud similarly believes that affects involve subjective experience of both unpleasure/pleasure and action, writing:

> And what is an affect in the dynamic sense? It is in any case something highly composite. An affect includes in the first place particular motor innervations or discharges and secondly certain feelings; the latter are of two kinds— perceptions of the motor actions that have occurred and the direct feelings of pleasure and unpleasure which, as we say, give the affect its keynote.
>
> *(Freud, 1916–1917, p. 395)*

60 The biological foundations of personality

A case can also be made for viewing affective experience as Intentional (directed towards objects) since, as Brentano (1874) observes, to be angry, or in love, both implicate an object that one is angry or in love with (Brentano, 1874, pp. 88–89). More recently, Panksepp and Biven (2012) are explicit on this point, writing that "affects are intentional—they are always 'about' something. They are 'propositional attitudes' that arise from 'emotional appraisals'" (p. 20), which suggests that affects, in some respects are relational, whereby a person, for instance, feels angry or in love with some object. There is thus some merit to Zepf's (2001) claim that "affects constitute relations" (p. 479), since, and in line with the anticipatory nature of Panksepp's basic emotions described earlier (e.g. Panksepp & Biven, 2012; Wright & Panksepp, 2012), the relation between drive and object appears affective Zepf (2001), in fact, even writes that "from the very beginning of a drive-determined action, there must be an affective relationship with what is desired" (p. 478; cf. Zepf, 2010, p. 11). This relation can thus be described as an affective propositional attitude, and such attitudes are necessarily cognitive since, as others have recognised, we cannot feel something towards an object without cognition: "As soon as we spell out what frightens, irks or gratifies the person, our report of his emotion will imply that he is thinking in some manner about the item" (Thalberg, 1977, p. 35).

However, the precise nature of this affective relationship can be developed further. To illustrate this, Solms and Zellner (2012b) believe that affects are, in fact, the primary state of consciousness given that they constitute the first experience of subjectivity: "'I feel like *this*' is the origin of consciousness ... in fact it is the essence of consciousness", they write (p. 136, their italics). However, Solms and Zellner further note that with experience, these primary feelings become further related to the world such that a person begins to feel a certain way about specific states of affairs:

> vital needs (represented as deviations from homeostatic set-points) can only be satisfied through interactions with the external world ... Therefore, affects, although inherently subjective, are typically directed towards objects: 'I feel like this *about that*' (cf. the philosophical concept of Intentionality or 'aboutness').
>
> *(Solms, 2013, p. 7, his italics; cf. Solms, 2014)*

What this indicates is that affects are particular ternary relations involving an experiencing subject (S) feeling x about some state of affairs y, and this feeling x about y is necessarily psychological, although whether affects are 'conscious', as is commonly assumed, will be addressed in Chapter 4. However, the basic point here is that as ternary relations, any satisfactory account of affects requires addressing the terms of the relations, and so rather than obscuring the mind's emotional activities, drives provide an important explanatory foundation since

The biological foundations of personality **61**

it is motivation and affect that imbue the world with psychological meaning. As Mackay (2002) writes:

> Psychological meaning (meaningfulness) is motivational salience, that where some object, event, experience has particular salience to a person's interests, established, it is important to note, via the person's construing those objects consciously or unconsciously as means for effecting desires. Now, something does not have psychological meaning just because it stands for something else. Rather, it is meaningful in that it plays some special part in the person's motivational economy. It is because a person hates, fears, or desires something that it has psychological meaning (salience) for that person.
>
> *(p. 7)*

The relation between drives and affective relations is further reflected in the long-standing observation that affects typically arise in relation to frustration and gratification (Arlow, 1977; Jacobson, 1953; Rosenblatt & Thickstun, 1977; Zepf, 2001), where the relationship between drives and affects is generally seen to centre upon drive gratification being associated with *pleasure*, while drive frustration is associated with *unpleasure*. Solms and Zellner (2012a), for instance, write

> that there does seem to be some predictable relationship between oscillations in drive tension and oscillation in the feeling of pleasure and unpleasure; to put it simply, we can say that generally it feels good to have our needs met and feels bad to have our needs go unmet for too long.
>
> *(p. 56)*

In this respect, affects thus appear to be the drives' embodied experience of their relations towards objects, which has far-reaching implications for an integrated psychoanalytic theory, as well for addressing supposed divisions between impersonal drives and experienced affects.

For a start, such embodied experience for regulating the drives is important theoretically, since affective processes confer feedback to the organism about how various aspects of the world relate to the primary motives, which, in turn, has been related to the evolutionary context within which affective systems most likely arose (Rosenblatt & Thickstun, 1977; Solms, 2014; Solms & Panksepp, 2012; Solms & Zellner, 2012a; Watt, 2012; Zepf, 2001). In a similar respect, affects (or feelings[8]) act as important feedback conditions in Bowlby's theory, too, and thus provide an area of convergence between a revised drive theory, neuropsychoanalysis and attachment theory. Bowlby (1969), for instance, writes that "[n]o form of behaviour is accompanied by stronger feeling than is attachment behaviour" (p. 209), and for Bowlby, affects, feelings and emotions arise in relation to an individual's appraisal of organismic states and urges to act, and environmental situations, providing a

62 The biological foundations of personality

valuable source of feedback: "Because an individual is often aware of these processes, they commonly provide him with a monitoring service regarding his own states, urges, and situations" (Bowlby, 1969, p. 105). Not unlike Freud and Maze's position, too, Bowlby even proposes that the resulting changes in the organism's own state resulting from behavioural acts are often experienced as pleasurable/painful, liked/disliked, good/bad (p. 115), while satisfaction and frustration itself is determined by whether a set-goal has been achieved or not. Solms and Zellner (2012b) appear to also have something like this in mind when they write:

> Drives tell the apparatus of the mind—which brings us into contact with the things we need, out there in the world—what the body needs. Now, how do we know that we need something? And how do we know whether the need has been met? In both cases, we have to register the state of our drives (their satisfactions or frustrations); we have to *feel* them. This is the heart of Freud's theory of affect. Emotional feelings (at their most basic, experiences of pleasure versus unpleasure) ultimately register the state of our drives. To the extent that our drives are being met, that is to say, satisfied, we feel pleasure. To the extent that they are not being met, or frustrated, we feel unpleasure.
>
> *(p. 136, their italics)*

On this specific point, the affects appear to help regulate the drives and their behaviours through acting as a set of environmental conditions themselves. Panksepp (2003) writes that "affective/emotional processes provide intrinsic values ... for the guidance of behaviour" (p. 6), and in this respect, any affect produced by the drive-environment relationship provides a new set of environmental (including bodily) conditions within which the drives operate, and which may go on to act as a set of exciting or satiating conditions themselves. Rather, then, than as 'mere by-products', our emotional lives, serve to act as a set of determining conditions, which in turn may explain the ongoing activity of the drives, since such bodily environments may act to trigger or add impetus to any given drive behaviour.

Accordingly, all of this indicates that affects reflect our embodied, motivated relationship with the world, and while drive sources are brain structures that are not open to direct experiences, we can subjectively experience the drive-vicissitudes via affective relations. Rather than the drives obscuring emotional experience, affects provide an indication of the relevant significance of situations to our motivational states and can thus be considered the experienced element of our motivational processes. As Panksepp (2003) suggests, "[a]ffects reflect our internal feelings of goodness and badness ... typically through organismic interactions with the outside world" (p. 6), while Zepf (2001) notes that "affects ... should be regarded as forms whereby drives can attain consciousness, be experienced and act as motives" (p. 478). Viewed in this manner, affects are complex phenomena incorporating drive, bodily, and cognitive-evaluative processes, appearing to have a direct regulatory

The biological foundations of personality **63**

function in accounts of human behaviour and subjectivity, and taken as such, there does not appear to be any necessary barrier to integrating Freud's more sophisticated drive position (divested of its economics), with neuropsychoanalysis and attachment theory, in this particular regard.

Summary

Freud's theory of motivation, when divested of the problematic drive-discharge economics, provides a coherent explanatory foundation for understanding motivational policy and human subjectivity in relation to states of affairs in the world. More specifically, the desire-belief model of explanation can be salvaged by accounting for the motivational 'desire' component with the concept of 'drive', as well as showing how affection and cognition are in the service of our motivational states. As biological creatures, our minds are necessarily embodied and integrated with motivational, affective and cognitive states, rather than existing as separate 'faculties' in competition with one another. The position developed here also accommodates the feedback component of Bowlby's (1969) theory of motivation, as well as integrating current neuropsychoanalytic views, and thus provides a common foundation for the motivational bases posited in these accounts. However, while the discussion thus far has considered the motivational foundations for understanding action, what is still missing from the discussion is motivational conflict, which is a further tenet of psychoanalytic metapsychology and for understanding human behaviour more generally. Conflict is particularly important for understanding complex, 'higher' human activity, since rather than just acting on impulse, for example, we learn to delay gratification and think through various actions and consequences, or even *not* act upon desire. However, how best to conceptualise conflict requires elaboration. Behavioural neuroscience, for its part, appears to underplay the significance of motivational conflict, and Berridge's (2004) review of motivation and drives, for instance, make no explicit reference to either motivational conflict or how conflict may be important for explaining any given action. On the other hand, neuropsychoanalysis typically proposes that conflict is between the 'lower' drives and higher processes, the latter providing the "top-down control of drives" (Solms & Zellner, 2012a, p. 61), a responsibility typically attributed to the prefrontal cortex:

> This capacity for thought allows for more nuanced responses to drive demands in relation to prevailing conditions, as mediated by attention and memory. Free will, in this sense, arises from the freedom not to act which ventromedial prefrontal inhibition allows.
>
> *(Solms & Zellner, 2012a, p. 61)*

However, attributing decision-making to higher functions leads to questions about the motivational policy of such top-down control, and how such processes relate

64 The biological foundations of personality

to other components in psychoanalytic metapsychology, and to address this further requires an exposition of the dynamic view of Freudian metapsychology.

Notes

1 For a discussion of various positions on the relationship between desires and wishes see Pataki (2014a, pp. 4–5).
2 Bowlby (1969) notes that since 'purpose', 'aim' and 'goal' carry teleological associations, he prefers the term 'teleonomic' (from Pittendrigh, 1958; see Thompson, 1987) "to denote any system, living or mechanical, that is so constructed that, when activated in its environment of adaptedness, it achieves a predictable outcome" (p. 139).
3 However, terminating stimuli are different from what Bowlby refers to as 'inhibitory stimuli', the latter preventing a sequence of behaviour from occurring: "Such inhibitory stimuli usually originate in some other behavioural system that is also on the brink of activity" (Bowlby, 1969, p. 96).
4 Bowlby (1969) acknowledges that there may have been a feedback component in Freud's theory but it was eclipsed by other aspects of the theory and never received a clear exposition.
5 The problem concerning the arbitrary assignment of behavioural systems is apparent when contrasting Bowlby (1969), who posits multiple systems underlying attachment, and Mikulincer and Shaver, who posit a single system underlying attachment (Mikulincer & Shaver, 2003, 2008; Shaver & Mikulincer, 2002, 2005).
6 See Pataki (2014a, 2015) for an extensive discussion of Freudian wish fulfilment.
7 Watt notes that such affective anticipation implies that the brain can be said to act as a 'predictive engine', as proposed by the Bayesian brain position discussed earlier (cf. Carhart-Harris & Friston, 2010; Friston, 2009, 2010). However, unlike that account, such prediction is substantiated in terms of primary drives and basic emotions, rather than unspecified sources of 'preference'.
8 Bowlby (1969) prefers the term 'feeling' to either 'affect' or 'emotion' since it is the only one of the three terms directly derived from a verb ('to feel'), "having exactly the same meaning as itself" (p. 105), and thus less likely to be reified (cf. p. 123).

3
REPRESSION AND THE METAPSYCHOLOGY OF DEFENCE

Introduction

While, for Freud, drives and affects provide the foundations of personality, it is conflict, repression, and defence that provide the foundations for psychoanalytic theory generally and his metapsychology specifically. Freud declared that the "theory of repression is the corner-stone on which the whole structure of psychoanalysis rests" (Freud, 1914d, p. 16; cf. Freud, 1925d, p. 30) and a simple reason for this concerns the effects of repression. Freud (1915d) writes that "*the essence of repression lies simply in turning something away, and keeping it at a distance, from the conscious*" (p. 147, his italics), and the targets of repression are typically desires and wishes ('instinctual representatives'—Freud, 1915d) that invoke anxiety and are blocked from both awareness and being acted upon. These targets, however, fuelled by their endogenous sources, are not thereafter destroyed but instead persist and remain causally active (Freud, 1900a, p. 577; 1915e, p. 166; 1919g, p. 260; 1933a, p. 68; 1939a, p. 95), which then allows Freud to explain the symptoms of the psychoneuroses and other phenomena, such as dreams and slips, in terms of repressed wishes, blocked from primary sources of gratification, acquiring substitutive ones (e.g. Freud, 1926f, p. 267; 1939a, p. 127). Conflict and repression thus provide Freud with a *dynamic* explanation of psychoneurotic symptoms, and indeed the mind generally:

> We seek not merely to describe and to classify phenomena, but to understand them as signs of an interplay of forces in the mind, as a manifestation of purposeful intentions working concurrently or in mutual opposition. We are concerned with a *dynamic view* of mental phenomena.
>
> (*Freud, 1916–1917, p. 67, his italics*)

66 Repression and the metapsychology of defence

The mind is thus pictured as an economy of competing motives, underlying both normal and pathological behaviour. In fact, writes Freud, given that impulses are generally not afforded free reign, "the maintenance of certain internal resistances is a *sine qua non* of normality" (Freud, 1940a[1938], p. 161), and thus repression is part of everyday human existence and even necessary for adaptive functioning. However, if there was any room left for doubting the centrality of repression in Freud's thinking, repression is also a cornerstone in terms of clinical practice. From very early, Freud recognised that repression manifests itself in therapy as *resistance* to making the repressed conscious, and given that psychoanalytic therapy "aims at ... nothing other than the uncovering of what is unconscious in mental life" (Freud, 1916–1917, p. 389), overcoming resistances becomes a central therapeutic concern (Freud in Breuer & Freud, 1895d, pp. 269–270; Freud, 1910k, p. 225; 1913c, pp. 141–142; 1919a, p. 159; 1937d, p. 257).

Be this as it may, whether repression is actually still a central concern in psychoanalysis is not at all clear. On the one hand, Zepf (2012) writes that "[r]epression is one of the few Freudian concepts that is accepted by most psychoanalysts of different orientations" (p. 397), and Auld, Hyman and Rudzinski (2005) believe that "[r]esistance is ubiquitous in analytic therapy and is inherent in every aspect of the client's participation" (p. 120). On the other, the Blum/Fonagy debate on the clinical relevance of repression (see Blum, 2003a, 2003b; Fonagy, 1999b, 2003) indicates that much of current psychoanalysis views repression as anachronistic and irrelevant to current clinical theory and methods. Approaches emphasising mentalisation, for instance, appear generally uninterested in dynamic repression and view psychopathology as a developmental failure rather than as a consequence of active defence (e.g. Fonagy & Target, 2000). For example, Fonagy and Campbell (2015) believe that the apparent 'repression' of sexuality and aggression is simply a result of neglect rather than resulting from active defence: "sexuality and aggression are the least marked mirrored states in development, thus always remaining somewhat alien, and so prone to acting out" (p. 241). However, while such a 'deficit' account may have its merits, conflict is presumably necessary for explaining why mirroring does not occur in the first place, and so the explanatory value of such deficits appears less than satisfactory, as well as prone to circular explanation. Alternatively, and following a direction in Freud's own thinking (see Petocz, 1999 and Chapter 4 following), a variety of approaches attempt to explain 'repression' by appeal to the notion of qualitatively different processes, where the repressed is unknowable simply because it is in a form incompatible with conscious knowing (e.g. Gardner, 1993; Martindale, 1975; Matte-Blanco, 1975), a view often claiming that the repressed is non-verbal, while consciousness requires language (e.g. Frank, 1969; Frank & Muslin, 1967; Jones, 1993). One problem, however, with such accounts is that they fail to explain how repression operates as a *selective* process, targeting only specific content, since such accounts simply explain a general lack of awareness for a whole class of mental process (e.g. all mental life before the onset of language)(Boag, 2007b, 2012), and

Repression and the metapsychology of defence **67**

so, as Maze and Henry (1996) note, if this were the case then repressions could never be lifted. Nevertheless, the latest manifestation of this approach is reflected in the growing trend in psychoanalysis to embrace 'cognitive neuroscience', which has led to re-positioning psychodynamic processes within cognitive theory (e.g. Bucci, 1997; Davis, 2001; Gabbard & Westen, 2003; Mancia, 2006; Pugh, 2002; Westen & Gabbard, 2002), with further shift towards non-dynamic conceptualisations of repression. Repression no longer requires an active, dynamic rejection of targets and is instead viewed in terms of implicit, procedural and non-declarative processes whereby certain mental contents are simply in a form inaccessible to consciousness. Talvitie and Ihanus (2002) accordingly deduce, "if we treat repressed contents in terms of implicit knowledge, the idea of becoming conscious of the repressed should be abandoned" (p. 1312; cf. Talvitie, 2009).[1]

However, possibly the biggest concern for developing a coherent general theory is that the logical coherency of repression theory remains a matter of dispute (e.g. Talvitie, 2009), and, in particular, Macmillan (1991) disputes Freud's claim that repression can have causal efficacy, writing that repression is logically precluded from referring to any actual process. The specific problem, says Macmillan, is that the repressive process is "uncharacterised and only expresses a relation. We know what it *does* but we do not know what it *is*" (p. 160, his italics), and so description is being confused with explanation. In other words, if repression means nothing more than a 'failure of awareness', then to say that repression causes a 'failure of awareness' is simply to re-describe what is in need of explanation. Repression is thus a circular pseudo-explanation where the effect is being used to explain itself (*a* causes *b*, when *a=b*), and, at best, repression is simply a *post hoc* reification derived from the observation of certain effects. Macmillan subsequently concludes that repression "has no potential for referring to real processes" (Macmillan, 1991, p. 166; cf. Boag, 2007a).

Given the logical requirements set out in Chapter 1, Macmillan is proposing a valid philosophical point here since any satisfactory explanation requires that causes and effect are logically distinct (Mackay, 1996; Maze, 1983) for to say otherwise is to be left saying that the cause somehow brings itself about. Consequently, if repression is said to be capable of explaining a 'lack of awareness', then it needs to be characterised independently of a 'lack of awareness', and there are *prima facie* indications that the effects of repression are all too often re-labelled and used fallaciously to 'explain' the supposed repressive effects. For instance, Solms (2013) writes: "This could be the mechanism of repression: it could consist in a *premature* withdrawal of reflexive awareness (of episodic 'presence'), *premature automatization* of a behavioural algorithm, before it fits the bill" (p. 17, his italics). However, since either 'premature withdrawal' or 'premature automatisation' are redescriptions of the effect of repression, any actual mechanism is left uncharacterised, and thus Solms's position appears to succumb to Macmillan's (1991) criticism. What instead is required then is an account of repression that provides a workable mechanism logically independent of the effects explained. This chapter will address the theory of repression and its

68 Repression and the metapsychology of defence

role in a general metapsychology, and whether the process can be conceptualised independently of its effects (*viz.* independently of 'failure of awareness'). The role of repression in human functioning generally will also be considered, with the aim of showing the repression and response selection can be integrated into an everyday account of human psychology, and one consistent with an account in terms of foundational drives.

Repression and motivated ignoring

Despite any question mark over repression, postulating conflict generally and repression more specifically is essential given the account of bodily grounded foundational drives developed in the previous chapter; the foundational drives are numerous and so some mechanism is required for resolving conflict and competing demands. In this respect, repression is a form of motivated ignoring (selective inattention—see Boag, 2015b) and premised upon Freud's postulated general motivating principle that underlies both normal and pathological behaviour. In the *Project*, Freud writes that "[t]he nervous system has the most decided inclination to a *flight from pain*" (Freud, 1950[1895], p. 307, his italics) and this forms the basis of what Freud initially referred to as the *unpleasure* principle (Freud, 1900a, p. 600). Just as "psychical activity draws back from any event which might arouse unpleasure" (Freud, 1911b, p. 219), repression is comparable to a "flight-reflex in the presence of painful stimuli" (Freud, 1901b, p. 147), involving a *turning away*, or withdrawal of attention from unpleasurable perceptions (Freud, 1900a, p. 600). Thus, rather than 'seeking pleasure' whereby a person acts in order to achieve pleasure, as interpreted by Zepf (2001), which lapses into teleological thinking, repression instead is a response to painful stimulation such as intense anxiety. In this respect, repression is thus comprehensible within a framework of pain-responsive activities, and Freud (1936a) believes that there are various such defensive activities:

> There are an extraordinarily large number of methods (or mechanisms, as we say) used by the ego in the discharge of its defensive functions ... The most primitive and thorough-going of these methods, 'repression', was the starting point of the whole of our deeper understanding of psychopathology. Between repression and what may be termed the normal method of fending off what is distressing or unbearable, by means of recognising it, considering it, making a judgement upon it and taking appropriate action about it, there lie a whole series of more or less clearly pathological methods of behaviour on the part of the ego.
>
> *(pp. 245–246)*

While the relation of repression to defence continues to be dissected (e.g. Zepf, 2012), it is generally accepted (see Boag, 2012, 2015b) that Freud appears to initially

Repression and the metapsychology of defence **69**

use the terms 'repression' and 'defence' synonymously (e.g. Breuer & Freud, 1895d, p. xxix), and then later he describes repression as a distinct mechanism of 'defence' characterised by *hysterical amnesia*, standing in contrast to other defences such as reaction-formation, isolation, undoing and projection: "[Defence] can cover all these processes that have the same purpose—namely, the protection of the ego against instinctual demands—and for subsuming repression under it as a special case" (Freud, 1926a, p. 164). However, while the view that repression is a specific form of defence has many adherents (e.g. Arlow & Brenner, 1964; Brenner, 1957; A. Freud, 1968; Nesse, 1990; Sjöbäck, 1973; Willick, 1995), Madison (1956, 1961) notes that all defences typically include motivated ignoring, and so what distinguishes the various defences is the *target* that is denied awareness: memories are denied in hysteria, logical connections in obsessional neurosis, and ownership of thoughts and impulses in projection (cf. Freud, 1894). Hence, argues Madison (1956), "[r]epression (in the sense of unawareness) is not *one* of a number of defences, it is the essence of all defences" (p. 78, his italics), and so conceptualised, repression can be seen as the basis of all defences (Gillett, 1988; Kinston & Cohen, 1988; Slavin & Grief, 1995), a view again recently promoted by Zepf (2011) who writes that repression is "a generic term referring to the common element of all defences" (p. 59; Zepf, 2012, p. 400). Bazan and Snodgrass (2012) similarly note that while a specific defence, repression "can be considered a universal psychic process insofar as it is constitutive of the dynamic unconscious" (p. 309).

The protagonists of repression

However, how motivational conflict and defensive processes fit into an account of foundational drives requires elaboration. 'Conflict' requires at least two protagonists conflicting (i.e. x conflicts with y), and motivational conflict itself, such as desiring incompatible responses (as with approach-avoidance conflict) is both core Freudian theory, and a phenomenon recognised throughout diverse areas of psychology (e.g. Carver, 2006; Elliot, 2006), and thus this concept potentially unites diverse areas of psychology with psychoanalytic thinking. However, here Freud further provides two incompatible views on the nature of the conflicting forces, and, as will be shown, these diverse views lead to different models of the mind that then provide a further source of pluralism in psychoanalysis. One of Freud's proposals, at first glance, appears straightforward enough. Freud proposes a dynamic interplay of forces underlying repression involving the foundational drives, whose motivated interests could both combine and compete with one another. Freud here writes that

> [p]sycho-analysis derives all mental processes (apart from the reception of external stimuli) from the interplay of forces, which assist or inhibit one another, combine with one another, enter into compromises with one

70 Repression and the metapsychology of defence

> another, etc. All of these forces are originally in the nature of *instincts*; thus they have an organic origin.
>
> *(Freud, 1926f, p. 265, his italics)*

In this account, given that there are multiple drives with varying interests, the mind is pictured as an economy of competing drive-motives where both the repressed and repressing forces spring from the foundational drives. As Freud (1910i) further writes, "instincts are not always compatible with one another; their interests often come into conflict. Opposition between ideas is only an expression of struggles between the various instincts" (pp. 213–214; cf. 1925d, p. 23; 1933a, p. 57), and thus the protagonists of repression can be described in motivational terms, such as "a struggle between motive forces of different degrees of strength or intensity" (Freud in Breuer & Freud, 1895d, p. 270), a "volition ... opposed by a counter-volition" (Freud, 1900a, p. 337) or a "conflict between two opposing impulses" (Freud, 1909d, p. 192).

As noted earlier, positing endogenous motivational sources is consistent with a foundational drive account and has explanatory value since it allows Freud to account for the repressed content's 'upward drive' and subsequent symptom formation in terms of frustrated drive states remaining causally active and forced to acquire substitutes (Freud, 1915c, p. 149). This position further led Freud to develop an initial working hypothesis contrasting the self-preservative drives with the libidinal ones, reflecting the "common, popular distinction between hunger and love" (Freud, 1914c, p. 78) and the 'twofold' function of the individual (*viz.* self- and species-preservation) (Freud, 1913j, p. 182). Freud believed that such a distinction was necessary for addressing psychoneurotic conflict, which was typically between libidinal strivings and the drives constituting the ego:

> The primal conflict which leads to neuroses is one between the sexual instincts and those which maintain the ego. The neuroses represent a more or less partial overpowering of the ego by sexuality after the ego's attempts at suppressing sexuality have failed.
>
> *(Freud, 1913j, p. 181; cf. Freud, 1911c, p. 67)*[2]

Freud's distinction between the self-preservative and libidinal drives will be discussed further in Chapter 5, but while the specific nature of the drives involved in any instance of conflict with one another is an empirical question, Freud's view that the repressed and repressing forces are on the same motivational footing as one another is by no means standard psychodynamic theory. Instead, and resulting from a distinct line in Freud's own thinking, the protagonists of conflict are typically the drives pitted against some 'higher agency' of the mind, acting as inhibiting forces of the foundational drives, a position epitomised in Freud's account of the censoring agency.

A different account of repression: Freud's censor

While Freud provides one account of repression in terms of conflicting drives, another explanation of repression involves a repressing 'censor', which, as will be demonstrated, is also an explanatory strategy to explain repressive processes found in both the self-deception literature (e.g. Pears, 1984, 1986) and attachment theory (e.g. Bowlby, 1980). As discussed elsewhere (Boag, 2006b, 2012), the censorship first appears in the Fliess correspondence where Freud compares the dynamics of the mind to the political oppression in late nineteenth-century Russia (Freud in Masson, 1985, p. 289, his italics[3]). Soon after, Freud draws a similar analogy in *The Interpretation of Dreams* (1900a) where he describes a 'ruthless censorship' that acts exactly like the censorship of newspapers at the Russian frontier (p. 529). Later the censor becomes personified as a 'watchman' preventing wishes in the *Ucs.* from accessing the *Pcs.*, the latter within which consciousness resides: "on the threshold between these two rooms a watchman performs his function: he examines the different mental impulses, acts as a censor, and will not admit them into the drawing room if they displease him" (Freud, 1916–1917, p. 295; cf. 1900a, p. 567). While clearly metaphorical, Freud (1916–1917) writes that such a position "must nevertheless be very far-reaching approximations to the real facts" (p. 296) and Freud's metapsychological paper similarly describes "the rigorous censorship exercises its office at the point of transition from the *Ucs.* to the *Pcs.* (or *Cs.*)" (Freud, 1915d, p. 173; cf. Freud, 1900a, pp. 177, 553, 617; 1915c, p. 153; 1915d, pp. 191–194; 1917a, p. 225). This censor is then carried over into the theory of the superego:

> I might simply say that the special agency which I am beginning to distinguish in the ego is conscience. But it is more prudent to keep the agency as something independent and to suppose that conscience is one of its functions and that self-observation, which is an essential preliminary to the judging activity of conscience, is another of them. And since when we recognise that something has a separate existence we give it a name of its own, from this time forward I will describe this agency in the ego as the '*super-ego*'.
>
> *(Freud, 1933a, p. 60, his italics; cf. Freud, 1914c, p. 95;*
> *1916–1917, pp. 428–429)*

This special agency is specifically a higher examining function that determines what can and cannot become conscious. Freud (1913j) writes,

> [w]e find that there is a 'censorship', a testing agency, at work in us, which decides whether an idea cropping up in the mind shall be allowed to reach consciousness, and which, so far as lies within its power, ruthlessly excludes anything that might produce or revive unpleasure.
>
> *(Freud, 1913j, pp. 170–171; cf. Freud, 1932c, p. 221)*

72 Repression and the metapsychology of defence

Since Freud, accounts implicating censors have proliferated throughout the literature, whether it be in reference to a 'scanning function' (Sandler & Joffe, 1969) or 'appraisal function' (Shill, 2004), the common function being to scan mental content before they are allowed to become conscious (see also Boag, 2012, pp. 152–154).

Why such accounts may have appeal is that they appear to address a particular logical difficulty with Freud's theory repression, whereby repression appears to require knowing the repressed in order not to know it (Maze, 1983; Maze & Henry, 1996). As discussed earlier, in Freud's view, 'wishes' are repressed because they provoke anxiety, and since anxiety requires threat evaluation (see Boag, 2012), the person (or ego) must know the target of repression—on at least one occasion—for repression to occur (Boag, 2007b, 2012; Maze & Henry, 1996). If this were the end of the matter then no problem would arise, but as noted earlier, the repressed persist (e.g. Freud, 1900a, p. 577; 1915e, p. 166; 1919g, p. 260; 1920g, p. 19; 1933a, p. 68; 1939a, p. 95), acquiring substitute aims that may, in turn, also become further targets of repression (Freud, 1909a, p. 124; 1912–1913d, p. 30; 1915c, p. 149), or manifesting as resistance. As Freud (1940a[1938]) writes, "the unconscious ... has a natural 'upward drive' and desires nothing better than to press forward across its settled frontiers into the ego and so to consciousness" (p. 179), and so successful repression appears to require 'screening' mental content for suitability before such content becomes known by the 'ego'. Otherwise, without such censoring, the ego must continuously guard against intrusions of the repressed and thus repression appears to require the repressing subject (the ego) re-knowing the target in order not to know it. A censor, standing as a screen between the repressed and the ego, thus appears to account for how repression can occur unknowingly.

Repression and the problem of self-deception

The logical difficulty with explaining repression is essentially a paradox of self-deception, and repression is at times described as a form of self-deception (e.g. Baumeister, Dale, & Sommer, 1998; Johnson, 1998; Nesse, 1990; Neu, 1988; Slavin, 1985, 1990; Slavin & Grief, 1995). While accounts of self-deception are diverse (see Mele, 1987), self-deception is typically modelled on *interpersonal* deception whereby person A deceives person B into believing that p, when person A believes that not-p. With self-deception, a person believes that p and yet deceives him- or herself that not-p is the case. Freud discusses repression in precisely such terms:

> I must draw an analogy between the criminal and the hysteric. In both we are concerned with a secret, with something hidden ... In the case of the criminal it is a secret which he knows and hides from you, whereas in the case of the hysteric it is a secret which he himself does not know either, which is hidden even from himself.
>
> *(Freud, 1906c, p. 108)*

A similar difficulty in explaining Freudian repression arises in Mele's (2001) discussion of self-deception, where he attempts to explain standard 'garden variety' cases of self-deception involving situations where a person falsely believes that some state of affairs obtains despite evidence to the contrary. A person, for example, may believe that his or her partner is not having an affair when the available evidence would indicate otherwise. For Mele, there is no actual paradox of self-deception since the belief is held simply because the person wishes to believe that this is the case, and while this believing is motivated, there is no necessary implication that the person believes that not-p ($\sim p$) and then comes to deceive him- or herself that p obtains. Mele provides several examples of how desiring that p can lead to the belief in p through misinterpreting relevant evidence. A person desiring p, for instance, may dismiss evidence for $\sim p$ (e.g. an academic might use *ad hominem* attacks to discount a critic's argument) or even interpret evidence of $\sim p$ as supporting p (e.g. the more that someone denies wanting sex, the more this is taken as evidence of his or her sexual desiring). Alternatively, a person may focus on confirmatory evidence via selective evidence-gathering while ignoring disconfirming evidence.

However, as discussed elsewhere (Boag, 2015b), while wishful thinking may explain how confirmatory evidence is selected (which may be fairly simple: I desire that p and thus am sensitive to instances of p in the environment), ignoring otherwise available disconfirmatory evidence requires some further explanation. More specifically, an explanation is required for how critical reflection is prevented from occurring. Mele refers to this lack of critical reflection as *blindness*: "Selective evidence-gathering may be analysed as a combination of hypersensitivity to evidence (and sources of evidence) for the desired state of affairs and blindness—of which there are, of course, degrees—to contrary evidence (and sources thereof)" (p. 27). A person may believe that p because p is desired but the difficult question then becomes one of how the person remains *blind* to evidence to the contrary.

An initial approach here could be to simply propose that we turn our attention from beliefs and evidence that cause us unpleasure. This could be a simple defensive response, premised upon Freud's proposal earlier that "psychical activity draws back from any event which might arouse unpleasure" (Freud, 1911b, p. 219). Mele appears to have this in mind when he writes that "[b]ecause favourable hypotheses are more pleasant to contemplate than unfavourable ones and tend to come more readily to mind, desiring that p increases the probability that one's hypothesis testing will be focused on p rather than $\sim p$" (p. 30). Mele further offers three possible "sources" of such biased belief based on psychological research (*vividness of information*, the *availability heuristic*, and *confirmation bias*), but it can be shown that these sources cannot explain self-deception, since these 'sources', if anything, appear to be descriptions of what is in need of explanation. For instance, 'confirmation bias', says Mele, is the finding that "[p]eople testing a hypothesis tend to search … more often for confirming than for disconfirming instances and to recognize the former more readily …" (p. 29). This 'tending to search for confirmation rather than

74 Repression and the metapsychology of defence

disconfirmation' is, however, what is precisely in need of explanation, and thus to say that people attend to *x* rather than *y* due to 'confirmation bias' is simply a circular explanation (as discussed in Chapter 1). Instead, what requires consideration is explaining *selective inattention* whereby ignoring unpleasant facts cannot preclude the awareness of those same facts, and in the case of Freudian repression, the difficulty is amplified since the repressed persist and push towards conscious thinking.

Does the censor stand up to scrutiny?

Taking Freud's account of the censor literally, Freud is proposing that an *examining* agency cognises and evaluates other mental processes (impulses and desires) before either allowing or forbidding them from entering consciousness. This requires the censor both knowing which wishes and desires are forbidden and acceptable, deciding whether such targets may become conscious or not, as well as knowing appropriate strategies for censoring and distorting repressed material in such a way as to make the offensive material appear innocuous to the conscious system. In this respect, many authors note that the censoring agency thus operates as a sophisticated, *rational* agent, "having beliefs and desires and exercising rational capacities" (Gardner, 1993, p. 49; cf. De Sousa, 1976; Gouws, 2000; Sartre, 1956; Thalberg, 1982).

There are, however, a number of problems with Freud's account of the censor, including logical difficulties with the teleological homunculus (see Boag, 2012, Chapter 9 for further discussion), but what makes Freud's account especially indefensible is that the censoring agency must be a cognising entity *superior* to the normal personality, since, to fulfil its duties, the censor must have unfettered access to all mental acts and be capable of manipulating the workings of the mental apparatus to prevent impulses deemed unlawful (Gardner, 1993; Mirvish, 1990). For example, in Freud's account, the censoring agency transcends the need to sleep, remaining vigilant ('awake') while the ego sleeps (Freud, 1900a, p. 505, added 1914; Freud, 1914c, pp. 97–98), and thus exists beyond any ordinary capacities associated with personhood. As Gardner (1993) thus rightly concludes, the censor "must have a greater capacity than any other part of the mind for (i) representing the contents of other mental parts, and (ii) controlling mental events" (p. 48), which allows critics such as Bonanno and Keuler (1998) to dismiss Freud's theory of repression as requiring a deity-like entity in the mind:

> If our conscious mind cannot bear to process certain memories, then the decision to keep these memories repressed elsewhere, in 'the' unconscious, could only originate in the unconscious. Consequently, 'the' unconscious must have an autonomous quality—an inner 'homunculus' which must somehow possess the omnipotence or wisdom to 'know' what is best for the conscious self.
>
> *(p. 439; cf. Rofé, 2008, p. 66)*

While one strategy here, in response to such criticisms, might be to try and salvage the censor in terms of the drives and some account of mental plurality (see Boag, 2005), any such account, based on the analysis in the preceding chapter, must provide a coherent account of the censor's origin that is consistent with the foundational drive account of mind (cf. Boag, 2006b, 2012; see also Gardner, 1993). Appealing to the theory of the superego does not explain how a *transcendental* agency could develop, since, as will be discussed in Chapters 5 and 6, the superego itself, if anything, is accounted for in terms of both biological and social pressures, whereby drive renunciation based on fear of punishment is associated with identification and compensatory narcissistic gratification (Freud, 1939a, pp. 116–117). While Freud's account here of the superego involves comprehensible 'normal' developmental processes, the postulation of a transcendental independent agency finds no justification.

Freud's account of the censor also does not address Macmillan's (1991) criticism of repression as a pseudo-explanatory term, precluded from referring to 'real processes'. The censor appears to be simply another instance of reification and circular explanation whereby the only evidence for the censoring agency is the censoring act itself, and given that the censor is inferred from the effects of apparent censorship, the 'censor' thus simply renames the phenomenon to be explained (Boag, 2007a, 2012; Macmillan, 1991). As Anspach (1998) notes, "to say that the unconscious drive is repressed by an agent of repression called the 'censor' amounts to no more than putting a name on the phenomenon to be explained" (p. 67; cf. Sartre, 1956, p. 53).

The censor in David Pears' account of self-deception

Problems with the censor and the origins of such an agency are exemplified by David Pears' (1984, 1986) attempt to explain self-deception and irrationality in terms of proposing a protective sub-system. Pears' strategy is to invoke internally consistent sub-systems to account for how a person maintains a belief that p despite evidence that not-p is the actual state of affairs. This, he says, can be achieved through dividing the person into several, distinct rational agencies: "When the relation between certain elements in a single, unified system would be too irrational to be credible, we mark off a subsystem, which rids the main system of the troublesome elements and combines them in a way that is internally rational" (1986, p. 72). Here Pears divides the mind into two independent, intentional systems "crediting each of them with the same kind of internal organization as a whole person" (1984, p. 86). The two protagonists are the *main system* (MS) and *protective system* (PS[4]), each of which is "entirely rational" (p. 87; cf. Pears, 1986, p. 64). The MS generally corresponds to the 'person' or 'ego'; it is the "tolerably rational system of interacting desires and beliefs that maintains its diachronic identity through inner stability and memory and occupies the hot seat between perceptual input

76 Repression and the metapsychology of defence

and behavioural output" (Pears, 1986, pp. 69–70). The MS ordinarily pays attention to reality and forms 'cautionary' beliefs preventing irrationality occurring, so even if the MS desires that p be the case, if the evidence supports not-p, then the undesired cautionary belief (the undesired not-p) is believed. However, anxiety complicates matters: despite not-p being the case, if the MS anxiously wishes that p be the case, this may give rise to the formation of a protective system (PS). Pears (1986) is explicit on this point: the MS's "wish to believe p, … is the force that produces the secession of S [the PS] and motivates all its operations" (Pears, 1986, p. 74), and the PS thereafter becomes an independent system, both dominating the MS and manipulating its beliefs: "dominance and manipulation are the *raison d'être* of the sub-system" (Pears, 1984, p. 89). The PS thereafter "directly attacks the thought-processes of the main system" (Pears, 1986, p. 66) and prevents the cautionary belief forming, so that the irrational belief is held to be true by the MS (Pears, 1986, p. 77).

However, Pears' proposal suffers from similar difficulties to Freud's account of the censor, since, and as with Freud's theory, the account fails to provide a satisfactory account of the origins of the PS. A 'wish' alone, cannot create an independent agency since some independent action must follow-up the wish, and in this case, some activity needs to bring about the creation of a super-ordinate independent agency that, and like Freud's censoring agency, traverses the various systems of the mind (see Pears, 1984, p. 89; Pears, 1986, p. 76), having privileged access to the MS's problems and beliefs, while the MS remains ignorant of the PS's operations (see also Boag, 2005). How the MS could produce a superior agency thus remains inexplicable, and provides no basis for a coherent account of the protagonists of repression.

Repression and defence in attachment theory

While the self-deception literature might be dismissed by some as simply 'philosophy', a version of the censor is similarly found within Bowlby's attachment theory account of repression and defence, and thus presents a hurdle for integrating attachment theory with any general psychoanalytic theory. Bowlby (1980) clearly sees dynamic repression as important for understanding responses to attachment threat, and he proposes a distinction between 'selective exclusion', which simply involves ignoring irrelevant stimuli, and 'defensive exclusion', which is akin to repression:

> the effects of repression are regarded as being due to certain information of significance to the individual being systematically excluded from further processing. Like repression, defensive exclusion is regarded as being at the heart of psychopathology. Only in their theoretical overtones is it necessary to make any distinction between the two concepts.
>
> *(Bowlby, 1980, p. 65; cf. Bowlby, 1982, p. 674)*

Defensive exclusion is generally considered maladaptive, and equated with the defensive deactivation of behavioural systems (Bowlby, 1980, 1982; Mikulincer & Shaver, 2003, 2008; Shaver & Mikulincer, 2002, 2005), and can be contrasted with hyperactivation strategies, entailing preoccupation with attachment figures (Mikulincer & Shaver, 2003, 2008; Shaver & Mikulincer, 2002, 2005). For defensive exclusion to work, since behavioural systems become active due to specific attachment-related information, defensive exclusion must prevent such information from activating the systems: "the system must be immobilized, together with the thoughts and feelings to which such inflows give rise" (Bowlby, 1980, p. 65). Consequently, deactivating strategies must occur both automatically and unconsciously, so that unconscious threat detection occurs independently of the 'person', who remains unaware of any such censoring activity:

> cognitive theory not only gives unconscious mental processes the central place in mental life that analysts have always claimed for them, but presents a picture of the mental apparatus as well able to shut off information of certain specified types and of so doing selectively without the person being aware of what is happening.
>
> *(Bowlby, 1982, p. 674)*

> automatic activation of the attachment system by appraisals of threats and dangers can occur unconsciously and can shape a person's state of mind and behaviour before he or she recognizes the activation in the stream of consciousness.
>
> *(Shaver & Mikulincer, 2005, p. 28; cf. Mikulincer & Shaver, 2003)*

However, while there is evidence that such defensive exclusion can occur unconsciously (e.g. Fraley & Brumbaugh, 2007), what is at issue here is the actual explanation of how this occurs. To explain how unconscious threat detection occurs independently of the 'person' (or ego, etc.), Bowlby (1980, 1982) adopts Erdelyi's (1974) information processing approach whereby 'control systems' internally regulate the flow of information in the system. The specific control system or systems relevant here for explaining repression is the Principle System(s):

> The mental apparatus can be thought of as made up of a very large number of complex control systems, organized in a loosely hierarchical way and with an enormous network of two-way communications between them. At the top of this hierarchy we postulate one or more principal evaluators and controllers, closely linked to long-term memory and comprising a very large number of evaluation (appraisal) scales ranged in some order of precedence. This system, or possibly federation of systems, I shall call the Principal System(s), thus leaving open the question whether it is best regarded as singular or plural.
>
> *(Bowlby, 1980, p. 52)*

78 Repression and the metapsychology of defence

These Principal System(s) take the role of censor, scanning information prior to the rest of the personality and then allowing the information to either move through the system or preventing it:

> On the inflow side the task of these Principal System(s) is to scan all raw data as it becomes available (for fractions of a second or at most a second or two in 'sensory register'), undertake a preliminary analysis and evaluation of it in terms of stored knowledge and relevant scales, and then send commands to an encoder regarding what should be selected for further processing and what should be discarded.
>
> *(Bowlby, 1980, p. 53)*

As with Pears' (1984, 1986) account, Bowlby is essentially shifting the responsibility of defensive exclusion onto a sub-system(s), and these Principal System(s) take on the role of the censor determining what becomes conscious or not. However, and as with Pears' account and Freud's, shifting the responsibility of repression or censorship to either a 'society of demons' (Erdelyi, 1974) or any other set of homunculi provides only a pseudo-explanation since sub-systems can be invented to explain any psychological phenomenon and thus is simply another instance of *ad hoc* speculation. Consequently, the problems associated with Freud's censor are relevant here: the Principle System(s) is a homunculus invoked simply to explain repression and thus attachment theory is without a coherent account of defence.

How do we explain repression?

If repression is not to be explained with respect to a censor then questions arise with respect to how repression occurs and is initiated and maintained. There are actually two facets that require addressing for this: one involves providing a plausible mechanism for repression that is logically independent of its effects (addressing Macmillan's 1991 criticism), and the other involves addressing the role of conscious and unconscious processes so that repression is logically coherent and not self-defeating (Maze & Henry, 1996). The latter will be addressed in the next chapter, while the former will be addressed by examining the concept of anticathexis and recent attempts to explain repression in terms of substitutive investments.

Anticathexis and substitute investments

While Freud appeals to a censor to explain repression, he also employs the concept of 'anticathexes' or 'counter-cathexes' (*Gegenbesetzungen*) to explain how repression is maintained. Unlike the censor account, entailing a teleological, transcendental homunculus, this alternative explanation employs Freud's problematic economic approach. In this respect, when discussing the metapsychology of repression, Freud

Repression and the metapsychology of defence **79**

writes that withdrawing a cathexis from the repressed—such as turning away from an impulse, "as though in an attempt at flight" (1915e, p. 182)—effects only a short-term solution since "the same performance would go on endlessly" given the persistence of the repressed (p. 180). For this reason, says Freud, an anticathexis must be assumed:

> What we require, therefore, is another process which maintains the repression … and … ensures its being established as well as continued. This other process can only be found in the assumption of an *anticathexis*, by means of which the system *Pcs*. protects itself from the pressure upon it of an unconscious idea … It is this which represents the permanent expenditure [of energy] or a primal repression, and which also guarantees the permanence of that repression.
>
> *(Freud, 1915e, p. 181, his italics; cf. Freud, 1916–1917, p. 411; 1925d, pp. 29–30)*

According to Freud, after the initial act of repression (or withdrawal of 'cathexis'), the anticathexis acting as 'counter-force' or 'counter-pressure' prevents the repressed idea breaking through into conscious thought: "[Since] the repressed exercises a continuous pressure in the direction of the conscious, … this pressure must be balanced by an unceasing counter-pressure. Thus the maintenance of a repression involves an uninterrupted expenditure of force …" (Freud, 1915d, p. 151; cf. Freud, 1917d, p. 225; 1926d, p. 157). Freud (1926d) provides a sense of what this force actually entails when describing resistance, where the anticathexis "appears … as a reaction-formation in the ego, and is effected by the reinforcement of the attitude which is the opposite of the instinctual trend that has to be repressed" (p. 157). The anticathexis acts as a 'substitutive investment', where the energy withdrawn from the repressed idea is invested onto another idea, which in turn prevents the repressed idea from emerging into conscious awareness. In the *Project*, Freud refers to this substitute as an "excessively intense idea" (Freud, 1950[1895], p. 349), and the position formally emerges in his early account of conversion hysteria, obsessional neurosis and paranoia. After repression, the affective excitation is channelled either totally or partially into sensory or motor innervation related by association to the traumatic experience (the mnemic symbol), or the affect suffuses a substitute idea, forcing it to take on both a compulsive and irrational character, as found with obsessional thoughts or paranoid distrust (Freud, 1894). As a result of this substitution, the repressed affective memory is no longer accessible since the substitute stands in place of the original memory: the substitutive idea "now plays the part of an anticathexis for the system *Cs*. (*Pcs*) by securing it against an emergence in the *Cs*. of the repressed idea" (Freud, 1915e, p. 182), which provides a substitute-blocking account whereby the repressed idea can no longer be known since the substitute usurps the place in

80 Repression and the metapsychology of defence

consciousness that the repressed would otherwise occupy. Freud (1950[1895]) explains:

> For there has been an occurrence which consisted of $B + A$. A was an incidental circumstance; B was appropriate for producing the lasting effect. The reproduction of this event in memory has now taken a form of such a kind that it is as though A had stepped into B's place. A has become a substitute, a *symbol* for B. ... We [can] convince [ourselves] that whenever anything is evoked, from outside or by association, which should in fact cathect B, A enters consciousness instead of it.
>
> *(p. 349, his italics)*

However, while the preceding explanation describes the formation of the substitute in terms of incidental association, in other instances Freud (1905e) treats anticathexis as synonymous with reaction-formation, writing that

> [t]his process I call *reactive* reinforcement, and the thought which asserts itself with excessive intensity in consciousness and (in the same way as a prejudice) cannot be removed I call a *reactive thought* ... The reactive thought keeps the objectionable one under repression by means of a surplus intensity.
>
> *(p. 55, his italics; cf. Freud, 1908b, p. 171)*

Accordingly, Brenner views reaction-formations as synonymous with anticathexes, writing that Freud's "concept at that time was *not* that reaction formation was evidence of a countercathexis, or a manifestation of a countercathexis, but rather that it *was* the countercathexis" (Brenner, 1957, p. 35, his italics).

An account similar to anticathexis has been recently developed by Zepf (2012), who challenges the position that substitutes form *after* repression, writing instead that "repression is to be understood as the general outcome of forming substitutes" (p. 415). Unlike Freud's general account whereby a drive target is prevented from expression and then forced to find round-about means of gratification (substitute satisfactions), for Zepf the act of substituting one thought with another causes repression: "The original is not crossed through and *afterward* substituted by a different text; it is immediately typed over, by means of which the original is made unreadable" (p. 415, his italics).[5]

However, it is not difficult to see problems with the basic suggestion that repression (as an anticathexis) involves occupying the mind with substitutes, symptoms, or reaction formations so that the repressed cannot emerge. To begin with, the account appears to primarily describe what occurs rather than providing any actual mechanism that is logically independent of the effects, and so Macmillan's (1991) criticism of repression remains unaddressed. Additionally, Zepf's approach is particularly problematic given his explicit teleological stance, since he proposes that a person maintains substitutes *in order to* avoid knowing the repressed and the associated unpleasure. Zepf (2011) writes:

> By virtue of the unpleasure that would be experienced as a result of the instinctual interaction, its mental representation is removed from consciousness, and because of the unpleasure that would again arise if the repressed material were to reappear in consciousness, the individual holds fast to his or her substitute formations.
>
> *(p. 52)*

However, aside from the teleological stance, which precludes coherent explanation, Zepf's account further requires the repressing agent knowing the repressed in order to anticipate prospective unpleasure, which obviously requires knowledge of the repressed, and so would make the process appear self-defeating. This notwithstanding, the general substitute-blockage account fails to explain how repression and resistance occur *without* substitutes, such as with failures of association and gaps in memory, and similarly does not address the active, dynamic, selective nature of secondary repression and resistance (Boag, 2007a). In fact, accounting for resistance is altogether ignored in Zepf's (2012) account of repression, and while he appears to be aware that the 'return of the repressed' creates difficulties for his position, he fails to develop the implications of this. He instead proposes a paradoxical situation where "the repressed is excluded from and remains included in the representational world. In both cases there are substitutive formations and repressions" (p. 406), and while precisely how the repressed is both 'excluded' and 'included' is not made clear, in another paper Zepf appears to mean that the return of the repressed is expressed in the compromise formation, which both reflects the repressed and repressing activities: "in substitute formation repression and the return of the repressed take place simultaneously in one and the same process—in terms of Freud's analogy: the original text is not only crossed through but immediately typed over" (Zepf, 2011, p. 58). However, if this is Zepf's meaning, his account is problematic since we are left again simply with a description of the state of affairs to be explained and we are thus still in need of a mechanism for explaining repression (cf. Macmillan, 1991).

A possible neural mechanism underlying repression

To address Macmillan's (1991) criticism that repression is without potential for referring to a real process, an immediate starting place to look for a possible mechanism for resolving conflict and repression is in terms of neural processes (cf. Maze & Henry, 1996). The advantage of such a strategy is that neural processes stand logically independent of the effects to be explained, and there appears to be ample evidence that unconscious threat evaluation is associated with subcortical processing (e.g. Öhman, 2005, 2009; Öhman, Carlsson, Lundqvist, & Invar, 2007; Phelps &

82 Repression and the metapsychology of defence

LeDoux, 2005). Inhibitory brain processes also appear implicated in various accounts, whether it be along the lines of "the embodied, instinctual brain ... constrained by the cognitive brain with its predictive modelling" (Solms, 2013, p. 18; cf. Solms & Panksepp, 2012, p. 171), or as, for instance, Hopkins (2012) writes that "we can start to understand the Freudian unconscious as the natural product, in our conflicted species, of the management of conflict by the Bayesian brain" (p. 262; cf. Pataki, 2014a, p. 41). However, whether such accounts, as they stand, are coherent or not, requires further attention (and will be addressed in Chapter 5) but for present purposes, it is simply noteworthy that such a direction is *prima facie* plausible for identifying a potential, possible neural mechanism that addresses Macmillan's (1991) claim that repression has no potential for referring to a 'real process'.

Returning to Freud's view of the foundational drives, if we reject postulating a censor standing over and above one's desires and choosing which content to allow to become conscious and acted upon, and instead accept an account of an interaction between multiple drives giving rise to behaviour and repression, then some explanation is required for accounting for what does and does not find expression in behaviour that we commonly refer to as 'choice', as well as selective attention and inhibitory repressive processes. Given both the logical necessity and evidence of drives, the relevant causal antecedents will entail drives and a mechanism for explaining how one desire rather than another is acted upon and another repressed. An example of a suitable mechanism is provided by behavioural neuroscience approaches proposing neural inhibitory/disinhibitory mechanisms, where, for any action to occur, competing actions must also be restrained and prevented from interfering with the action's execution. On this viewpoint, when there are two competing courses of action, X and Y, for X to occur, X must be activated while Y must be inhibited and prevented from accessing the relevant motor execution systems (although not necessarily prevented from non-relevant ones) (Redgrave et al., 1999). It is noteworthy that this behavioural neuroscience framework is congruent with the Freudian one, since both accounts postulate multiple motivational sources and potential conflict, and thus require a mechanism for resolving such competition.[6] Consider, for instance, Mink's (1996) claim that "during any given movement, a multitude of potentially competing motor mechanisms must also be inhibited to prevent them from interfering [with] the desired movement" (p. 382), and while not a case of repression *per se*, there are nevertheless competing actions requiring restraint during any given action. For instance, simply reaching for something requires selective inhibition of posture-holding motor mechanisms, which would otherwise interfere with and prevent the reaching movement. Consequently, as with repression which requires competing impulses being prevented from finding their way into action, Mink proposes that other movements "which had previously been active or that might otherwise compete with the intended movement must also be turned off" (p. 383). Consequently, without some type of inhibitory mechanism, competing motor pattern generators acting simultaneously "would result in

Repression and the metapsychology of defence **83**

ineffective action and cause inappropriate muscular cocontraction and abnormal postures and movements" (Mink, 1996, p. 414; cf. Diamond et al., 1963, p. 81). Neuropsychoanalysis recognises a similar state of affairs, where Wright and Panksepp (2012), for example, note that any general account of successful functioning must address how distinct motivational systems either converge or inhibit one another, in such a way so as to allow adaptive functioning: "in a well-regulated mind, a single coherent behavioral response toward a particular end commonly emerges, diminishing the likelihood of running about in circles in an attempt to carry out competing motivations" (p. 24; cf. Watt, 2012).

Accordingly, both psychoanalysis and these behavioural neuroscience accounts recognise the plurality of potentially competing motivational sources, which indicates that inhibitory mechanisms are required for addressing the outcome of response-competition, of which repression is an example. However, while inhibition may be necessary for understanding response selection it remains an uncharacterised descriptive term until an actual operative mechanism is specified (cf. Macmillan, 1991). To address this matter, an initial response could postulate some type of neural system for reconciling divergent demands, and so, as Watt (2012) proposes with respect to competing motives, "[o]ne cannot do all of these things simultaneously, and the internal competition between goals must be mediated in a neural clearinghouse where all needs, risks and rewards can register and be weighed in some fashion, generating the 'hedonic calculus'" (Watt, 2012, p. 104). Similarly, Wright and Panksepp (2012) propose that the SEEKING system could act as a "central processing unit" providing "an integrative system ..., where drives come together and are thereby intersystemically regulated in order to experience specific drive states" (p. 18).

However, while such neural systems presumably exist, an actual mechanism for conflict and response inhibition is still required, and one possible mechanism underlying apparent choice and response selection has been discussed within the context of what is described as the 'selection problem'. The selection problem "arises whenever two or more competing systems seek simultaneous access to a restricted resource" (Redgrave et al., 1999, p. 1010), and as with repression, the selection problem entails resolving conflict between competing motives. One set of findings suggests that the basal ganglia provide the neural underpinnings of both selection of desired movement and inhibition of competing action. The basal ganglia consist of a group of subcortical nuclei involving the striatum, the pallidum, the subthalamic nucleus, and the substantia nigra (Groenewegen, 2003; Mink, 1996; Redgrave et al., 1999; Stephenson-Jones et al., 2011), and are believed to provide a mechanism mediating "the competition between incompatible inputs" (Redgrave et al., 1999, p. 1016) whereby "selected movements are enabled and competing postures and movements are prevented from interfering with the one selected" (Mink, 1996, p. 414). Since, basal ganglia pathology appears associated with various diseases related to failures of inhibitory control, including difficulties in switching

84 Repression and the metapsychology of defence

between behaviours, and competitive interruptions during actions (e.g. Parkinson's disease, Tourette's syndrome, Huntington's disease) (e.g. Bodden, Dodel, & Kalbe, 2010; Groenewegen, 2003; Kravitz et al., 2010; Mink, 1996; Redgrave et al., 1999; Redgrave et al., 2010), such structures may, indeed, be implicated.

However, whether the basal ganglia, or SEEKING system, or some other brain area is necessary for inhibition is an empirical question, and more to the point here is the actual proposed mechanism. The specific mechanism that could potentially underlie repression, as well as apparent choice and behaviour selection, is a winner-takes-all mechanism entailing competing inputs, thresholds and shut-off mechanisms (cf. Boag, 2007a; Cisek & Kalaska 2010; Hopkins, 2013). The mechanism works along the following lines: when there are competing motivational inputs, any given behavioural outcome results from one input reaching a threshold that shuts off competing inputs and allows execution of the action. While the threshold is at this stage still descriptive, it is not beyond any stretch of the imagination to propose that different responses will take precedence over one another in varying circumstances, since it appears clear that certain motivational states have priority over others according to various circumstances (cf. Rosenblatt & Thickstun, 1977, p. 553). Presumably motivational priority will be a function of relevant deprivation and urgency (what Redgrave et al. describe as the 'salience' of the competing behaviours) so, for example, 'eating' could be expected to occur when both 'hunger' is somatically activated and food is available, while in the absence of immediate threat. However, should a threat arise, responding to the threat could be expected to take priority over eating, causing the termination of eating behaviour and the activation of fleeing behaviour (i.e. a switching of behaviour). Such a neural system does not obviate a role for beliefs and affects, and should such a mechanism apply also to repression, there is no need then for a censor deciding what can or cannot become conscious and acted upon. Instead, repression is explained deterministically, whereby intense anxiety triggers the winner-takes-all threshold, precluding the repressed desire from accessing the relevant motor systems, as well as preventing knowledge of that same desire (Boag, 2007a, 2012). What this demonstrates is that it is possible to find a plausible mechanism for explaining repression independent of its effects and capable of characterising repression as a real (cf. Macmillan, 1991).

The winner might take all but who competes?

What all of this further indicates is that both Freud and the behavioural neuroscience accounts discussed here recognise that conflict—a foundation of psychoanalytic theory—is necessarily a basic component within any theory of mind given the existence of multiple motivational sources with competing aims, and viewed in this light, the selection problem applies to a range of inhibitory-related activities ranging from everyday 'choice' to defensive processes. Nevertheless, behavioural neuroscience accounts are yet to characterise the nature of the competitors involved,

Repression and the metapsychology of defence **85**

and here integration with (neuro)psychoanalysis might be profitable. For instance, Redgrave et al. (1999) ascribe the competing behaviours to an amorphous set of "predisposing conditions" (e.g. Redgrave et al., 1999, p. 1010), which indicates that what is missing from their account is a satisfactory description of the competing motor programs involved in conflict. An account of foundational drives helps fill the gaps in accounts of voluntary or intended movement by providing an account of the sources of conflicting actions *and* the motivational policies of the conflicting systems themselves with respect to the foundational drives. However, while a neural mechanism for repression addresses Macmillan's (1991) criticism, a major gap nevertheless remains in providing a coherent explanation of repression: what precisely is conscious and unconscious when talking about repression?

Notes

1 The evidential standing of repression is also disputed (e.g. Erwin, 1996, 2015; Grünbaum, 1983, 2015). However, with respect to the empirical evidence, repression is commonly conceived in terms of 'motivated forgetting' (as seen in the so-called 'memory wars'—Crews, 1995), and evidence for or against the possibility of forgetting unpleasant stimuli is typically furnished by the proponents of the respective positions (see Boag, 2006a). Be this as it may, given the motivational foundations of personality discussed in the previous chapter, the 'repressed memory' literature generally addresses a truncated account of repression that fails to take into account the greater dynamic picture (consider, for instance, Freud's (1900a) hungry baby example and the role of memory in the formation of wishes (pp. 565–566)), and thus the validity of these findings either for or against repression is questionable.

2 In Freud's view, the sexual drives "are numerous, emanate from a great variety of organic sources, act in the first instances independently of one another and only achieve a more or less complete synthesis at a late stage" (Freud, 1915c, p. 125). Freud believes that the sexual aims are typically targets of repression because of dangers associated with their expression (Freud, 1916–1917, p. 413), but as he points out, although the sexual drives are subjected to repression more than any other drive, this is an empirical rather than an *a priori* assertion: "Theoretically there is no objection to supposing that any sort of instinctual demand might occasion the same repressions and their consequences: but our observation shows us invariably, so far as we can judge, that the excitations that play the pathogenic part arose from the component instincts of sexual life" (Freud, 1940a[1938], p. 186). On the other hand, while the aims of non-sexual drives might be targeted by repression, such aims "could not be permanently and totally repressed while still allowing the subject to live" (Maze, 1993, p. 466).

3 Letter to Fliess dated 22 December 1897.

4 Pears refers to the 'subsystem' or simply 'S' (Pears, 1984, 1986). The term 'Protective system' is from Johnston (1988) based on the system's proposed motivation.

5 As discussed elsewhere (Boag, 2007b), a similar explanatory strategy is proposed in Billig's (1997, 1999) 'dialogic' account of repression. On Billig's view, repression involves occupying the mind so fully with language that forbidden thoughts cannot emerge: "No speaker can be making two utterances at once. Every utterance, which fills a moment of conversational space, is occupying a moment which might have been filled by an infinity of other utterances" (Billig, 1999, p. 52; cf. Billing, 1997, p. 153). Since, on the Freudian model, desires repeatedly force themselves upon the mind, on Billig's (1999) account, the person would have to be *continuously* speaking (e.g. Billig),

86 Repression and the metapsychology of defence

and although Billig's account of desires differs from Freud's—for Billig desires are socially constructed rather than biologically generated—the situation is equally difficult since according to Billig social inhibition and dialogue create desires that need to be repressed: "Repression can be seen to be dialogic, for dialogue involves both the creation of desires and their routine repression" (Billig, 1999, p. 100).

6 In fact, the recognition that competing responses must be prevented from access to the relevant motor execution systems, although not necessarily prevented from non-relevant ones (Redgrave et al., 1999), provides a platform for appreciating how psychoneurotic symptoms can occur as displaced actions.

4

THE METAPSYCHOLOGY OF THE UNCONSCIOUS

Introduction

A fundamental element of any account of mind is addressing the nature of consciousness and the possibility of unconscious mental processes. This is particularly so for psychoanalysis since, as Fonagy and Target (2000) write, "[t]he hallmark of psychoanalytic theory is the attention to unconscious mental processes and unconscious motivation in the explanation of complex and often paradoxical human behaviour" (p. 414) and, as discussed earlier, the very nature of Freud's metapsychology can be described as the psychology of the unconscious (Brenner, 1980). However, there is clearly something difficult in conceptualising unconscious mentality. Searle (2004), for example, writes that "[t]he notion of the unconscious is one of the most confused and ill-thought-out conceptions of modern intellectual life. Yet it seems we cannot get on without it" (p. 256). Furthermore, Freud's theory is considered particularly problematic (e.g. Greenwald, 1992; Uleman, 2005), and complicated by his dissection of unconscious mentality into descriptive, dynamic, and systematic senses (Freud, 1912g, 1915d, 1915e). The difficulties with conceptualising unconscious mentality are compounded by the proliferation of apparent synonyms for the term 'unconscious', including nonconscious, aconscious, or implicit processes, as well as varieties of 'the unconscious', including the 'past' and 'present' unconscious (Sandler & Sandler, 1983, 1994), or the 'cognitive', 'emotional', 'behavioural', 'procedural', 'principle' unconscious systems, etc. (see, for instance, Northoff, 2012).

Nevertheless, the emergence of the so-called 'new unconscious' in the 1980s (e.g. Kihlstrom, 1987) by and large legitimised discussion of unconscious mentality, and the wealth of empirical evidence makes the possibility of unconscious mental processes incontrovertible (see, for instance, Brakel, 2015; Westen, 1999).

88 The metapsychology of the unconscious

Nevertheless, as in Freud's time, mentality is still often equated with consciousness, making 'unconscious mentality' an oxymoron (Searle, 1992, 2004; Talvitie, 2009, 2015; Talvitie & Ihanus, 2003a, 2003b, 2005, 2011; Talvitie & Tiitinen, 2006), and philosophical questions persist concerning what kind of 'thing' unconscious mentality might be (Talvitie, 2009, p. 13; Talvitie & Ihanus, 2011, p. 1589). Given that conceptual clarity is required for sound empirical research in this area (Oppenheim, 2012), coherently conceptualising both unconscious and conscious mentality is essential. As will be argued, it is possible to provide a coherent account of mind that addresses the nature of both unconscious and conscious mentality to serve as a foundation for psychoanalytic theory, not through introducing new terminology, but by examining the distinction between psychological and physiological processes with respect to Brentano's (1874) thesis of Intentionality (i.e. the 'aboutness' or 'ofness' of mental acts). Analysis of Brentano's thesis demonstrates that not only is unconscious mentality defensible, it is logically necessary when the distinction between conscious acts that *know*, and ones that are *known*, is taken into account. However, there are problematic elements of Freud's theory (most notably, his treatment of 'the Unconscious'), and Freud's systemic view of unconscious mentality appears to both reify the cognitive relation and propose a dualism between conscious and unconscious processes that cannot be coherently maintained. This notwithstanding, both Freud's descriptive and dynamic unconscious are defensible and provide a basis for a modified systemic account in terms of primary and secondary mental acts.

The nature of consciousness: Intentionality and mental acts

A useful starting point for addressing the nature of mentality and consciousness is the concept of Intentionality as found in the writings of the Austrian philosopher Franz Brentano (1874). Brentano, following the Scholastics, believes that mental acts could be distinguished from physical processes by virtue of their having a "direction toward an object" (p. 88), which he describes as *Intentionality*. Just as we speak of a perception *of* light or a belief *about* the future, mental acts are always *of* or *about* something and so can be said to *intend objects*. For Brentano, Intentionality distinguishes mentality from physical objects, and this position is accepted by many as the defining criterion of mentality (e.g. Searle, 2004; Solms, 2013, 2014; Zepf, 2011).[1] Brentano (1874) writes:

> Every mental phenomenon includes something as an object within itself, although they do not do so in the same way. In presentation something is presented, in judgement something is affirmed or denied, in love loved, in hate hated, in desire desired and so on ... No physical object exhibits anything like it. We can, therefore, define mental phenomena by saying that they are those which contain an object intentionally within themselves.
>
> *(pp. 88–89)*

Brentano's thesis of Intentionality may have influenced Freud's understanding of the mind and his employment of the term *Besetzung* in psychoanalysis. Freud knew Brentano personally and attended his lectures at the University of Vienna (Fancher, 1977; Merlan, 1945; Jones, 1953; Frampton, 1991; Wollheim, 1991), and Freud appears to have adopted Brentano's concept of *Vorstellungen* ('presentations') (Brentano, 1874, p. 5), translated by Freud's editor Strachey as 'idea', and covering the English terms 'idea', 'image' and 'presentation' (in Freud, 1915d, p. 174).[2] Ideas, in turn, could be invested with affect/psychical energy/attention, reflected in Freud's term *Besetzung*, which Freud's editor Strachey rendered as *cathexis* from the Greek *catechein* meaning 'to occupy'. However, Freud's use of *Besetzung* straddles both phenomenological and economic senses, the latter as a synonym for psychic energy (Laplanche & Pontalis, 1973; Ornston, 2002), whereas with the former, *Besetzung* is more akin to emotional investment, preoccupation, or attention (Ornston, 2002; Pataki, 2014a; Zepf, 2001, 2011), and Freud's own translation of *Besetzung* (in a letter to Ernest Jones) was "interest" (see Gay, 1988, p. 465*n*). The specific similarity between Brentano's thesis of Intentionality and Freud's use of *Besetzung* is that terms such as 'interest', 'emotional investment', 'preoccupation', and 'attention' can all be viewed as certain types of *relations*, where, for example, a person invests in x, or is preoccupied with y, or attends to z, and so on. The same holds true for Brentano's thesis—a person judges x, loves y, or desires z, and this all points to a relational structure of mentality where, more generally, cognition involves a relation between a knower (the subject term of the knowing relation) and the situation known (the object term of the knowing relation[3]). Given the logic of relations described in Chapter 1, in any instance of knowing (where S knows p), there is: (i) a *subject S* that knows something, and; (ii) the something known (p). S's knowing p is entailed by neither (i) nor (ii) alone, and thus any account of cognition thus requires stipulating the subject term (the knower) and object term (the known) involved in the cognitive relation (Anderson, 1962; Boag, 2008b, 2012, 2015c; Maze, 1983). Consequently, taken as a relation, cognition cannot be reduced to anything less than a relation (i.e. mental acts cannot be reduced to either the subject or object term), and so, as Petocz (2006) recognises, "neural processes are necessary but not sufficient for mental processes, and the neurophysiological data pertain to the *subject term only* of the cognitive relation" (pp. 50–51, her italics). That is, although neural processes may constitute one term of the cognitive relation (i.e. the knower) and are even foundationally (structurally) necessary for knowing to occur, the cognitive relation itself is not reducible to them, in the same manner as an entity's activities are not reducible to the entity performing them. Freud essentially makes the same sound distinction concerning the embodied brain and its activities when he writes: "We know two kinds of things about what we call our psyche (our mental life): firstly, its bodily organ and scene of action, the brain (or nervous system) and, on the other hand, our acts of consciousness ..." (Freud, 1940a[1938], p. 144).

90 The metapsychology of the unconscious

Additionally the concept of mental *act* further invokes the concept of motivation, and while (capital-I) Intentionality is commonly treated distinctly from the ordinary conception of 'purposive' Intentionality, Solms (2014) rightly points out that 'aboutness' involves volition—a 'reaching for' objects—and so cognition needs to be understood as 'purposive' within a broader motivational account of mind and cognition. In this respect, acts of knowing, in turn, implicate an engaging and motivated mind, as Passmore (in Anderson, 1962) observes:

> [Knowing] ... is never ... the bare reception of a given object by an act of awareness. Rather, it is an attempt to come to terms with ourselves (in self-knowledge) or the things around us ... In any adequate theory of knowledge the knowing mind must be regarded as a complex entity with its own demands, which are partly satisfied by, partly encounter obstacles in, the complex behaviour of other things, including other people and other tendencies within the same mind.
>
> *(p. xiii)*

Consequently, cognition involves not only the brain/nervous and perceptual systems, but also the motivational ones (the foundational drives and affects), and so our cognitive relation with the world is motivated.

Brentano's thesis of Intentionality and the possibility of unconscious consciousness

While Intentionality is generally seen as the mark of the mental, Brentano's thesis is also used to rule out the possibility of unconscious mentality. The argument goes like this: if mental processes are necessarily Intentional (i.e. conscious of something) then an *unconscious* mental process appears to imply an oxymoronic non-Intentional mental state: "An unconscious mental state is exactly like a conscious mental state only minus the consciousness" (Searle, 2004, p. 238). Consequently, says Searle, since Intentionality means that mental acts necessarily involve awareness, and unconscious processes by definition do not involve awareness, we have then, according to Searle, a paradox:

> Once one adopts the view that mental states are both *in themselves* mental and *in themselves* unconscious, then it is not going to be easy to explain how consciousness fits into the picture. It looks as if the view that mental states are unconscious in themselves has the consequence that consciousness is totally extrinsic, not an essential part of any conscious state or event.
>
> *(Searle, 1992, p. 170, his italics; cf. Searle, 2004, pp. 238–239)*

If anything then, given that mental states, *by definition*, involve awareness, and unconscious states, *by definition*, do not involve awareness, so it follows, argues

The metapsychology of the unconscious **91**

Talvitie (2009), that "the unconscious is only the brain and its neural processes" (p. 94; cf. Searle, 1992, 2004; Talvitie & Ihanus, 2003a, 2003b, 2005, 2011; Talvitie & Tiitinen, 2006). Talvitie subsequently attempts to reformulate unconscious processes in biological non-mental terms, where 'unconscious mentality' is at best a metaphor or clinical tool actually referring to neural states (Talvitie, 2009, 2012). In a comparable manner, Searle (1992, 1995, 2004) distinguishes 'nonconscious' states involving non-mental physical properties from conscious ones that are Intentional (e.g. where S believes that p) and similarly concludes that since unconscious processes are non-Intentional (i.e. without objects) they must be brain states. Such brain states give rise to a 'dispositional unconscious' whereby unconscious states are in fact neural ones that are mental only by virtue of their power to bring about conscious mental states: "Unconscious beliefs are indeed dispositional states of the brain, but they are dispositions to produce conscious thoughts and conscious behaviour" (Searle, 1992, p. 161; cf. Searle, 2004, pp. 248–249).

Brentano similarly rejects unconscious mental processes but for quite different reasons to Searle and Talvitie above. In fact, Brentano sees such arguments above as missing the mark, since the distinction between the *object* of a mental act and the *mental act* itself requires greater consideration. Brentano reasons that while any mental act necessarily involves knowing the intended object, it is of course logically possible for the mental *act* itself to remain un-reflected upon, so that the act itself can be described as unconscious. In other words, Brentano acknowledges a distinction between knowing something and knowing that you know it, and he further addresses an important logical distinction between an unconscious mental process lacking any Intentionality whatsoever (such as a non-red redness) and an Intentional mental act that is simply unknown. He writes:

> We use the term 'unconscious' in two ways. First, in an active sense, speaking of a person who is not conscious of a thing; secondly, in a passive sense, speaking of a thing of which we are not conscious. In the first sense, the expression 'unconscious consciousness' would be a contradiction, but not in the second. It is the latter sense that the term 'unconscious' is used here.
>
> *(Brentano, 1874, pp. 102–103n)*

While Searle and Talvitie appear to be attacking the 'passive' (non-red redness) sense of unconscious mental process, which they quite rightly note is problematic, their arguments against unconscious mentality do not extend to Brentano's 'active' sense whereby, in knowing something it might be possible to not know that same mental act of knowing. In this active sense, there is no logical paradox when proposing unconscious Intentional processes. As Brentano (1874) writes,

> a person who raises the question of whether there is an unconscious consciousness is not being ridiculous in the same way he would be had he asked

92 The metapsychology of the unconscious

> whether there is a non-red redness. An unconscious consciousness is no more
> a contradiction in terms than an unseen case of seeing.
>
> *(Brentano, 1874, p. 102)*

Nevertheless, Brentano rejects such active unconscious mentality, believing that
mental acts are also self-reflexively known insofar as any mental act is incidentally
directed towards itself. A mental act not only intends its object but also itself, so
that in knowing x a person also knows that x is known, sustaining the orthodox
Cartesian view whereby knowing necessitates knowing that we know. Descartes
(1641), for instance, proposes:

> As to the fact that there can be nothing in the mind, in so far as it is a think-
> ing thing, of which it is not aware, this seems to me self-evident. For there
> is nothing that we can understand to be in the mind, regarded in this way,
> that is not a thought or dependent on a thought. If it were not a thought
> or dependent on a thought it would not belong to the mind *qua* thinking
> thing; and we cannot have any thought of which we are not aware at the very
> moment when it is in us.
>
> *(p. 171; cf. Descartes, 1648, p. 357)*

Consequently Brentano (like Descartes) denies the possibility of unconscious
mental acts, not because unconscious mental processes are without Intentionality
but rather because mental acts are self-reflexively known, and so in all practical
senses, unconscious acts are never to be found. The reason for this is that Brentano
assumes "that there is a special connection between the object of inner presentation
and the presentation itself, and that both belong to one and the same mental act"
(p. 127), and he illustrates this with an example of a case of hearing, where both the
sound and the act of hearing the sound are known simultaneously:

> The presentation of the sound and presentation of the presentation of the
> sound form a single mental phenomenon; it is only by considering it in its
> relation to two different objects, one of which is a physical phenomenon
> and the other a mental phenomenon, that we divide it conceptually into
> two presentations. In the same mental phenomenon in which the sound is
> present in our minds we simultaneously apprehend the mental phenomenon
> itself.
>
> *(p. 127)*

Hence, Brentano notes that we can distinguish between two different objects in the
example above: (i), the *primary object* of hearing (the sound; a physical phenomenon),
and; (ii) the *secondary object* which is the mental *act* of hearing (i.e. a mental
phenomenon), and so what appears (according to Brentano) to be a 'single mental

The metapsychology of the unconscious **93**

phenomenon' actually includes two known objects occurring simultaneously, even if the sound must logically occur first:

> sound is the *primary object* of the *act* of hearing, and … the act of hearing itself is the *secondary object*. Temporally they both occur at the same time, but in the nature of the case, the sound is prior. A presentation of the sound without a presentation of the act of hearing would not be inconceivable, at least *a priori*, but a presentation of the act of hearing without a presentation of the sound would be an obvious contradiction.
>
> *(p. 128, his italics)*

However, as discussed elsewhere (Boag, 2015c), an immediate problem here for Brentano (and one that he was aware of) follows from claiming that knowing x further involves knowing that x. This problem involves an infinite regress: if knowing p involves also necessarily knowing that I know it, then I would need to know that, too, and so on, *ad infinitum* (see Maze, 1983, p. 90; Michell, 1988, p. 236). Brentano is cognisant of this threatening infinite regress of knowing acts, and his response is simply to assert that "[f]ar from having to absorb an infinite series of presentations which become more and more complicated, we see the series ends with the second member" (p. 130). That is, Brentano makes an empirical claim that in knowing that x is known, the series simply terminates and the possibility of regress is thus avoided.

On the other hand, Searle (1992) also appreciates a distinction between knowing and knowing that one knows, and even comes to the sound logical conclusion that any mental act is itself unconscious until it becomes the object of a second mental act. However, he does not pursue the matter given that he is also aware of the threat of an infinite regress:

> What about the act of perceiving—is this a mental phenomenon? If so, it must be 'in itself' unconscious, and it would appear that for me to become conscious of that act, I would need some higher-level act of perceiving of my act of perceiving. I am not sure about this, but it looks like an infinite regress argument threatens.
>
> *(Searle, 1992, p. 171)*

However, as noted elsewhere (Boag, 2012, 2015c), Searle's concern here is unfounded. There is only the threat of an infinite regress if the first mental act by *necessity* entails a second, which is precisely the problem for Brentano's (and Descartes') position that knowing necessitates knowing that we know. Put differently, if we accept that mental states involve awareness (of something) it does not logically follow that that same awareness is itself known. Brentano even admits that logically, unconscious mental acts could occur in principle (p. 128), and he

94 The metapsychology of the unconscious

is simply proposing that phenomenologically we experience the object and the act simultaneously. Whether this is the case or not is partly an empirical question, although we need to first consider further what it means to become conscious of a mental act.

Becoming conscious of mental acts

Freud provides an empirical account of how we come to know our own minds:

> In psycho-analysis there is no choice for us but to assert that mental processes are in themselves unconscious, and to liken the perception of them by means of consciousness to the perception of the external world by means of the sense-organs.
>
> *(Freud, 1915e, p. 171; cf. Freud, 1924f; p. 198; 1940a[1938], p. 161)*

That is, the mind's contents are not automatically known and need to discovered, in the same manner as we come to learn about any other situation. Freud's position here appears to have been influenced by Lipps,[4] and on numerous occasions Freud writes that any mental act is initially unconscious: "Everything conscious has an unconscious preliminary stage: whereas what is unconscious may remain at that stage and nevertheless claim to be regarded as having the full value of a psychical process" (Freud, 1900a, pp. 612–613). Moreover, Freud explicitly states that 'psychical acts' begin unconsciously—"every psychical act begins as an unconscious one, and it may either remain so or go developing into consciousness" (Freud, 1912g, p. 264; cf. Freud, 1915e, p. 171; Freud, 1916–1917, pp. 143, 295)—indicating that he is talking of psychological rather than neural processes.

Implied in Freud's position above is the logically sound view that *psychical acts* must exist *logically prior* to any reflection upon them and so mental acts are necessarily unconscious in the first instance until attention is turned to them (cf. Maze, 1983). Freud is on sound logical ground here because, as will be shown, no mental act can be 'conscious' without first having been unconscious as a primary mental act, since a second mental act is required for making any primary mental act known (conscious). More specifically, when S knows (or is conscious of, etc.) p (which can be signified as SRp), that relation of knowing SRp is itself unconscious and does not become conscious unless it becomes the object of a *second mental act* such that S knows SRp (Maze, 1983; Michell, 1988; see also Boag, 2012, 2015c). A person, for instance, will generally hold the belief that the earth is round, but for the most part not be directly or currently aware of holding this belief, and thus here is no logical problem with describing such an unattended belief as an unconsciously held one. Upon reflection, however, a person can typically make such beliefs the present object of attention, and so become conscious of holding the belief, and this act of reflection constitutes a second mental act, reflecting

The metapsychology of the unconscious **95**

upon the first. Furthermore, given that any mental act must logically exist prior to any reflection upon it, Freud is justified in claiming that all mental acts begin unconsciously (unreflected upon), and, moreover, since at any moment we have numerous beliefs, memories (etc.) which we are not currently aware of, Freud recognises that this fact provides indisputable evidence for unconsciously held mental processes:

> We can go further and argue, in support of there being an unconscious psychical state, that at any given moment consciousness includes only a small content, so that the greater part of what we call conscious knowledge must in any case be for very considerable periods of time in a state of latency, that is to say, of being psychically unconscious. When all our latent memories are taken into consideration it becomes totally incomprehensible how the existence of the unconscious can be denied.
>
> *(Freud, 1915e, p. 167; cf. Freud, 1912g, p. 260;*
> *1933a, p. 70; 1939a, p. 95)*

Freud's position is thus consistent with the distinction between 'knowing' and 'knowing that one knows', where mental acts are unconscious when not reflected upon, and conscious when attended to by a second mental act. Consequently, when Freud (1916–1917) writes that psychoanalysis "defines what is mental as processes such as feeling, thinking and willing, and it is obliged to maintain that there is unconscious thinking and unapprehended willing" (p. 22), this can be understood in terms of the distinction between a primary mental act involving knowing or being conscious of x, and a second mental act that is required for knowing that x is known.

The logical distinction between 'knowing' and 'knowing that one knows' is not a new one and has been variously described as the distinction between 'primary' consciousness and a 'secondary reflective' consciousness (Brakel, 2013, p. 41), as well as 'simple awareness' and 'reflexive awareness' (Solms & Turnbull, 2002, p. 82),[5] and so the distinction can possibly provide a foundation for a coherent, integrative account of unconscious mentality. Solms (2014), for example, appears to be proposing the logically sound view that psychical acts remain unconscious until a secondary mental act attends to them, when writing that "[r]emembering, recognizing, judging, navigating, thinking, etc., go on all the time, but these processes only become conscious when we pay attention to them" (p. 178). Nevertheless, Solms is not consistent on this point, especially since his position is conflated with dual-aspect monism, whereby unconscious mental processes refer to some kind of unknowable reality (e.g. Solms, 2003; Solms & Turnbull, 2002). How dual-aspect monism takes into account the distinction between 'knowing' and 'knowing that one knows' is not clear, but the distinction between primary and secondary mental acts finds application for

96 The metapsychology of the unconscious

making sense of various puzzles within psychoanalysis, whereas the same cannot be said for the dual-aspect position.

Can affects be unconscious?

One such puzzle is that of the possibility of unconscious affects. Freud (1915e), like many after him, believes that affects, by definition, are necessarily conscious since they are intimately bound to subjective experience:

> It is surely of the essence of an emotion that we should be aware of it, i.e. that it should become known to consciousness. Thus the possibility of the attribute of unconsciousness would be completely excluded as far as emotions, feelings and affects are concerned. But in psycho-analytic practice we are accustomed to speak of unconscious love, hate, anger, etc., and find it impossible to avoid even the strange conjunction, 'unconscious consciousness of guilt', or a paradoxical 'unconscious anxiety'.
>
> *(p. 177; cf. Freud, 1923b, pp. 22–23)*

While Freud's position has been widely criticised (e.g. Brenner, 1974; Emde, 1999; Pulver, 1971, 1974; Rangell, 1995; Rosenblatt & Thickstun, 1977; Schur, 1969), there is still a puzzling dimension to this (see Lacewing, 2007). After all, it is reasoned, affects are *felt* and thus necessarily conscious (Hatzimoysis, 2007). However, feeling x about y is distinct from *knowing that you feel* x about y and there is no logical objection to *feeling* x about y without reflecting upon it, in the same way that no logical objection exists with knowing y without knowing that you know it. Instead, coming to reflect upon such states (a second mental act) is necessary for becoming conscious of those first (conscious) mental acts (Maze, 1983).

Furthermore, various *elements* of the affective relation may also remain unknown, even if the relationship (or elements thereof) are reflected upon. As Freud (1915e) notes,

> it may happen that an affective or emotional impulse is perceived but misconstrued. Owing to the repression of its proper representative it has been forced to become connected with another idea, and is now regarded by consciousness as the manifestation of that idea.
>
> *(pp. 177–178)*

So, for example, if rage towards one's father is repressed, it would generally not be possible to remain ignorant of the 'father' term of the relation, nor 'rage', even if the rage cannot be brought into connection with the father (i.e. 'father' and 'rage' would remain capable of being known independently of one another). Should the rage be displaced upon a substitute (for instance, such as someone in authority) then what manifests as 'conscious rage' towards that substitute belies the rage held towards one's father *unconsciously*, indicating that unconscious affects, and elements thereof, are essential clinical considerations. By extension, one may feasibly be angry with x, without knowing that one even knows x, or simply angry, without even knowing that one is angry (as in so-called strong cases of unconscious affects—Berridge & Winkielman, 2003, p. 184). Similarly, one may know a bodily response, without knowing that it is an affective response, and so on, due to factors such as repression discussed earlier (accounting for so-called weak instances of unconscious emotion—Berridge & Winkielman, 2003). *Alexithymia*, for instance, appears to involve knowing bodily states, yet not their emotional relationship to other things (Hyer, Woods, & Boudewyns, 1991), and while it may be retorted, as Hatzimoysis (2007) points out, that something is nevertheless 'felt', there are nonetheless unconscious aspects of the affective relation to provide a basis for conceptualising unconscious affects.[6]

The dynamic unconscious

The distinction between 'knowing' and 'knowing that one knows' is also particularly useful for conceptualising the dynamic unconscious. As noted earlier, "*the essence of repression lies simply in turning something away, and keeping it at a distance, from the conscious*" (Freud, 1915d, p. 147, his italics), and Freud (1923b) states that "we obtain our concept of the unconscious from the theory of repression. The repressed is the prototype of the unconscious for us" (p. 15). As described in the previous chapter, Freudian repression is not a passive process, and instead, the dynamic unconscious is actively prevented from becoming known by opposing forces in the mind:

> 'Repressed' is a dynamic expression, which takes account of the interplay of mental forces: it implies that there is a force present which is seeking to bring about all kinds of psychical effects, including that of becoming conscious, but that there is an opposing force which is able to obstruct some of these psychical effects, once more including that of becoming conscious.
>
> *(Freud, 1907a, p. 48)*

For instance, a person might anxiously hold hostile desires towards someone but be unable to reflect upon such desires due to repression. As described previously, dynamic repression entails a paradoxical situation of knowing in order not to know, since such anxiety-laden targets persist and require continual repressing (see Boag, 2007b, 2012; Maze & Henry, 1996). The paradox is particularly apparent with 'resistance', which acts as a selective and discriminative process, actively opposing some, though not other, mental contents from becoming conscious, while concurrently the analysand ostensibly attempts to discover what is

98 The metapsychology of the unconscious

unconscious (Freud, 1910a, p. 30; 1912b, p. 103; 1914g, p. 155; 1923b, p. 17). Repression and resistance thus require unconsciously knowing the repressed, and Freud appreciated the theoretical complexity with this since he writes that it was 'resistance' that led him to "revise the relation between the ego and the unconscious" (Freud, 1933a, p. 108) and propose unconscious aspects of the ego to account for resistance and defence: "Now these resistances, although they belong to the ego, are nevertheless unconscious and in some way separated off within the ego" (Freud, 1937c, pp. 238–239; cf. Freud, 1923b, p. 17). Of course, simply attributing repression and resistance to unconscious aspects of the ego provides no actual explanation of how this process actually occurs, and instead, what is needed is an account of how it is possible to both know and ignore some event simultaneously.

To address this, it is useful to dispense with any strategy that treats the dynamic unconscious as a dungeon-like location where repressed content are banished. Critics such as Loftus (1993), for instance, write, "[a]ccording to the theory, something happens that is so shocking that the mind grabs hold of the memory and pushes it underground, into some inaccessible corner of the unconscious" (p. 518). Taken literally, this spatial metaphor involves viewing unconscious mental processes as existing *somewhere* different from (pre)conscious ones, prompting Talvitie and colleagues (e.g. Talvitie, 2009; Talvitie & Ihanus, 2003a, 2003b, 2005; Talvitie & Tiitinen, 2006) to write that psychoanalysis has failed to satisfactorily address where such repressed contents are specifically located. Since repressed ideas are not stored in the brain (since the brain simply consists of physical properties), these authors conclude that "[t]he obvious logical conclusion is that when ideas are missing from consciousness, they are not 'hiding' anywhere, but are prevented from being formed in the domain of consciousness" (p. 91). That is, repressed contents are not psychical but rather physical states that potentially give rise to mental states (cf. Searle, 1992).

However, on the relational view offered here, as Eagle (2000) proposes, "[t]he essence of repression lies in its interference with one's ability to reflect on one's mental state" (p. 173), and so, rather than banishing the repressed into a location called "the unconscious", repression prevents mental content from becoming the object of a second mental act. As developed elsewhere (Boag, 2015c), Freud's likening consciousness with an act of perception is instructive here in terms of the spotlight analogy: shining a spotlight onto an object does not change the object's spatial location, just as when shining the light elsewhere, the object does not shift spatial location either. Similarly, if I turn my attention towards or away from some state of affairs, x, then x does not move anywhere: my attention changes but the objects that are either attended to, or unattended to, remain exactly where they are. Accordingly, if I turn my attention to my beliefs they do not 'enter consciousness' as if entering a room, and when ignoring something (whether it be an irritating person or my own beliefs), the repressed does not change location: only the second mental act of reflection is interfered with (see Boag, 2015c). Consequently, there is no difficulty in locating the repressed since the repressed exists in the same place as so-called conscious mental states.

Nevertheless, the situation with repression is more complex since repression does not simply interfere with reflection, and instead the difficulty is "explaining how the ego contrives not to know something when the contriving requires that it does know it" (Maze, 1983, p. 149; cf. Maze & Henry, 1996). Explaining how it is possible to unconsciously know some fact without also knowing it can be addressed in terms of repression preventing knowing (or acknowledging) that the repressed is known (Boag, 2007b, 2008b, 2012, 2015b, 2015c). The resolution of the apparent paradox hinges upon the recognition that repression inhibits knowledge of knowing the repressed, mediated by neural inhibition (see the previous chapter), which further prevents the repressed aim from being acted upon. Viewed as such, maintaining repression and resistance does involve knowing the repressed, which prompts anxiety and resistance, while also allowing the repressor to maintain denial or ignorance in the face of evidence to the contrary. To illustrate this further, various neuroclinical phenomena suggest that such unconscious knowing is both possible and necessary for explaining similar states of affairs.

Mental relations and neuroclinical phenomena

The distinction between 'knowing' and 'knowing that one knows' can be extended to a range of clinical phenomena including blindsight (e.g. Weiskrantz, 1986; Weiskrantz, Warrington, Sanders, & Marshall, 1974), and various neuroclinical phenomena such as Korsakoff's syndrome, Alzheimer's dementia, split-brain procedures, as well as 'syndromes of unawareness' including anosognosia (e.g. Eslinger et al., 2005; Hartman-Maeir, Soroker, Oman, & Katz, 2003; Kaplan-Solms & Solms, 2000; Rankin, Baldwin, Pace-Savitsky, Kramer, & Miller, 2004; Salmon et al., 2006; Vallar & Ronchi, 2006). With all of these phenomena a subject ostensibly knows certain things, but is incapable of coming to know that she or he knows them. For example, with the phenomenon of "blindsight" (Weiskrantz et al., 1974; Weiskrantz, 1986), subjects with visual cortex lesions report being unaware of objects in their blind visual field yet appear to perceive the objects nonetheless, as evident in success on discriminatory tasks. Consistent with the earlier discussion, Bowers (1984) writes, "[o]ne implication of this finding is that different parts of the brain may be responsible for detection of stimuli on the one hand, and consciousness of them on the other" (pp. 233–234), which could be taken to mean that neural registrations of 'knowing' are distinct from ones involved in 'knowing that one knows'. In this respect, the distinction between 'knowing' and 'knowing that one knows' is also consistent with theories proposing unconscious/conscious hierarchies of brain functioning, where, for instance, Solms and Panksepp (2012) distinguish between 'unconscious awareness' associated with the brainstem on the one hand,

100 The metapsychology of the unconscious

and 'cognitive consciousness' associated with the neocortex, the latter a necessary condition for the former. They write:

> Neocortex without a brainstem can never be conscious. Although [the] neocortex surely adds much to refined perceptual awareness, initial perceptual processing appears to be unconscious in itself (*cf.* blindsight) or it may have qualities that we do not readily recognise at the level of cognitive consciousness.
>
> *(Solms & Panksepp, 2012, p. 164)*

This can be taken to mean that secondary mental acts require higher brain regions associated with the cortex, and if so, then a range of phenomena can be understood in terms of higher brain regions failing to allow secondary reflective mental acts from occurring, while not interfering with primary ones.

Anosognosia and motivated ignoring

Cases of anosognosia are well-documented and typically occur after physical trauma to the brain's right hemisphere, resulting in various physical deficits (e.g. paralysis) (Kaplan-Solms & Solms, 2000; Ramachandran, 1994, 1996; Solms & Turnbull, 2011; Turnbull, Fotopoulou, & Solms, 2014; Turnbull, Jones, & Reed-Screen, 2002). The anosognosic individual, while otherwise cognitively intact, appears unaware of his or her physical symptoms (Turnbull et al., 2014), and yet nevertheless appears to have unconscious awareness of their deficit, as indicated in both retrospective awareness of the deficit, as well as displacement of emotion onto other events (e.g. a stroke patient might feel disproportionate distress about losing her spectacles, substituting for the distressing paralysis—Kaplan-Solms & Solms, 2000; Turnbull et al., 2014). As Turnbull et al. note, such patients thus paradoxically demonstrate 'implicit awareness' or 'implicit knowledge' of their symptoms (Turnbull et al., 2002; Turnbull et al., 2014), which is simply another way of stating that the patients know their symptoms but are incapable of acknowledging or reflecting upon them. Kaplan-Solms and Solms (2000) similarly write: "unconsciously these patients do perceive and remember that they are paralysed, notwithstanding the facts that they are unable to direct their conscious attention to these facts" (Kaplan-Solms & Solms, 2000, p. 159). Turnbull et al. (2014) conclude that while not sufficient, a motivated element to the denial of symptoms appears to be present, whereby otherwise catastrophic symptoms are "misconstrued in accordance with the patient's wishes" (p. 21). Freud describes something similar to anosognosia when he writes that repression "even prevents the patient from becoming aware of the products of the disease itself" (Freud, 1909b, p. 124), and yet a person might also say that he or she knew the repressed all along after lifting the repression (Freud, 1914a, p. 207). Such phenomena are explicable with a primary/secondary mental act account, whereby it is possible to know something without knowing that you know it.

The metapsychology of the unconscious **101**

Mental acts, primary/secondary processes, and the systemic view of unconscious mentality

While both the descriptive and dynamic views of unconscious mentality are logically defensible, Freud's systemic view raises its own set of problems. Freud (1926f) writes: "*Topographically*, psycho-analysis regards the mental apparatus as a compound instrument, and endeavours to determine at what points in it the various mental processes take place" (p. 266), and his first topographic model emerges within the Fliess correspondence (see letter to Fliess dated 6 December 1896) and his *Project* (Freud, 1950[1895]), before being formally published in *The Interpretation of Dreams* (1900a). However, unlike the neurological focus of his *Project*, Freud's (1900a) account presents a psychological approach where mental processes possess particular qualities and operate according to certain laws pertaining to their respective system, which includes the much celebrated distinction between primary and secondary processes (see also Freud, 1912g, 1915e). Freud's topographic line of thinking crosses over into the structural theory (e.g. Compton, 1972; Wiedeman, 1972; Wollheim, 1991; Boesky, 1995; Petocz; 1999), and much of the difference between the models is in name only: "the criteria of *Ucs.* and *Pcs.* are the same as those of id and ego" (Gill, 1963, p. 53; cf. Wiedeman, 1972; Compton, 1981; Wollheim, 1991; Brenner, 1994; Petocz, 1999).

Freud describes the system *Ucs.* as "a particular realm of the mind with its own wishful impulses, its own mode of expression and its peculiar mental mechanisms which are not in force elsewhere" (Freud, 1916–1917, p. 212; cf. Freud, 1912g, p. 266; 1915e, p. 186), and its characteristics specifically include *primary process* mentation, *exemption from mutual contradiction, timelessness*, and *replacement of external by psychical reality* (Freud, 1915e, p. 187). Primary process psychical energy is *highly mobile* (Freud, 1900a, p. 600) whereby mental content ('wishes') are subject to *condensation* and *displacement*:

> The cathectic intensities [in the *Ucs.*] are much more mobile. By the process of *displacement* one idea may surrender to another its whole quota of cathexis; by the process of *condensation* it may appropriate the whole cathexis of several other ideas. I have proposed to regard these two processes as distinguishing marks of the so-called *primary psychical process*.
>
> *(Freud, 1915e, p. 186, his italics)*

Ucs. processes subsequently possess an *irrational* character since the meaning and relation of ideas to reality is neglected (Freud, 1900a, p. 597; 1915d, p. 187), leading Freud to depict the system *Ucs.*'s operations as governing all that is *irrational* and *illogical* in the mind:

> The governing rules of logic carry no weight in the unconscious; it might be called the realm of the Illogical. Urges with contrary aims exist side by side

102 The metapsychology of the unconscious

in the unconscious without any need arising for any adjustment between them. Either they have no influence whatever on each other, or if they have, no decision is reached, but a compromise comes about which is nonsensical since it embraces mutually incompatible details.

(Freud, 1940a[1938], pp. 168–169; cf. Freud, 1900a, p. 598;
1905e, p. 61; 1915e, p. 186)

Nevertheless, if left to its own devices, the functioning of the system *Ucs.* is unsatisfying and ultimately detrimental since there is no inhibition of hallucinatory satisfaction associated with the primary process, wish-fulfilling character of the mind. Secondary processes subsequently develop due to the need for attending to 'indications of reality', which determine whether the wished for situation is in fact real or not, and further inhibiting hallucinatory satisfaction (Freud, 1911b, p. 219). Secondary processes here are said to follow the 'reality' principle, a reality-tempered modification of the primitive pleasure principle, where actual conditions of satisfaction and frustration are taken into account before initiating action:

Under the influence of the ego's instincts of self-preservation, the pleasure principle is replaced by the *reality principle*. This latter principle does not abandon the intention of ultimately obtaining pleasure, but it nevertheless demands and carries into effect the postponement of satisfaction, the abandonment of a number of possibilities of gaining satisfaction and the temporary toleration of unpleasure as a step on the long indirect road to pleasure.

(Freud, 1920g, p. 10, his italics; cf. 1900a, p. 601;
1915c, p. 120; 1925i, p. 127)

The system *Pcs.* thereby develops where the more reality-oriented *secondary* processes gradually replace or cover the earlier, primitive, primary processes, preventing the free discharge of excitations into hallucinations and delaying discharge until the required conditions for satisfaction are present (Freud, 1900a, p. 599; 1915e, p. 188). The fundamental relationship between the systems then is that wishes in the system *Ucs.* press for immediate discharge, which in turn are inhibited by system *Pcs.* processes (Freud, 1900a, p. 599; 1915e, p. 188), leading Freud to propose a critical distinction between primary and secondary processes in terms of economics: "psychical energy occurs in two forms, one freely mobile and another, by comparison, bound" (Freud, 1940a[1938], p. 164), where the 'mobility' refers to whether processes are inhibited from discharge or not (see Laplanche & Pontalis, 1973, pp. 172–173). This account, for Freud, was of major significance and he writes that "this distinction represents the deepest insight we have gained up to the present into the nature of nervous energy, and I do not see how we can avoid making it" (Freud, 1915e, p. 188), and carries over into the id and the ego respectively (Freud, 1923b).

Recent extensions of the primary/secondary process distinction

The primary/secondary process distinction has been recently extended by Linda Brakel (2009, 2010, 2015) who equates primary processes with a-rational mentality. A-rational mentality, says Brakel, typically involves phantasy, in contrast to rational secondary process thinking, where belief generally resides. In contrast to irrationality, says Brakel, which requires the possibility of rational thought, a-rationality is developmentally prior to rational thinking and lacks the constraints of logic and internal consistency: "[It] is a form of thinking that operates *outside* (rather than in violation) of rationality and its principles" (Brakel, 2010, p. 56). More specifically, whereas secondary process rational mentation is tensed (occurs in time), is reality tested, originates from a single agent's viewpoint, and "tolerates no contradiction" (Brakel, 2015, p. 131), primary process a-rational mentation involves "only a tenseless and unexamined present", an absence of reality-testing ("no attempt to regulate representations for considerations of truth"), is developmentally prior to a stable self "capable of grasping (in any fashion) continuity-in-experience ..." (p. 132), and is without the constraints of standard logic ("Most notably, contradictions are tolerated"—p. 132). Primary process thinking is nevertheless psychological insofar as it is Intentional (has 'content') (Brakel, 2015).

The primary/secondary process distinction is also advanced within the free energy principle approach described earlier in Chapter 2. Carhart-Harris and Friston (2010, 2012) believe here that their model parallels Freud's with respect to the secondary process ego minimising (inhibiting/binding) 'free energy': "In both accounts, higher cortical areas are trying to organize (and thereby explain) activity in lower levels through suppression of their energy" (2012, p. 221; cf. Friston, 2013, p. 39). Carhart-Harris & Friston (2012), in fact, make a direct comparison to Freud's theory, writing that "the unconscious could be understood more explicitly as a *system* subserving a *specific mode of thinking*" (p. 225, their italics), whereas the *Pcs./Cs.* system reflects top-down inhibition: "The analogy between ... Helmholtzian suppression of free energy and Freudian free energy is self-evident: the binding of free energy (prediction errors) corresponds to a top-down suppression, which necessarily entails an explanation or resolution of violated predictions" (Friston, 2013, p. 39).

Now, whether such account can be sustained depends upon two critical factors. One of these, that will be addressed here, is whether there is justification for proposing qualitatively distinct processes as Freud's (and Brakel's) systemic accounts propose. The second factor involves the purported hierarchy between 'lower' and 'higher' agencies of the mind and will be addressed in the next chapter.

Problems with the systemic account of mentality

Problems with Freud's systemic position have been discussed elsewhere (e.g. Boag, 2012, 2015c; Petocz, 1999) and only a summary is presented here. The systematic

104 The metapsychology of the unconscious

account rests on the assumption that various processes are exclusively associated with some systems and not others, and so, as Petocz (1999) has cogently argued, if a quality of a process is unique to a particular mental system as Freud suggests, then such qualities should not be found in the other systems' processes. However, and as has long been recognised, the theory simply does not hold since processes that should exclusively reside in some systems are nevertheless found in the other systems (Arlow & Brenner, 1964; Gill, 1963; Macmillan, 1991; Petocz, 1999; Weintraub, 1987). For instance, Freud's claim that illogical thinking and irrationality are the hallmarks of *Ucs.* processes (in contradistinction to rational, logical *Pcs./Cs.* thinking) (Freud, 1900a, p. 615; 1915b, p. 187) is unsustainable since (pre)conscious thought activity may also be illogical or irrational (Arlow & Brenner, 1964; Weintraub, 1987). In fact, attempting to maintain the systemic distinction leads to problems with explaining dreams and symptom formation in terms of products of the repressed since, as unconscious products, there should be no logical order or structure when obviously there is (Beres, 1962; Macmillan, 1991). On the other hand, it is precisely the defensive processes associated with the *Pcs./ego* that lead to distortions of reality, rather than holding fast to the 'reality principle', as should be the case. In fact, Petocz (1999) further notes that a basic problem with the primary/secondary process distinction is that hallucination requires first attending to reality, rather than the other way around, a point similarly noted by Bohleber et al. (2015), who write, "if there is no element of reality, then fantasy as a whole would be a complete illusion, or delusion" (p. 713). Consequently, it appears impossible to sustain an account of qualitatively distinct systems with their own specific processes not found in the other, and attempting to force the distinction simply annuls other essential aspects of psychoanalytic theory.

Can we rescue the primary/secondary process distinction?

Given the problems associated with the primary/secondary process distinction, Petocz (1999) advocates abandoning these terms, even if some sense of the distinction holds with respect to the infant's initial intolerance of frustration leading to hallucinatory wish-fulfilment and *subsequent* attention to reality for gratification. However, the distinction might have some usefulness in terms of the distinction between primary and secondary mental *acts* (Boag, 2015c). As noted earlier, Freud depicts the system *Ucs.*'s operations as governing all that is *irrational* and *illogical* in the mind (Freud, 1900a, p. 598; 1905e, p. 61; 1915e, p. 186; 1940a[1938], pp. 168–169) whereas the development of the system *Pcs.* and the more reality-oriented *secondary* processes replace these earlier, primitive, primary processes. On the relational view, a primary mental act is unconscious because it occurs necessarily prior to reflection upon it (cf. Freud, 1900a, pp. 612–613; 1912g, p. 264; 1915e, p. 171; 1916–1917, p. 295), and since determining whether a belief is true or false (rational or otherwise) requires an act of critical examination, such scrutiny requires a secondary act of reflection. Thus, prior to reflection we might hold logically incompatible beliefs which, should they be subject to scrutiny, might reveal logical contradictions. Such reflective critical examination is probably initially absent in infancy and likely does not arise until maturational processes allow, and then helped along by sources of discomfort (e.g. hallucinatory wish-fulfilments not leading to actual satisfaction— Freud, 1911b), as well as aspects of socialisation, which lead to monitoring of thoughts and actions (e.g. punishment for certain acts). Freud's primary/secondary process distinction could thus be seen then as simply a distinction between primary mental acts lacking critical reflection, and secondary mental acts reflecting upon and correcting those, rather than qualitatively distinct mental processes pertaining to various mental systems.

Summary

Any general metapsychology providing foundations for psychoanalytic theory must address the nature of unconscious and conscious processes. While legitimate questions arise concerning the nature and location of unconscious mental processes, there are no metaphysical mysteries associated with unconscious mentality: unconscious mental acts are simply Intentional mental acts not reflected upon. This is not to say that there are not genuine problems with the Freudian account, and in particular, the systemic/topographic point of view associated with Freudian metapsychology is *prima facie* incoherent. Nevertheless, the primary and secondary process distinction may still hold *temporally* and some mechanism for understanding the difference between these processes is proposed in terms of uncritical, primary mental acts. This being said, as the relational view makes clear, the subject term of the cognitive relational (the knower) must also be accounted for, and given that consciousness is typically considered bound to various agencies, whether it be the 'person', 'self', or ego, discussion of the nature of personality structure is further required.

Notes

1 Intentionality as the mark of the mental is not universally accepted given apparently non-Intentional mental states. Pataki (2015), for instance, writes: "Mental states such as bare awareness …, moods, pain and other sensations fail to have Intentional objects: a headache, for example, it not about pain, it is pain" (*n*3, p. 37). Nevertheless, by its very description, to have a headache is to stand in a painful relationship with the head, where the intended object may be any number of sources of discomfort (e.g. ruptured blood vessels, sinusitis, or muscular tension). On the other hand, the counter-examples of so-called 'bare awareness' and 'moods' require further consideration with respect to whether the objects are simply unconscious. More will be said later on this matter.
2 On the other hand, MacIntyre (1958) compares Freud's notion of 'idea' with the British empiricist tradition's atomic view (e.g. Locke, 1690/1947, p. 34). It is fair to say that both positions are present in Freud's account, though this atomist position is especially problematic (see, for example, McMullen, 1996).

106 The metapsychology of the unconscious

3 This view of cognition as a certain type of relation has a long history (e.g. in Aristotle; see Petocz, 1999), medieval scholasticism (see Pasnau, 1997), and is found in the American new realists (e.g. E. B. Holt) and the British Realists (e.g. G. E. Moore), J. Laird and Samuel Alexander (see Michell, 1988, 2011). Further discussion of this position can be found in Anderson (1962), Boag (2005, 2008a, 2010a, 2012, 2015b, 2015c), Hibberd (2014), Mackay and Petocz (2011), Maze (1983), McMullen (1996), Michell (1988), and Petocz (1999).

4 Freud had marked out the line in Lipps's work: "We would rather assume that unconscious processes lie at the root of all conscious ones and accompany them" (in Masson, 1985, p. 325*n*).

5 Given that Freud's use of *Besetzung* captures some sense of Intentionality in terms of what one is occupied or invested in (i.e. attention to the intended object), the distinction between 'knowing' and 'knowing that one knows' appears to also parallel Freud's account of 'cathexis' and 'hypercathexis' (e.g. Freud, 1939a, p. 97), while the inverse applies for 'anticathexis' discussed in the previous chapter.

6 Similarly, the relational view helps appreciate how it is possible to hold unconscious phantasies. Bohleber et al. (2015) write that "[u]nconscious phantasy is one of the central concepts in psychoanalytic theory and practice" (p. 706), although the concept varies according to theories and overlaps with others such as wish-fulfilment, internal objects, enactment, etc. Some theoretical approaches deny that phantasy can ever become conscious. Fonagy (1999), for example, writes that "fantasy may be thought to exist in the non-experiential realm of implicit memory" (p. 219). However, on the relational view it is possible to conceptualise unconscious psychical phantasy in a manner that does not preclude becoming conscious of phantasy and Freud provides a valuable direction here. For Freud, phantasies are substitute satisfactions (wish-fulfilments) which may occur unnoticed, or, if noticed, then become repressed: "Unconscious phantasies have either been unconscious all along and have been formed in the unconscious; or—as is more often the case—they were once conscious phantasies, day-dreams, and have since been purposely forgotten and have become unconscious through 'repression'" (Freud, 1908a, p. 161). While Bohleber et al. (2015) interpret Freud's reference to "unconscious all along" above as a reference to phylogenetically transmitted primal phantasies from human prehistory, as the relational view indicates it is possible to have phantasies that have been fully blown psychological acts and simply never reflected upon.

5
THE METAPSYCHOLOGY OF THE SELF

Introduction

While repression is accountable in terms of motivational conflict preventing reflection upon certain mental acts, such a picture nevertheless requires integration into a larger framework involving the 'person', ego and identity. Personality development typically involves the emergence of an apparent agent—the 'person'—and a comprehensive general theory must address the relation of this person to the various parts, including the drives and their relation with the 'cognising subject' or ego. This is no small feat, since 'sub-personal' drive accounts typically appear to undermine the role of the 'person', which underscores the tension between whether we should understand humans mechanistically or as 'agents', and whether psychoanalysis should be seen as a natural science or some kind of privileged human science. Consequently, unless an integrative account of drives and persons can be provided, then the apparent division between impersonal drives and 'persons' provides a further source of pluralism in psychoanalysis.

Freud, himself, appears to have been in two minds about the role of human agency, and it has been long observed that Freud's theory straddles both person-level and sub-personal-level explanation (Grossman & Simon, 1969; Nagel, 1959; Sartre, 1956; Thalberg, 1982). 'Agency' particularly comes to the fore in Freud's (1923b) 'structural' theory of id, ego and superego, where the ego initiates action and interacts with the other agencies, and thus questions arise concerning the precise relation between the ego and the drives. However, addressing the issue agency and personality structure within psychoanalytic theory is not altogether easy since there is a tendency to define structures in terms of what they are said to do (i.e. their 'functions') rather than in terms of *what* it precisely is, that is said to be

108 The metapsychology of the self

performing those same functions. Beres (1965), in fact, writes that Freud's model would have been better termed the 'functional theory of id, ego, and superego', and some authors prefer abandoning talk of structures altogether and referring only to 'functions' (e.g. Arlow, 1975). Nevertheless, any discussion of functions (processes or activities) implicates 'something' performing those same activities (i.e. some kind of structure) (Maze, 1983), and thus purely functional definitions are both incomplete and lend themselves to a number of problems including reification and circular explanation, whereby a set of activities becomes treated as an entity performing those same activities, and then used to explain those same processes with respect to the concocted entity (Boag, 2011a, 2011b, 2015a; Maze, 1983). It is precisely in this respect that the structural theory has been criticised for reifying various activities into entities performing those same activities, which in turn, become personified into homunculi (see Boesky, 1995). Viewed as such, not only do we then have to account for the 'person', we now also need to explain the activities of multiple persons (Grossman & Simon, 1969; Maze, 1983, 1987; Talvitie, 2012; Wegner, 2005; Wiedeman, 1972), and while anthropomorphic descriptions of the psyche might be appropriate in the context of identification and object relations (see Beres, 1965; Gardner, 1993; Gillett, 1990; Hopkins, 1995), such descriptions nonetheless require being compatible with causal explanation. More specifically, as the discussion in Chapter 1 proposes, any explanation must be in terms of causal antecedents and mechanisms, and proposed structures must be logically independent from their activities (or their functions). While the analysis in Chapter 2 indicates that drives provide a coherent foundation for explaining motivation—for instance, the drives are logically independent of their activities—whether the structural theory meets these same criteria remains to be seen.

The structural theory of personality

While Freud's early theory equates the repressed with the system *Ucs.* and the repressing forces with the *Cs.* and *Pcs.*, he comes to recognise that this division is problematic since aspects of the repressing forces, particularly the defences, are themselves unconscious in the deeper, systematic sense (Freud, 1923b, p. 18). Based on this insight, Freud formulates what has become known as the 'structural theory', postulating three main structures or agencies: the id, ego and superego. The id and ego, by and large can be understood in terms of how they differ from one another in four principle ways. First, the ego is that which knows and that which can be known (even if some aspects of ego functioning such as defences are unconscious—Freud, 1923b, pp. 17–18), whereas the id consists of "the dark, inaccessible part of our personality" (Freud, 1933a, p. 73). Second, the ego is structured, organised, and possesses a synthetic character while the id does not: "what distinguishes the ego from the id quite especially is a tendency to synthesis in its contents, to a combination and unification in its mental processes which are totally lacking in the id" (Freud, 1933a, p. 76). Third, the id operates via the primary process *pleasure* principle whereas the ego is motivated by the *reality* principle: "Just as the id is directed exclusively to obtaining pleasure, so the ego is governed by considerations of safety. The ego has set itself the task of self-preservation, which the id appears to neglect" (Freud, 1940a[1938], p. 199; cf. Freud, 1923b, p. 56), which implicates the fourth principle difference involving motivation, which will be discussed below. On the other hand, the superego is "the representative … of every moral restriction, the advocate of a striving towards perfection" (Freud, 1933a, p. 67).

The different natures of the ego and id can be generally superimposed upon the topographic theory (see Boag, 2012 for further discussion), and as with Freud's topographic theory, a major criticism with Freud's structural demarcation is that the supposed distinctions between the id and ego cannot be sustained since so-called ego-processes can be found in the id and vice versa. Brenner (1994), for example, rightly points out that "the ego is by no means as consistent, as integrated, as mature, and as immune from primary process functioning as the ego is supposed to be" (p. 477). Equally, the id is organised, since, for instance, any id-impulse or urge can only be conceptualised as a propositional attitude (*S* has an impulse to do *x*) and thus id-impulses cannot be any less organised or structured compared to any other mental act since a content-less 'urge' or 'impulse' is incoherent (see Boag, 2014). Moreover, Freud's distinction between the id and ego invalidates other aspects of his theory given that, as Beres (1962) notes, an 'organised repressed content' must somehow belong to the ego rather than the id:

> If we assume that the fantasy which is unconscious retains its organization, to whatever degree, we must grant the continued activity of ego functions. 'The ego is an organisation', Freud has said, 'and the id is not'. An 'id fantasy', then, is by definition a contradiction in terms, and to speak of a fantasy being 'repressed into the id' is, in my opinion, a complex of logical fallacies.
>
> *(Beres, 1962, p. 324; cf. Slap & Saykin, 1984, p. 110)*

However, one further problem with Freud's demarcation between id and ego involves motivation, and as will be discussed, Freud's theory here provides another source for psychoanalytic pluralism.

The horse-and-rider analogy

The fourth major difference between the id and ego is with respect to sources of motivation, and here Freud invokes an ancient metaphor that goes at least as far back to Plato's comparison of reason as a charioteer, steering the horses of spirit and desire. In Freud's version, the ego is the controlling entity responsible for mediating between the 'irrational' id, superego demands, and constraints of the external

110 The metapsychology of the self

world, whereby the ego assumes the role of an *executive agent*, attempting to satisfy the id through activity in the world:

> As a frontier-creature, the ego tries to mediate between the world and the id, to make the id pliable to the world and, by means of its muscular activity, to make the world fall in with the wishes of the id.
>
> *(Freud, 1923b, p. 56; cf. Freud, 1924c, p. 167; 1933a,*
> *p. 75; 1940a[1938], p. 199)*

According to Freud, the ego principally functions here via cognitive activity and perception, anticipating danger, and both preparing responses and inhibiting action (Freud, 1940a[1938], p. 199). As Freud (1923b) writes,

> in each individual there is a coherent organization of mental processes; and we call this his *ego*. It is to this ego that consciousness is attached; the ego controls the approaches to motility ... it is the mental agency which supervises all its own constituent processes.
>
> *(p. 17, his italics)*

With respect to sources of motivation, Freud proposes that the 'irrational' id is the source of energy, distinct from the ego as a rational executive agent that instead decides how to act. Freud compares the relation of the id and ego to the relation between a horse and rider: "The ego's relation to the id might be compared with that of a rider to his horse. The horse supplies the locomotive energy, while the rider has the privilege of deciding on the goal and of guiding the powerful animal's movements" (Freud, 1933a, p. 77; cf. Freud, 1923b, p. 25). In this respect, whereas the id is constituted by the 'blind' drives ("instinctual cathexes seeking discharge— that, in our view, is all there is in the id"—Freud, 1933a, p. 74), the ego's attachment to perception and consciousness allows it to manage the drives, taking into account indications of reality: "For the ego, perception plays the part which in the id falls to instinct. The ego represents what may be called reason and common sense, in contrast to the id, which contains the passions" (Freud, 1923b, p. 25; cf. pp. 55–56; Freud, 1933a, p. 76).

This horse-and-rider analogy has major theoretical implications for conceptualising personality and provided impetus for the emergence of divergent psychoanalytic schools. Maze (1983, 1987), for example, notes that the horse-and-rider analogy paved the way for the development of ego psychology, whereby the ego is distinct from the drives, and consists of a set of functions inhibiting the drives, controlling motility and directing perceptual processes (Hartmann, 1950, 1958; Rapaport, 1951). The ego's autonomy from the drives has subsequently become orthodox ego psychology and a position prominent within psychoanalytic theorising generally (e.g. Arlow & Brenner, 1964; Beres, 1962, 1971, 1995; Gill, 1963; Hartmann,

The metapsychology of the self **111**

1950, 1958; Hartmann, Kris, & Loewenstein, 1949; Hopkins, 2013; Horowitz, 1977; Madison, 1961; Rangell, 1988; Ritvo & Solnit, 1995; Stolar & Fromm, 1974; White, 1963), and taken to its extreme, leads to proposing that the ego has a "fundamentally autonomous, self-generating nature" (Lettieri, 2005, p. 377), which essentially views the ego as a disembodied, Cartesian rational faculty.

However, the horse-and-rider analogy also finds its way into neuropsychoanalysis where sub-cortical id processes are contrasted with higher cognitive processes, the latter typically associated with the prefrontal cortices involved in controlling the lower sub-cortical ones (e.g. Fotopoulou, 2013; Solms, 2013; Solms & Turnbull, 2002; Yovell, 2008a). Solms (2013), for instance, refers to "the embodied, instinctual brain—which must of necessity be constrained by the cognitive brain with its predictive modelling" (p. 18; cf. Solms & Panksepp, 2012, p. 171), while Solms and Zellner (2012b) describe "[t]he dynamic tension between reality-constrained executive function and a compulsive pleasure principle-driven affective life which is at the core of the analytic model of the mind" (Solms & Zellner, 2012b, p. 139). Wright and Panksepp (2012) similarly appear to disconnect the lower drives from the higher complex systems of the mind, writing

> in early bottom-up development, the lower powers of the mind (basic bodily drives and brain emotions) govern how systems get organized. At maturity, the higher order (top-down) systems govern complex decision-making based upon what is happening in lower brain systems.
>
> *(p. 19)*

Accounts discussing free energy and hierarchical cortical systems similarly invoke the horse-and-rider analogy by positing cognitive ego-functions, which constrain and control desire (Carhart-Harris & Friston, 2010, 2012; Fotopoulou, 2013; Hopkins, 2012, 2015; Solms, 2013). In that account the inhibiting high-level ego-function activity is associated with the default-mode network (DMN), involved in both self-reflection and anticipating future events. In this manner, Carhart-Harris and Friston (2010, 2012) believe that their model parallels Freud's with respect to the secondary process ego minimising (inhibiting or binding) primary process 'free energy': "In both accounts, higher cortical areas are trying to organize (and thereby explain) activity in lower levels through suppression of their energy" (2012, p. 221; cf. Friston, 2013, p. 39). These higher cortical areas are principally equivalent to the ego controlling the energies of the id: "the ego *constrains* all energy impinging upon it" (Carhart-Harris & Friston, 2012, p. 223, their italics) and "is the constraining edge of our desires" (p. 224; cf. Solms, 2013). Thus, all of these positions propose that higher cognitive processes act to control the lower drives and so are all functionally equivalent to the ego controlling the id, which essentially replicates the horse-and-rider distinction proposed by Freud.

112 The metapsychology of the self

Problems with the horse-and-rider analogy

The intuitive appeal of the horse-and-rider analogy likely follows from the common-place observation that humans have both desires and passions on the one hand, and 'higher' rational cognitive activity on the other, the latter needed to keep the former in check. Furthermore, if one takes a top-down approach to understanding behaviour, the 'person's" mental activities, in many instances, appear totally disconnected to biological drives and affects. As White (1963) writes, the "activities of the ego are clearly not instinctual" (p. 1), and so a challenge for any foundational drive account is adequately addressing the ostensibly non-biological character of such 'higher activities' of the person. However, the main problem with such a distinction—*viz*. the horse-and-rider analogy—is that it fails to adequately account for the ego's motivation (Maze, 1983, 1987, 1993). Since the ego is said to arbitrate between different desires and demands—between the id, superego and external world (Freud, 1923b, p. 56)—then some account of the ego's motivational policy must be provided. For example, not all desires are inhibited in equal measure, and so some determinant of this differential selection is required since otherwise Freud's 'rider' is left without direction. As developed in Chapter 2, cognition in isolation does not imply motivational policy, so if the ego's motivation is entirely perceptual or cognitive in character, then there is no explanation for its actions. Why, for instance, does the ego pay attention to p rather than q, or choose to do x rather than y, or inhibit a rather than b? Claiming that the ego merely controls or neutralises drive energy to use for its own purpose (e.g. Hartmann, 1950, p. 85) provides no basis for explaining why any given behaviour will be chosen over another, while appeal to 'adaptation' as an explanatory strategy suffers similar difficulties. As Maze (1987) writes, adaptation is relative to both subject and situation, and a behaviour considered adaptive to one person may be considered maladaptive by another, and thus "adaptation" can not be used as a means for determining motivational policy. Thus, the horse-and-rider position invariably lacks the motivational foundations to account for the activity of the 'rational ego' (or 'cognitive brain') and its constraining actions upon desire, and essentially paves the way for reinstating the Cartesian rational faculty which psychoanalysis generally fought so hard to demonstrate was false. Instead, a motivational account ultimately based on some biological deterministic mechanism is required for explaining both the direction and activity of any behaviour and avoid postulating a disembodied rational agency.

The conscious id

One promising direction that avoids the problems associated with the horse-and-rider analogy positions the id, rather than ego, as the seat of consciousness (the so-called 'conscious id'). While consciousness is typically believed to be reliant on 'higher' cortical processes, evidence instead indicates that the functional neural

The metapsychology of the self **113**

substrate of consciousness is located in deeper brainstem structures (Solms, 2013; Solms & Panksepp, 2012). One upshot of this position is the view that consciousness is intrinsically affective-motivational rather than merely perceptual: "Consciousness is not generated in the cortex; it is generated in the brainstem. Moreover, consciousness is not inherently perceptual; it is inherently affective. And in its primary manifestations, it has less to do with cognition than with instinct" (Solms, 2013, p. 12).

Solms and Panksepp realise that this turns Freud's structural theory on its head: rather than a conscious ego, on the one hand, and an intrinsically unconscious 'blind' id, on the other, the id is fundamentally conscious. The id, writes Solms (2013), "constitutes the primary stuff from which minds are made" (p. 16), and so, if anything, the id rather than the ego is the embodied subject of cognition. Solms refers to this embodied subject as the 'internal body', which includes the autonomic body acting as the knowing *subject*, monitoring and regulating the states of the body: "This primary subject of consciousness (the body-as-subject) is the id" (Solms, 2013, p. 15). In contrast to this internal body, what we generally take to be our ego or sense of self is referred to as the 'external body', which is associated with cortical processes, including the cortical homunculus body-image map. This self as external body is essentially something known (an object of cognition) rather than a knower, in the same manner as any other object external to the organism: "The external body is not the owner or locus of consciousness. It is not really the subjective self; it is an objective representation of the self" (Solms & Panksepp, 2012, p. 167). This theory is essentially proposing a relational view of cognition whereby the knowing subject term is the internal body (body-as-subject) and the external body is something known (body-as-object) (Solms, 2013; Solms & Panksepp, 2012). Since "[t]he external body corresponds to the 'ego', the internal body is the 'id'" (Solms & Panksepp, 2012, p. 158), the id is thus essentially the experiencing subject, while the ego is something known:

> My major conclusion can now be restated: the internal self, synonymous with Freud's 'id,' is the fount of all consciousness; the external self, synonymous with Freud's 'ego,' is a learnt representation that is unconscious in itself, but can be consciously 'thought with' when cathected by the id; the abstracted self, which provides the reflexive scaffolding for the 'superego,' is likewise unconscious, but it can consciously 'think about' the ego.
>
> *(Solms, 2013, p. 16)*

This accordingly inverts the general association of consciousness with the ego and unconsciousness with the id: "... *consciousness is generated in the id*, and the ego is fundamentally unconscious" (Solms, 2013, p. 12, his italics).

The theoretical upshot of this position is that there is no longer a division between motivation and consciousness since consciousness is bound up with the embodied id, while the ego itself is something known (the self) rather than an

114 The metapsychology of the self

actual agency. What this means is that while we typically believe that our self is a cognising agency, it is instead something cognised—"the self of everyday experience is largely an abstraction" (Solms, 2013, p. 16)—and so our sense of agency as a separate self is false. How this arises is explicable with respect to identification: given that the "[t]he subject of consciousness identifies itself with its external body (object-presentation)" (Solms, 2013, p. 15), the false sense of selfhood arises from the internal body identifying itself with the external body, and hence the illusion of external body selfhood.

Motivation and embodied cognition

The essential relation between motivation and consciousness has long been underappreciated (Maze, 1983; Watt, 2012), and the conscious id proposal could be taken to mean that the motivational systems—the foundational drives—are the knowing and experiencing subjects. Such a position has the immediate advantage of accounting for the motivational policy of any cognitive act, while also reflecting Freud's (1915c) recognition that drives are *psychobiological* systems. As psychobiological systems, the drives engage cognitively with the environment in their quest for gratification and avoidance of frustration, and so, to use a simple example, the hunger drive instigates awareness of available food sources, activates motor systems related to ingestion, while also being sensitive to metabolic feedback involved in eating (Watt, 2012; cf. Passmore, 1935). There is thus a "fundamental reliance of cognition on motivational drives and emotional presses 'from underneath'" (Watt, 2012, p. 88), which, as Watt recognises provides an integrated perspective for addressing cognitive and sensory processes, motor activity and motivation (p. 93). As he writes: "It seems very difficult to create any kind of heuristic model for conscious states in the brain without considering how the brain might integrate sensory processing and motor processing with motivational/homeostatic processing" (Watt, 2012, p. 93).[1]

In some respects, the 'conscious id' position was foreshadowed by Maze (1983, 1987) who, following Freud's lead, proposes that the knowers within personality are psychobiological drive structures. Maze proposes a strongly partitive view of personality where each individual is made up of a small community of these drives, "each of which is a knower and a doer" (Maze, 1987, p. 197). While the drives are knowers, these are biomechanical systems utilising cognition and not anthropomorphic homunculi ('little persons'), and so rather than a 'person' (or persons) acting rationally and deciding upon when and how to act, each drive is simply a mechanistic system (literally a psychobiological engine) that, once activated, impels the organism's cognitive activity and behaviour until other factors intervene to terminate or arrest the activity (including conflict and repression) (Maze, 1983; see also Chapter 2 and Boag, 2005, 2012, 2014). The behaviour of the 'person' results from both facilitating and inhibiting influences emerging from the interaction of these drives, shaped by their interaction with the world around them.

While neuroscientific evidence for the conscious id provides preliminary support for Maze's position, Maze's account differs in an important respect to Solms's. Solms appear to treat the conscious id as a *singular* entity rather than a complex arena of competing drives and affects, when he writes, for instance, that "[t]his primary subject of consciousness (the body-as-subject) is the id" (Solms, 2013, p. 15; Solms & Panksepp, 2012). Whether this singularity is specifically meant or not is unclear, but any singular conception of this body-as-subject risks creating another executive agency which invokes the same homunculus problems already associated with the structural theory. Furthermore, the fact of psychological conflict forces upon us the view of there being multiple motivational systems constituting the conscious id, since, as Petocz (1999) points out, "in order to accommodate the facts of mental conflict, of a conflict of interests within a single mind, there must be a plurality of drives—at least two" (p. 221; cf. Boag, 2005, 2007b, 2012; Maze, 1983). Consequently, conflict requires an 'id' composed of multiple, independent motivational sources rather than treating the sub-cortical id as a singular unit.

Freud's ego-drives account

Maze (1983, 1987), in fact, notes that Freud, himself, provides an alternative to the horse-and-rider analogy when he writes that "[t]he ego is not sharply separated from the id; its lower portion merges into it" (1923b, p. 24; cf. 1933a, p. 75). On this view, the ego is constituted by the drives, providing a source of motivational policy for the ego in terms of these foundations. Freud (1925i) here writes that the

> ego developed out of the id, it forms with it a single biological unit, it is only a specially modified peripheral portion of it, and it is subject to the influences and obeys the suggestions that arise from the id. For any vital purpose, a separation of the ego from the id would be a hopeless undertaking.
>
> *(p. 133)*

This position is principally important since it accounts for the ego's motivation in terms of the drives, in the same manner as the id and thus provides a possible explanatory motivational basis for the ego's activities (Boag, 2012, 2014; Maze, 1983, 1987, 1993). Additionally, any conflict is accounted for then in terms of inter-drive conflict, rather than a 'lower' id and 'higher' cognitive functions, which is consistent with both the foundational drive account developed in Chapter 2 and the account of repression developed in Chapter 3, where repression was between competing impulses rather than functionally antithetical agencies.

The view that the ego is constituted by the drives (or subset thereof) initially appears in one of Freud's lesser-known works (*The Psycho-analytic View of the Psychogenic Disturbance of Vision*—Freud, 1910i), and as discussed earlier, the ego-drives

116 The metapsychology of the self

were broadly described as the 'self-preservative' drives ('hunger') which could be contrasted with the libidinal drives ('love'). Freud stresses that the distinction between the two sets of drives was developed partly to account for psychodynamic conflict, and while Freud's ego-drive account is only explicit in his writing for a relatively short period of time (approximately between 1910–1917), before being subsumed into the life and death drives (Freud, 1920g; see Laplanche & Pontalis, 1973), the ego/libidinal drive account has the advantage over the latter position since the life and death drives are without clear motivating structures and described teleologically. The theoretical significance of Freud's ego-drive account has hardly been recognised, however, although Laplanche and Pontalis (1973) write that while Freud had always postulated it was the ego that initiated repression, until the formulation of the ego-drives, "the ego had until now been assigned no specific instinctual support" (p. 146). In other words, Freud's ego-drive account formalises this repressing source as a set of self-preservative drives responsible for conflict and subsequent repressions. More than this, though, Freud's (1910i) ego-drive account fills a motivational void because the ego then is motivated by the foundational drives, in the same manner as the id (see Boag, 2014; Maze, 1983, 1993). The ego is not passive or separate from the drives but rather composed of them (Maze, 1983, 1987, 1993), and thus Freud's account of the ego-drives is thus theoretically welcome since it provides a biological foundation for all of the motivational systems involved in conflict and provides a non-homuncular view of the ego (cf. Boag, 2012, 2014; Maze, 1983, 1987, 1993).

As discussed elsewhere (Boag, 2014), when Freud (1910i) first mentions the ego in his paper introducing the ego-drives, he does so in scare quotes (i.e. 'ego'), referring to "the collective concept of the 'ego'—a compound which is made up variously at different times" (p. 213). As a 'collective' and a 'compound', Freud is indicating that the 'ego' is not a singular agency or entity, but instead composed of *multiple* motivational sources as knowers. Thus, in Freud's view, the ego is not an irreducible entity but rather composed of one set of instinctual drives of which membership is fluid. The apparent unity of the ego follows from a drive neither knowing itself directly (nor the other drives) and instead only knowing and identifying with the *whole* organism and its activities (Boag, 2005), in a similar manner as the proposed relation between the 'internal' and 'external' bodies (see Solms, 2013).

The view that the ego is simply a modified portion of the id is also consistent with Freud's qualification concerning the distinction between the pleasure and reality principle. Rather than the id blindly demanding gratification, while the dispassionate ego remains attentive to reality, Freud writes the 'reality principle' is but a modified version of the pleasure principle. As he writes, "[t]he id obeys the inexorable pleasure principle. But not the id alone. It seems that the activity of the other psychical agencies too is able only to modify the pleasure principle but not to nullify it" (Freud, 1940a[1938], p. 198; cf. Freud, 1911b, 1925i). The ego's supposed adherence to the reality principle is because self-preservation and reality-orientation (which is only ever more or less) is itself a means of gratification and

The metapsychology of the self **117**

frustration avoidance (see Boag, 2012; Maze, 1983, 1987; Maze & Henry, 1996; Newbery, 2011; Petocz, 1999). As Freud notes, the ego-drives are generally forced to take reality more sharply into account than the libidinal drives, which leads to the ego's modification of the pleasure principle:

> the ego-instincts, have the same aim to start with [i.e. pleasure]. But under the influence of the instructress Necessity, they soon learn to replace the pleasure principle by a modification of it. For them the task of avoiding unpleasure turns out to be almost as important as that of obtaining pleasure. The ego discovers that it is inevitable for it to renounce immediate satisfaction, to postpone the obtaining of pleasure, to put up with a little unpleasure and to abandon certain sources of pleasure altogether. An ego thus educated has become 'reasonable'; it no longer lets itself be governed by the pleasure principle, but obeys the *reality principle*, which also at bottom seeks to obtain pleasure, but pleasure which is assured through taking account of reality, even though it is pleasure postponed and diminished.
>
> *(Freud, 1916–1917, p. 357, his italics; cf. Freud, 1911b, pp. 222–223)*

Conflict, repression, and the id

While the ego-drive account situates conflict primarily between sets of drives, how the repressed fits with 'the conscious id' remains outstanding. Solms, in fact, writes that his proposal that the id is the seat of consciousness challenges the orthodox position that the repressed constitutes a portion of the unconscious id. Accordingly, he asks, he asks, if the id is conscious, "then what does the repressed consist in?" (Solms, 2013, p. 17), while Hopkins (2013) instead believes that the term 'id' should be reserved solely for 'the repressed'. At the same time, despite the theoretical importance of the conscious id position there remains a tendency in neuropsychoanalysis to characterise conflict as "[t]he dynamic tension between reality-constrained executive function and a compulsive pleasure principle-driven affective life" (Solms & Zellner, 2012b, p. 139). That is, conflict is between the 'higher functions' of the mind (the so-called 'cognitive brain') and the conscious id (or instinctual brain) (Solms, 2013; Solms & Panksepp, 2012; Solms & Zellner, 2012b), which invokes all the problems associated with the horse-and-rider analogy discussed earlier.

However, Freud is not entirely consistent in his treatment of the id since the id is conceptualised in two (not mutually exclusive) ways: one as the biological unconscious drives, the other as that which is repressed (Boag, 2014; Maze, 1983). With the former, the id is "a cauldron full of seething excitations. We picture it as being open at its end to somatic influences, and as there taking up into itself instinctual needs which find their psychical expression in it" (Freud, 1933a, p. 73; cf. Freud, 1940a[1938], p. 197), while the other component of the id is that of the repressed. As the repressed, the id consists of all those impulses subjected to

118 The metapsychology of the self

repression, which partake in the particular processes of the biological id (Freud, 1933a, p. 74). Nevertheless, Freud (1923b) further writes that "the repressed merges into the id as well, and is merely a part of it" (p. 24; cf. Freud, 1933a, p. 77), and one way of conceptualising this is by viewing the id as a subset of the drives, just as the ego is, with the principal difference entailing repression (Maze, 1983). Freud (1923b), in fact, writes that "[t]he differentiation between ego and id ... is the inevitable expression of the influence of the external world" (p. 38), and thus personality division arises from the interaction of the foundational drives and the environment, particularly relating to the social context. Following Freud here, Maze (1983) proposes that a dominating set of drives emerges in competition with and inhibiting wishes and desires associated with loss of love and danger, which instigate anxiety and primary repression:

> In general, all those instinctual drives whose gratification is dependent on the parent's good will and which is employed as reward by them are mobilised in opposition to the forbidden instinctual impulses. Thus, one subset of the instinctual drives becomes organised in competition with the remainder, and treats the blocking off of the remainder as an essential part of securing its own gratification.
>
> *(Maze, 1983, p. 171)*

As Freud often notes, the ego assumes a dominating position within the personality (Freud in Breuer & Freud, 1895d, p. 116; Freud, 1900a, pp. 594–595; 1907a, p. 58) and this particular position is not inconsistent with the developmental context postulated by attachment theory. Threats to attachment relations also involve danger associated with 'loss of love', and whether this involves complex understanding of the implications of such loss, or simply a more primitive anxiety response along the lines of what Bowlby (1969) believes, the same principle remains for understanding ego/id differentiation. There is no necessary tension between Freud's and Bowlby's account in this respect, and in fact, given the intense anxiety associated with threats to attachment (Bowlby, 1980; Hopkins, 2015; Shaver & Mikulincer, 2002, 2005), the conditions for repression of threat-associated impulses are ripe. Furthermore, taking into account the findings from affective neuroscience, the infant's activated RAGE system is likely to be an intense source of conflict and repression since it threatens those same attachment relations (Hopkins, 2013, 2015). In this regard, the findings of attachment research and neuropsychoanalysis are consistent with Freud's view that the social environment during infancy is the primary context for repression and thus personality division (Freud, 1914d, 1915b).

However, while Freud (1910i) initially contrasts the repressing self-preservative drives and the repressed libidinal drives (reflecting the classical conflict situation underlying the psychoneuroses), Freud further notes that in principle there is no objection to non-libidinal drive expressions becoming repressed, and it is not

The metapsychology of the self **119**

inconceivable that sexuality, for instance, could repress the aim of self-preservation (Bleichmar, 2004, p. 1387). As Freud (1940a[1938]) writes

> [t]heoretically there is no objection to supposing that any sort of instinctual demand might occasion the same repressions and their consequences: but our observation shows us invariably, so far as we can judge, that the excitations that play the pathogenic part arose from the component instincts of sexual life.
>
> *(p. 186)*

Viewed in this way there are no *a priori* 'id' drives and what becomes repressed is determined by prevailing social factors and inter-drive competition (Maze, 1983, 1987). With this in mind, a contextualised approach to id and ego is needed, since a particular drive manifestation may at different times be either prohibited or encouraged, depending upon the prevailing social environment:

> Although, according to the classical canon sexuality and aggression are id instincts ... nevertheless certain alignments of the sexual instinct are admitted to the ego as socially acceptable: in our society, sexual interest in a human being of the opposite sex and of a suitable age, provided there are no barriers of marriage or blood, is defined as legitimate. Again, aggression is not only permitted but demanded in certain situations against certain objects. Thus, the repressing instincts do not forbid all recognition or expression of the repressed: under special circumstances some sexual and aggressive impulses are allowed temporary membership of the ego.
>
> *(Maze, 1987, p. 196)*

In summary, an integrative position views both id and ego as constituted by the psychobiological drives, the former involving held back and repressed drive expressions, while the latter involves the repressing subset of psychobiological systems. The advantage of this position is that the problems of the horse-and-rider analogy are circumvented. The ego is not a higher agency divorced from the organism's motivational systems, and so explaining the behaviour of the 'person' is without appeal to a rational Cartesian ego devoid of biological and motivational bases. Furthermore, proposing that the repressed drive trends remain isolated and incapable of synthesis into the collective forming the ego (Freud, 1910i) is consistent with the account of repression in Chapter 3, where repression involves competition between drives, rather than between drives and some superordinate agency. This account further circumvents the criticisms of anthropomorphic homunculi associated with the structural theory (Boag, 2014; Maze, 1983). Neither the id nor ego constitute homunculi but instead reflect more or less fluid collectives of psychobiological drive trends that have or have not submitted to repression. Accordingly, there is no single executive entity called the ego acting as the agency of repression and instead

120 The metapsychology of the self

the protagonists behind repression are the psychobiological drives, guided by beliefs of frustration and gratification, while those succumbing to repression form the id. Consequently, given then that the ego is not divorced from the psychobiological drives, there is then a case for conceptualising the id principally in reference to the repressed subset of psychobiological drive expressions (cf. Hopkins, 2013).

Ego, identification and identity

While understanding the division between ego and the id is explicable in terms of inter-drive conflict and pressures from the social context, the story is nevertheless incomplete since important facets such as identity and character still require exposition. The ego is typically associated with the "I", whereas the id (the "it") is not, and so given that the proposal here that the ego is comprised of various motivational sources, some account is required for explaining how a sense of identity develops normatively to form a singular sense of 'self' as is typically the case. With respect to the earlier discussion, a first approach to understanding this is with respect to the distinction between the so-called 'internal body' (the psychobiological drives) and the 'known ego' (or 'external body'), where the internal body (here taken to be the drives) generally comes to identify itself with the external body—"[t]he subject of consciousness identifies itself with its external body (object-presentation)" (Solms, 2013, p. 15), and "arouses the external body to serve its vital needs in the external world" (Solms, 2013, p. 6; cf. Solms & Panksepp, 2012, p. 155). In addition to this, given that the drives are *brain structures* (connected nevertheless intimately with various physiological organs, the perceptual systems, etc.), there is ordinarily no possibility of direct awareness of the drives themselves. However, the expressions of the drives, their desires and affects, are knowable, and such expressions are realised through the singular body and its various activities (including cognition). Furthermore, as Freud (1910i) notes, both self-preservative and libidinal drives have an anaclitic relationship—"[t]he sexual and ego-instincts alike have in general the same organs and systems of organs at their disposal" (pp. 215–216; cf. Freud, 1912d, pp. 180–181)—and thus, the drives, *plural*, necessarily identify with a *singular* physical and mental apparatus, which includes knowing a shared pool of the 'person's' desires, beliefs, and actions (insofar as these have not succumbed to repression). Consequently, as Freud (1923b) recognises, the known ego "is first and foremost a body-ego" (p. 27) and "the ego is ultimately derived from bodily sensations" (p. 26n), since the body provides an initial identificatory object (cf. Solms, 2013). Consequently, since from the start the psychobiological drives perceive singularity rather than division, the apparent unity of the ego follows from a drive neither knowing itself directly (nor the other drives) and instead only knowing the general organism and its associated activities. Social interactions would further reinforce the development of this more or less coherent sense of self since we appear as a single organism to others and are treated as such accordingly. Consequently, as noted

The metapsychology of the self **121**

elsewhere (Boag, 2005), due to these factors, "[t]he resulting belief of a unified self is as *prima facie* plausible as the belief that the sun revolves around the earth" (p. 753). Nevertheless, the known self, ostensibly acting as the agent behind action, is essentially a fantasy—a false belief—based upon appearances (cf. Grossman, 1982; Solms, 2013; Solms & Panksepp, 2012).

However, Freud also recognises that one's sense of self can extend far beyond the boundary of the actual organism and can extend to family, possessions and beyond (cf. William James, 1890, p. 291) and thus 'personal identity' can be seen as a collective viewpoint whereby a subset of the psychobiological drives identifies (most commonly but not necessarily) with the body and its parts, as well as other people to various degrees, values, society, culture, etc. and, as Freud and others have recognised, the role of object relations and identification is essential for understanding this.

Note

1 The view that the drives are the cognitive subjects also emerges in affective neuroscience. Panksepp (1999), for example, implies that the drives engage both cognition and behaviour via the SEEKING system. By its very nature, the SEEKING system, guided by the drives, must navigate the world: "The SEEKING system, under the guidance of various regulatory imbalances, external incentive cues and past learning, helps take thirsty animals to water, cold animals to warmth, hungry animals to food, and sexually aroused animals towards opportunities for orgasmic gratification" (p. 167; cf. Panksepp & Moskal, 2008; see also Bazan & Detandt, 2013, pp. 6–7).

6
THE METAPSYCHOLOGY OF OBJECT RELATIONS

Introduction

The concept of object relations first emerges in Freudian theory, and the theory and significance of object relations has subsequently been addressed and extended by a number of theorists including Melanie Klein, W. R. D. Fairbairn, Donald Winnicot amongst others (see Ogden, 1983; Sandler, 1990). While object relational approaches are by no means a unified position (see Blum, 2010), they tend to be viewed as a major breakaway from Freudian theory, providing greater emphasis upon 'persons', both in contrast to Freud's 'impersonal' drives, as well as proposing an independent autonomous need for relationship based on more than simply self-gratification (Fonagy, 1999a). In this latter respect, motivational factors again provide a focal point underlying shifts away from Freud's theory (e.g. Bowlby, 1969, 1982; Fairbairn, 1952), and thus a discussion of the adequacy of motivational accounts in object relational positions is particularly pertinent for addressing pluralism in psychoanalytic theory. The necessity of a foundational drive account, developed in Chapter 2, indicates that object relational approaches require, at minimum, an account of what *drives* object relations.

Object relations in Freudian theory

Freud (1915c) proposes that given that organisms satisfy drive-states through various 'objects', drive activity necessarily involves object relationships. Accordingly, drives provide the motivational bases for understanding object relations and neither drives nor object relations can be satisfactorily appreciated in isolation, as Spruiell (1988) rightly notes:

> While it is true that Freud's concepts of drives and objects changed over the years, it is also fair to say that he *always* saw objects in terms of drives;

The metapsychology of object relations   **123**

by the same token, it would be almost impossible to imagine drives without objects. It would be like the Zen koan in which one tries to imagine one hand clapping.

(p. 598, his italics)

While drive-objects include various substances, such as food, it is drive relationships with both real and imagined persons that take on added significance in Freudian theory. Freud recognises that object relations set up in very early life are especially enduring and influential upon the individual, as epitomised by transference relationships (Freud, 1912b, 1915a), and it is generally accepted that object relations are especially relevant clinically given that projective and introjective identifications are tied up with transference and counter-transference processes (Maze, 1993; Ogden, 1983). However, object relations within Freud's theory are essentially consummatory relations whereby objects are gratifying or frustrating in relation to drive states. This state of affairs underlies both affective responses ("pleasure and unpleasure signify relations of the ego to the object"—Freud, 1915c, p. 137), as well as both approach and avoidance of objects:

> If the object becomes a source of pleasurable feelings, a motor urge is set up which seeks to bring the object closer to the ego and to incorporate it into the ego. We then speak of the 'attraction' exercised by the pleasure-giving object, and say that we 'love' that object. Conversely, if the object is a source of unpleasurable feelings, there is an urge which endeavours to increase the distance between the object and the ego and to repeat in relation to the object the original attempt at flight from the external world with its emission of stimuli. We feel the 'repulsion' of the object, and hate it; this hate can afterwards be intensified to the point of an aggressive inclination against the object—an intention to destroy it.
>
> *(Freud, 1915c, p. 137)*

Nevertheless, the psychological significance of these object relations extends far beyond simply consummatory acts because objects become internalised (introjected) through identificatory relationships: the individual comes to stand in various *intra*personal relationships, the most obvious within the structural theory being the relationship between the ego and superego. For Freud, the development of the superego specifically involves identificatory relationships set up within the resolution to the Oedipus complex. The young child's libidinal attraction towards one caregiver threatens loss of love and mutilation from the rival one (typically the father), and so the young ego subsequently identifies with, and internalises, the offended rival and their prohibitions, instigating repression of the libidinal impulse (Freud, 1923b, p. 36; 1933a, p. 63). Freud (1930b) writes:

> First comes renunciation of instinct owing to fear of aggression by the *external* authority. (This is, of course, what fear of loss of love amounts to, for love is a

124 The metapsychology of object relations

protection against this punitive aggression.) After that comes the erection of an *internal* authority, and renunciation of instinct owing to fear of it—owing to fear of conscience.

(p. 128)

The resulting 'internalised authority' becomes a more or less independent source of agency within the personality (e.g. Freud, 1923b, p. 51; 1933a, p. 60):

> In the course of an individual's development a portion of the inhibiting forces in the external world are internalized and an agency is constructed in the ego which confronts the rest of the ego in an observing, criticizing and prohibiting sense. We call this new agency the *super-ego*. Thenceforward the ego, before putting to work the instinctual satisfaction demanded by the id, has to take into account not merely the dangers of the external world but also the objections of the super-ego, and it will have all the more grounds for abstaining from satisfying the instinct.
>
> *(Freud, 1939a, p. 116, his italics; cf. Freud, 1914c, p. 95; 1916–1917, pp. 428–429; 1933a, p. 60)*

Personality structures, such as the superego, thus develop within the context of one's early relations with external objects, and, as Ogden (1993) points out, Freud provides the theoretical platform for subsequent developments in object relations theory, including the significance of 'internal objects' which will be discussed later.

However, as noted earlier, where object relational approaches chiefly differ from Freud's is with respect to the motivation underlying relationships: rather than mere consummation, object relations reflect a primary desire for relationship with others. This is particularly the case in W. R. D. Fairbairn's theory, where he writes, "relationship with the object, and not the gratification of impulse, is the ultimate aim of libidinal striving" (1943, p. 60). Bowlby similarly rejects the 'cupboard-love theory of object relations' (or 'Secondary drive' theory) whereby seeking relationships occurs as a secondary response to learning that the mother is a source of gratification (Bowlby, 1982, p. 667; see, for instance, Freud, 1926d, p. 137; 1940a[1938], p. 188).[1] In contradistinction to Freud, Bowlby consequently conceptualises a primary need for relationship: "attachment … [is] a fundamental form of behaviour with its own internal motivation distinct from feeding and sex, and of no less importance for survival" (Bowlby, 1982, p. 669), and with respect to this suggestion, Fonagy (1999a) proposes that attachment theory and object relations overlap in terms of motivation: "modern psychoanalysis shares the fundamental assumption of attachment theory that the infant-caregiver relationship is not based on physical need but rather on some kind of independent autonomous need for relationship" (p. 455).

Fairbairn and dynamic structures

Greenberg and Mitchell (1983) describe Fairbairn's theory as the "the purest and clearest expression of the shift from a drive/structure model to a relational/ structure model" (p. 151), and Bowlby (1969) similarly describes Fairbairn's object relational approach as "the most pure because of his explicit rejection of all non-object-relational concepts" (p. 17).[2] Fairbairn (1946) recognises that "Freud's whole system of thought was concerned with object-relationships" but he rejects Freud's view that "libido is primarily concerned with pleasure-seeking, i.e. with the relief of its own tension" (p. 149). That is, for Fairbairn, object relations are not essentially concerned with personal gratification, and instead, "[t]he real libidinal aim is the establishment of satisfactory relationships with objects; and it is, accordingly, the object that constitutes the true libidinal goal" (1946, p. 138). From the outset, it is clear that Fairbairn's position is more consistent with a teleological stance than a deterministic one, and thus requires an account of the driving causes of object relational activities. Fairbairn addresses motivation in terms of goals, as seen in his comparison of a child's seeking objects to a moth seeking a flame:

> It can hardly be said … that the moth is guided to the flame by pleasure. On the contrary, its behaviour is essentially object-seeking. What it is seeking, however, is not the flame but the light. Thus is it not actuated by a pleasure principle, but by a reality sense which is severely limited, since it cannot differentiate between one source of light and another.
>
> *(Fairbairn, 1946, p. 141)*

In some respects, Fairbairn's theory overlaps with Bowlby's, since environmental information guides the child's approach towards inherently valued objects (cf. Bowlby, 1969). However, Fairbairn is not entirely consistent on the matter, writing that 'tension relief' underlies object-seeking, which suggests some kind of efficient causality: "the tension which demands relief is the tension of object-seeking tendencies" (Fairbairn, 1946, p. 149). This notwithstanding, a closer inspection of Fairbairn's position demonstrates that his theory is, in part, a response to Freud's horse-and-rider analogy, and again, it is the differences in motivational stances that provide impetus for distancing object relations from Freudian theory, and thus contributing to psychoanalytic pluralism.

The horse-and-rider analogy revisited

Fairbairn is critical of Freud's proposal that the id, although without structure, contains the motivational impetus ('energy'), while the structured ego is without energy and simply controls and directs the id (Freud, 1923b, p. 25; 1933a, p. 77). Fairbairn is essentially here criticising Freud's horse-and-rider analogy discussed in

126 The metapsychology of object relations

the previous chapter, whereby the ego's motivation is left unaccounted for, a point that Fairbairn (1946) recognises, when he writes:

> the 'ego' is conceived as a structure without any energy in its own rights; and the 'id' is conceived as a source of energy without structure. As regards the 'super-ego', its behaviour is certainly described in terms which imply that it is a dynamic structure; but, since all energy in the psyche is regarded as proceeding ultimately from the 'id', it becomes obvious that the 'super-ego', like the 'ego', is really an energiless structure deriving energy from a source outside itself.
>
> *(p. 148)*

Freud's theory, says Fairbairn, is problematic here because the 'person' is left unaccounted for: both the person-like ego and superego are treated as passive structures, whereas the drives provide the real foundations, and thus personality, at its basis, is essentially impersonal. Fairbairn (1946) critically writes here that as a result of this "divorce of energy from structure", psychoanalytic theory "has been unduly permeated by conceptions of hypothetical 'impulses' and 'instincts' which bombard passive structures, much as if an air-raid were in progress" (p. 150).

Thus, for Fairbairn, the specific problem with Freud's theory is the dichotomy between (personal) structure and (impersonal) motivation, which essentially equates with Freud's horse-and-rider analogy, and which Fairbairn believes is simply false: since the 'ego' is *both* a structure and clearly motivated, "both structure divorced from energy and energy divorced from structure are meaningless concepts" (Fairbairn, 1946, p. 149). That is, persons are motivated, and so trying to attribute agency to the impersonal drives gives rise to a mistaken impulse-psychology, which does not adequately address the actual state of affairs. In response to this shortcoming, Fairbairn is prompted to replace the dichotomy between the structured-but-energiless ego and the structureless-but-energic id with a notion of 'dynamic structure', which has been subsequently amplified and extended by Ogden (1983, 1993). Although Fairbairn never explicitly defines either term 'dynamic' or 'structure' (Ogden, 1983; cf. Maze, 1993), within the context of his criticism of Freud's horse-and-rider analogy, dynamic structures can be taken to be person-level structures, with their own motivational sources (i.e. dynamism), and it is this response to Freud that leads Fairbairn to propose an alternative conception of personality development.

Personality structure and dynamic internal objects

In Fairbairn's theory, the ego is the primary dynamic structure, and unlike Freud (1923b), where the ego is initially absent, Fairbairn postulates that there is initially a unitary Central ego. However, as a consequence of frustrating object relations and subsequent repression, this original ego becomes split into separate dynamic

The metapsychology of object relations **127**

egos (most typically the Central ego, anti-libidinal/internal saboteur, and libidinal egos), each attached to (frustrating) 'internal' objects, and each persisting as dynamic (motivated) 'endopsychic structures' (Fairbairn, 1944). In contrast to Freud's horse-and-rider account of an unmotivated ego, Fairbairn (1946) writes that "all the ego-structures are conceived as inherently dynamic; and the Central ego represents the central portion of an original unitary, dynamic ego-structure, from which the subsidiary egos come to be subsequently split off" (p. 148). Personality later comes to consist in various intrapersonal relationships resulting from a fragmenting of the ego due to repression, which leads to a multiplicity of ego-structures with their own internal objects. For this reason, Ogden (1983) writes that object relations theory "is in fact fundamentally a theory of unconscious internal object relations in dynamic interplay with current interpersonal experience" (p. 227; cf. Ogden, 1993, p. 131), where 'internal' refers "not to a geographic locale, but to an intrapersonal event, (i.e. involving a single personality system) as opposed to an interpersonal interaction involving two or more different people" (Ogden, 1983, p. 227*n*).[3]

However, the precise relation between ego-structures and internal objects is not always clear in Fairbairn's theory and while Fairbairn generally treats ego-structures as dynamic he does not consistently do so with internalised objects (Maze, 1993; Ogden, 1993). Ogden (1993) writes that "Fairbairn only hesitatingly accepted the idea that internal objects are dynamic structures and was not able to delineate the relationship between the concept of internal objects and the concept of the ego" (p. 156). So, for example, whereas Freud treats the superego as a dynamic structure, Fairbairn in places explicitly does not (e.g. 1944, pp. 131–132; see also Maze's discussion, 1993, p. 463). Nevertheless, Fairbairn can also be found to grant autonomy to both various ego structures *and* internal objects, which he sees as an extension of Freud's position that the superego is an autonomous structure:

> the time is now ripe for us to replace the concept of 'phantasy' by a concept of 'inner reality' peopled by the ego and its internal objects. These internal objects should be regarded as having an organized structure, an identity of their own, an endopsychic existence and an activity [a capacity for thinking and feeling] as real within the inner world as those of any objects in the outer world. To attribute such features to internal objects may at first seem startling to some; but, after all, they are only features which Freud has already attributed to the superego … What has now emerged is simply that the superego is not the only internal object.
>
> *(Fairbairn, 1943, in Ogden, 2011, p. 938, Ogden's insertion)*

Ogden (2011) takes Fairbairn's position above to mean that internal objects are identical with ego-structures, writing that for Fairbairn, internal objects are not merely phantasy or simply ideational content: "Internal objects are not ideas—they are split-off parts of the ego with which the internal world is 'peopled'" (p. 938).

128 The metapsychology of object relations

Furthermore, according to Ogden, as dynamic agents, internal objects are consequently the subjects—the knowers—that engage in phantasying: "*phantasying is the product of internal objects (i.e. internal objects are the thinkers doing the unconscious thinking)*" (p. 139, his italics).

While Ogden appears to be conflating subject (ego) and (internal) object, his basic point here is that these various personalities are so identified with their objects that they believe themselves to be separate individuals and act accordingly: "This identification with the object is so thorough that one's original sense of self is almost entirely lost" (Ogden, 1983, p. 227). Again:

> The fact that this structure (the internal object) is experienced as non-self is accounted for by means of its profound identification with the object. Internalization requiring a splitting of the ego occurs only in early development and as a result, the identification with the object is of a poorly differentiated nature, i.e. the experiential quality of the identification is one of 'becoming the object' as opposed to 'feeling like' the object.
>
> *(Odgen, 1983, p. 234)*

Consequently, after splitting, what is originally a single, unitary subject term becomes (at least) three individual subject terms, each capable of cognitive acts and subjective experience, and Ogden explicitly states as such, describing internal objects as "dynamically unconscious suborganizations of the ego generating meaning and experience, i.e. capable of thought, feeling and perception" (p. 227). These internal objects are subsequently phenomenologically experienced as separate 'individuals', since the split-off ego-structures animate these personifications with their own dynamism. Consequently, Ogden's conceptualisation of internal objects goes beyond these as literally something known (in the way that the 'self and object mental representations' are). The primary difference between the various split-off ego structures is that some identify with external objects while others remain true to the original sense of ego:

> Such a dual split would result in the formation of two new suborganizations of the ego, one identified with the self in the external object relationship and the other thoroughly identified with the object. This formation accounts for the dynamic nature of the internal object and also defines the relationship between the concept of ego and the concept of internal objects. In brief, internal objects are subdivisions of the ego that are heavily identified with an object representation while maintaining the capacities of the whole ego for thought, perception, feeling, etc.
>
> *(Ogden, 1983, p. 234, his italics)*

Ogden's intention here is to clarify the relation between ego-structures and internal objects and address a shortcoming in Fairbairn's approach, *viz*. Fairbairn "did not explain how an internal object (presumably originally thought) achieves its dynamism" (Ogden, 1993, p. 148). While identifying ego-structures with the internal objects does not preclude differentiating them, "[t]his identification with the object is so thorough that one's original sense of self is almost entirely lost" (Ogden, 1993, p. 132), and hence the various internal objects are dynamic by virtue of their relation to these dynamic ego structures. Fairbairn (1951) similarly writes:

> Although I have spoken of internalized objects as structures, I have treated them simply as objects of dynamic ego-structures, and not as themselves dynamic. ... In the interests of consistency, however, I must draw the logical conclusion of my theory and acknowledge that, since internal objects are endopsychic structures, they must be themselves in some measure dynamic; and it should be added that *they must derive their dynamic quality from their cathexis by ego-structures.*
>
> (Fairbairn, 1951, p. 177; my emphasis)

Thus, both Fairbairn and Ogden could be taken here to be proposing an ego-structure/object relationship whereby the internal object is dynamic insofar as the respective ego-structure identifies with the phantasised object. Pataki (2014b) describes this as *personation* by which the ego-structures play the part of (i.e. personate) actual or phantasised individuals.

Drives and object relations

While Fairbairn's recognition that the ego is dynamic is theoretically welcome (in contrast to the horse-and-rider analogy), his position nevertheless raises several difficult theoretical questions. To begin with, as indicated earlier, Fairbairn's account of motivation is *prima facie* problematic given its teleological stance: at best, 'object-seeking tendencies' provide a description of what someone is likely to do in the presence of an object, leaving the actual explanation of such tendencies unaccounted for (cf. Boag, 2011a, 2015a). Furthermore, as we know from 'proximity seeking' in adults, any number of motives might be present (seeking security, sexual designs, providing comfort, a reaction to aggressive impulses, or any interaction of these—Yovell, 2008b), and all of these potential motives indicate that any number of drives and affective states might underlie one and the same behaviour. Furthermore, when Fairbairn does provide some indication of efficient causes, he never clarifies what he precisely means. For example, how are we to make sense of "the tension of object-seeking tendencies" (Fairbairn, 1946, p. 149)? Or what determines "the establishment of *satisfactory* relationships with objects" (Fairbairn, 1946, p. 138, emphasis added)? Fairbairn's phrases here suggest conditions possibly driving object-seeking behaviour, as well as some type of gratifying outcome related to those

130 The metapsychology of object relations

conditions, and Maze (1993) accordingly writes that to substantiate such claims, "[o]bject-relations theory implicitly assumes primary drives to cope with the fact that some kinds of transaction with objects are not gratifying but are feared and avoided" (p. 469). In other words, an account of foundational drives is necessary for explaining the motivational policy underlying frustration and gratification within object relationships, and thus drive accounts and object relations theory are not, as commonly supposed, antithetical (Maze, 1993). Instead, the obvious solution to account for both 'the tension of object-seeking tendencies' and 'satisfactory relationships with objects' would be to provide a foundational drive approach to account for the mechanics of driven object relations behaviour, as well as for accounting for both satisfying and frustrating object relations.

Thus, the essential problem for Fairbairn's account specifically, and object relational approaches more generally (including attachment theory), is that there is no adequate account of motivation. As developed earlier, some sort of driving system is necessary for providing a biologically grounded explanatory framework for understanding why a person is motivated to relate to certain objects and not others, and so an integrated position accounting for both the biological foundations (the drives) and their (object) relations is required. Bowlby, in fact, may have come to appreciate this, for while he initially rejected any suggestion of drives (and even the concept of motivation), proposing instead a behavioural system account of attachment behaviours ("The child's tie to his mother is a product of the activity of a number of behavioural systems that have proximity to mother as a predictable outcome"—Bowlby, 1969, p. 179), he later appears to have been aware of the inadequacy of such a proposal, attributing attachment to a drive-like motivational source, "conceived on the analogy of a physiological system organized homeostatically to ensure that a certain physiological measure, such as body temperature or blood pressure, is held between appropriate limits" (Bowlby, 1982, p. 670). However, as discussed in Chapter 2, identifying such drives based on behaviour is problematic, and substantiating Bowlby's claim requires fleshing out any such attachment drive, at least in some respects, neuroscientifically. Affective neuroscience research is highly relevant here (Panksepp, 1999; Panksepp & Biven, 2012; see, also, Hopkins, 2015) and while there are no clear answers yet concerning such primary drives (see Yovell, 2008a, 2008b and related commentaries), there is no theoretical objection to developing an integrated psychoanalytic, neuroscientific, attachment-oriented position that addresses precisely this.

The metapsychology of multiple personality

Fairbairn and Ogden's account of dynamic structures and internal objects provides a strong partitioning approach (i.e. multiple knowers—see Boag, 2005), and whether this fits with a foundational drive account also requires consideration. The possibility of multiple knowers has *prima facie* support from a variety of sources

The metapsychology of object relations **131**

(e.g. split-brain cases, for instance—e.g. Sperry, 1969, 1982), and the notion of multiple autonomous inner personalities is found in a variety of both ancient and contemporary theories (see Pataki, 2014b). Symington (1993), for instance, writes that "[w]e are all made up of parts, each part capable of functioning as a separate little person" (p. 23), which he links to object relations: "when we talk about an internalized mother, father, brother, sister, or whatever, these are internalized objects, and these objects act. They act within the personality. At certain points they may even take over the personality" (p. 20).

However, while Ogden (1993) claims that his account of internal objects "goes no further in the direction of demonology than did Freud in describing the formation of the superego" (p. 150), this is not necessarily a virtue. As noted earlier, Freud's theory of the id, ego and superego has been widely criticised for both reification and anthropomorphism (e.g. Boesky, 1995; Grossman & Simon, 1969; Laplanche & Pontalis, 1973; Talvitie, 2012), and as with Freud, both Fairbairn and Ogden are open to the criticism that their account of ego-structures and internal objects simply multiplies instances of reification since we are only told what the ego-structures *do* but not what they actually *are*, and so the 'ego-structures' are left uncharacterised and structure-less. Maze (1993), in fact, writes that "while it may appear that internal objects act autonomously," this is more apparent than real, since

> while this way of describing them may convey the patient's phenomenological experience very powerfully, it seems to me to obscure the fact that one is really dealing with the person's thoughts, wishes and fears, or more precisely, with the beliefs, wishes and fears of various parts of the person's mind.
> *(Maze, 1993, p. 464)*

Thus, for Maze (1993) "[i]nternal objects do not really initiate their own behaviour" (p. 464) and are simply imagined entities that have no actual autonomy, existing simply as objects of a person's desires and beliefs. If it is the case that internal objects are primarily beliefs, phantasies, and desires, as Maze (1993) believes, then such internal objects cannot exist as autonomous structures (or subject terms) simply because beliefs, phantasies, and desires are activities and so cannot also constitute the structures engaging in those same activities (Boag, 2005).

However, one limitation of Maze's counter-proposal is that it does not appear to account for the observed clinical phenomena (Boag, 2014). For example, Freud's descriptions of the superego suggest a motivated, independent agency (e.g. Freud, 1914c, p. 95; 1916–1917, pp. 428–429; 1933a, p. 60), and the question remains whether we can account for these apparent autonomous dynamic centres, without subscribing to the problems associated with the homunculus fallacy. One possible direction here is to link the drives with the various objects, where, for example, in the 'conscious id' account (Solms, 2013; Solms & Panksepp, 2012), the 'internal body' (the id) identifies with the 'external body' (the ego as self-representation). As was

132 The metapsychology of object relations

discussed previously, this internal body is best not considered a singular agent, since a multiplicity of drives is necessary to account for conflict and division between id and ego. In advancing such a multiplicity, the ego was conceptualised as a collective of drives identifying broadly with the self, and this position is not incompatible with Fairbairn's ego-structures and their internal objects as dynamic organisations, even if Fairbairn would reject substantiating the ego-structures with the ego-drives. If it is plausible (as suggested) for a single 'ego-structure' to be characterised in terms of a subset of the biologically grounded drives and their identifications, then this provides a basis for making sense of both personality differentiation and the motivational bases of ego-structures and their internal objects. As argued earlier, there is no logical difficulty in proposing various drive-combinations organised around various apparent centres of agency (self, identity, etc.), and thus Fairbairn's dynamic structures/internal object relationships could possibly reflect combinations of drives identifying with an imago, mistakenly identifying themselves as a 'person' that acts as a singular agent. Based on this, since Fairbairn's dynamic structures are without sufficient motivational foundations, and that Fairbairn (1944) aims to provide an explanatory system for the dynamics of endopsychic structures (pp. 128ff), Fairbairn's account gains everything from admitting a drive basis to account for the motivation of ego-structures and loses nothing with respect to providing his distinctive object relational approach (Boag, 2014).

If this position is granted then such 'persons' are not substantive entities but rather more or less stable and ultimately fluid personality positions. The dynamics of figures encountered in dreams provides some indication of such apparent structures or agents with their own dynamics which are nevertheless fluid and malleable. As discussed elsewhere (Boag, 2014), in an early analysis of a female patient with a physical genital abnormality (Fairbairn, 1931), Fairbairn describes two dream figures who appear to correspond to the id and superego ('the mischievous boy' and the 'critic', respectively—p. 217), and each of these dream figures were active, to the point where "invasion of waking life by [these] personifications did actually occur" (p. 219). For instance, at the onset of analysis "'the mischievous boy' took almost complete possession of her conscious life" (p. 219), and these figures were thus not simply passive phantasised figures (or objects of cognition) but also active subjects. Fairbairn further observed that the situation was not static: during the course of the analysis other figures (e.g. a 'little girl' and 'the martyr') also emerged, indicating that such 'structures' are not fixed and stable entities but rather fluid and flexible, leading Fairbairn to rightly ask whether Freud's tripartite division has been considered "too much in the light of entities" (p. 218).

This point was not entirely lost on Freud since he was also aware that "the ego can be split; it splits itself during a number of its functions—temporarily at least. Its parts can come together again afterwards" (1933a, p. 58), and Freud even recognises that the id, ego, superego were not the only possible personality divisions, commenting that "perhaps the secret of the cases of what is described as 'multiple

The metapsychology of object relations **133**

personality' is that the different identifications seize hold of consciousness in turn",
a position he describes as not necessarily pathological (1923b, pp. 30–31). Indeed,
although the id, ego, and superego are commonly observed personality structures,
Freud explicitly writes that variations may nevertheless be found:

> In thinking of this division of the personality into an ego, super-ego and an
> id, you will not, of course, have pictured sharp frontiers like the artificial ones
> drawn in political geography … After making the separation we must allow
> what we have separated to merge together once more … *It is highly probable that
> the development of these divisions is subject to great variations in different individuals.*
> *(Freud, 1933a, p. 79, emphasis added)*

That being so, Freud observes that the triadic structural theory is simply typical
rather than inevitable: various other personality divisions might arise and there is
no logical problem with the possibility of multiple 'egos' which, for all intents and
purposes, reflect 'multiple personalities', a possibility Freud briefly touches upon
in *On Narcissism* (1914c). Various subsets of drives constitute different 'egos', each
developing an independent and separate sense of identity or self-hood via various
object-identifications.

To take all of this into account, the integrative approach developed here for
addressing ego structures and internal objects is with respect to the foundational
drives and their shifting alliances and identifications. By linking ego structures/
internal objects with the foundational drives, motivational policy is accounted for:
divisions are instigated by frustrating drive-environments (object relations), whereas
personality consolidation entails drive-satisfaction, whether it be comfort, narcissism,
or some other fulfilment. Furthermore, this position avoids reifying personality
structures, since while the foundational drive sources are themselves substantive
psychobiological engines that remain relatively stable, the relative fluidity of drive-
subsets organising themselves around an imago (a fluidity which seems to be further
facilitated in dreaming) allows both splits within personality, as well as evolving
drive alliances, to give rise to any variety of emerging personifications. This position further contributes a dynamic framework for understanding a variety of normal
and clinical psychological phenomena related to 'multiple personalities', including
Dissociative Identity Disorder (DID) (Boag, 2014). Given that various drives can
join forces or be in conflict, then there is the possibility of divisions and further
sub-divisions of dynamic structures based around various identifications. Such divisions could give rise to an apparent multiplicity of 'personalities' and disruptions
in identity as found in DID, where two or more 'distinct personality states' (possibly experienced as 'possession') are associated with recurring gaps in remembering
(APA, 2013, p. 292). Developing a theoretical foundation for this is important since
there is persistent controversy as to whether DID is in fact an authentic disorder (see,
for instance, Boysen & VanBergen, 2013, 2014; see also Dalenberg et al., 2012, 2014;

134 The metapsychology of object relations

Lynn et al., 2014; Piper & Mersky, 2004a, 2004b), and a particular theoretical problem here concerns how best to conceptualise 'personality' within DID, an issue that also impacts upon clinicians working with DID with respect to both conceptualising the personalities ('alters'), as well as knowing how to engage with them in therapy. Kluft (2000) here writes, "[a]mong the major issues that arise in the treatment of DID are the relationship of the alters to the personality that the therapist may experience as his or her patient, and the relationship of the therapist to the alters" (p. 266). As a consequence of this uncertainty, many psychoanalytic clinicians (even if accepting that some version of alters exist), "are reluctant to address them [the alters] directly or to request or facilitate their participation in the process" (p. 270). On the theoretical position developed above, there is theoretical justification for treating alters in the same manner as one would treat the 'ego': both the ego and alters can be thought of as drive-object identifications, and consequently capable of acting as subjects and engaging with the world around them. Accordingly, and given the centrality of the therapeutic alliance (Meissner, 2007), there is justification for Kluft's (2000) proposal of forming therapeutic alliances with the alters, where the clinician addresses the alters as one would the 'ego' and engages with them in the therapeutic process. The integrative approach proposed here might also (at least, in principle) contribute to neuroscientific studies addressing the authenticity of DID (e.g. Reinders et al., 2012; Schlumpf et al., 2013), since given that the drives essentially entail neural sources, then their contribution to DID should be assessable, in the same manner as the motivational contributions to dreaming are presently being assessed (e.g. Colace, 2004, 2010, 2014; Colace & Boag, 2015).

Notes

1 Bowlby (1969) provides an extensive review of the cupboard love theory in an appendix titled 'The child's tie to his mother: review of the psychoanalytical literature'.
2 Interestingly, Greenberg and Mitchell (1983) also view Fairbairn's theory as closely related to Bowlby's.
3 There is nevertheless longstanding confusion surrounding the precise ontological status of internal objects and what is precisely meant by 'internal' when referring to internal objects (see, for instance, Brierley, 1942).

CONCLUSION

Freud's metapsychology, broadly speaking, was a grand attempt at developing a general psychology integrating motivation, cognition and affects. While Freud's specific metapsychology, entailing the *dynamic*, *topographic*, and *economic* points of view, has its fair share of problems, Freud's general metapsychological approach, nevertheless provides a sound platform and foundation for a general theory of both normal and pathological human activity. This book has attempted to demonstrate that a critical metapsychological approach, based on the sound insights of Freudian theory, is capable of providing a common foundation for the various strands and developments of psychoanalytic theory, both allowing the genuine insights from each approach to be appreciated, while dispensing with any theoretical claim that does not hold up to critical scrutiny. As Freud recognises, such a general theory is necessary for unifying disparate phenomena including dreams and neurotic symptoms, as well as for examining how the parts fit within the whole. Such an approach provides a more holistic and ultimately more fruitful picture of humanity, rather than examining any personality element in isolation. In this respect, even critics of Freud's specific metapsychology nevertheless appreciate the role and need of a general theory as a "hoped for alternative to metapsychology" (Holt, 1981, p. 130; cf. Holt, 1982, p. 251*n*), and Freud's general metapsychological account provides such a hoped for alternative, addressing the embodied inter-relationship of motivation, affects and cognition.

However, the intention here is not to provide a complete picture of personality. Such an account would not be presently possible, and the precise metapsychological components presented here will undoubtedly require revision (cf. Freud, 1915c). For instance, our understanding of drives and their role in the human system will presumably develop in sophistication according to further empirical and

136 Conclusion

theoretical research, even if their general role as motivational processes remains the same. Moreover, any such complete picture of personality, should it ever be realised—which is questionable given evolutionary selective pressures and the interaction with changing environments—requires delving further into (epi) genetics and the brain, which requires far greater understanding of the interaction between the body and the environment. Indeed, Freud was always sensitive to the fact that constitution and individual temperaments varied (Freud, 1888, p. 50; 1933a, pp. 149–150), and while he recognised that psychological analysis could not sufficiently address these, our increasing understanding of temperament and epigenetics underlying biopsychosocial development means that such new discoveries take on added significance and require synthesis within any comprehensive position.

Instead, the more modest aim here is simply to show that Freud's theory provides a foundation that, once divested of its problematic elements, accommodates the various coherent contributions provided by the various schools of psychoanalysis, as well as providing the basis for incorporating future insights and discoveries. What the present work points to is the possibility of an integrated psychoanalytic position incorporating the basics of Freudian theory, including a revised account of the foundational drives to replace the problematic drive-discharge theory, as well as appreciating the contributions of object relational approaches, including that of attachment theory and the role of internal objects. As Rangell (2000) notes, any comprehensive psychoanalytic general theory must embrace both drive and object relations, and to attempt to have one without the other can only ever provide an incomplete and truncated account of complex human activity. Nevertheless, not any drive account will do, and while drive-object relational approaches are, of course, already in existence (e.g. Kernberg, 2001; Meadow, 1989; Spruiell, 1988), including that of Melanie Klein, recognised as one of the earliest Object relations theorists (Bacal, 1987; Ogden, 1983), until a drive account is presented that is both logically sound and congruent with the neuroscientific evidence, drives will remain a source of pluralism in psychoanalysis. After all, it was problems with Freud's specific drive-discharge metapsychology that provided justification for the subsequent diversification of theoretical offshoots from Freudian theory, including attachment theory and Fairbairn's object relations. This subsequent pluralism, while instigated in part by problems with Freud's specific metapsychology, can nevertheless be reconciled by developing a common core of theory—a common metapsychology—which further helps integrate what is of value from any specific approach, while rightly rejecting problematic elements. In this respect, while it is true that problems with Freud's specific metapsychology contributed to the current state of theoretical pluralism in psychoanalysis, it is similarly the case that the solution is necessarily metapsychological in nature. What is needed is a coherent general theory, and by redressing faults in Freud's specific conception, a revised general metapsychology does provide a coherent theoretical basis for psychodynamic theory that is both grounded philosophically and empirically.

There is, of course, no shortage of hurdles to widespread acceptance of any general psychoanalytic theory, and it would be a mistake to blame pluralism purely on problems with Freud's theory. As pointed out in the beginning chapters of this work, any individual's metaphysical commitments contribute to division, at least in some measure, since criticisms of metapsychology are often presented in terms of 'persons' versus 'mechanisms', or causality versus freedom (or teleology). Freud's commitment to determinism thus prompts some to reject his position simply based on an opposing metaphysical stance, a problem that is particularly acute in psychology, since, as noted earlier, "psychology, in its broadest sense, represents a very natural last outpost for vitalistic and antideterministic viewpoints" (Immergluck, 1964, p. 274). Determinism conflicts with our apparent desire for freedom, and ironically, it was in fact Freud's psychology of the unconscious that provided us with the first real glimpse of the determinants lying behind the common naïve psychology of the 'person' where choice appears free and unconstrained by anything other than our spirit. While such issues are not easily resolved, if nothing else, this book hopefully demonstrates that any approach to substantive theorising in psychoanalysis requires much more than a casual glance at philosophical enquiry.

Of course, it is easy to dismiss any such philosophical enquiry as merely speculative 'metaphysics', or dismiss metapsychological considerations as abstract theory that is irrelevant to the needs of clinicians and psychoanalysts. But what are the needs of clinicians? Surely clinical theory needs to be grounded in a coherent general theory, not only for guiding current practice but for also incorporating future developments. In this respect, while drives, are believed to be remote from human experience and thus also from the clinical arena, nevertheless any clinician is dealing with a motivated individuals' hopes and fears, and surely future discoveries related to the biological foundations of human experience need to be carefully addressed and not dismissed as irrelevant. A general psychoanalytic metapsychology, in principle, provides such a foundation for incorporating future insights, and so, as Mackay (1996) notes, while drive-level considerations are not always relevant to any specific clinical need, a holistic picture requires them nonetheless. As he writes:

> The clinician is generally not concerned with giving a whole metapsychological explanation of the wishes, hopes and fears that motivate the patient's behaviour and shape the person's experience, but is rather more concentrated on the meaning, the content, of the wishes. Yet, ultimately, we need a full and coherent account of the origin and nature of motivation to make sense of motivated action. Freud's drive theory, for all of its flaws, is a better attempt to provide this than are the theories of many of his critics.
>
> *(p. 17)*

138 Conclusion

Thus, it is in the clinician's present and longer-term interests to work towards developing a comprehensive and coherent metapsychology, not simply for intellectual entertainment, but for the psychoanalytic discipline to retain integrity while accommodating the future. Such a metapsychological foundation also helps navigate the plethora of competing positions presently available, by allowing us to address what is most coherently formulated. While Freud's specific metapsychological account is problematic, his general metapsychology nevertheless provides such a foundation for psychoanalysis, and thus Freudian theory continues to provide a substantive foundation for psychoanalysis.

REFERENCES

Aarts, H. & van den Bos, K. (2011). On the foundations of beliefs in free will intentional binding and unconscious priming in self-agency. *Psychological Science*, *22*, 532–537.

Anderson, J. (1962). *Studies in empirical philosophy*. Sydney: Angus & Robertson.

Anspach, M. R. (1998). Madness and the divided self: Esquirol, Sartre, Bateson. In J.-P. Dupuy (Ed.), *Self-deception and Paradoxes of Rationality* (pp. 59–86). Stanford, CA: CSLI Publications.

Applegarth, A. (1971). Comments on aspects of the theory of psychic energy. *Journal of the American Psychoanalytic Association*, *19*, 379–416.

Arlow, J. A. (1975). The structural hypothesis: Theoretical considerations. *Psychoanalytic Quarterly*, *44*, 509–525.

Arlow, J. A. (1977). Affects and the psychoanalytic situation. *The International Journal of Psychoanalysis*, *58*, 157–170.

Arlow, J. A. & Brenner, C. (1964). *Psychoanalytic concepts and the structural theory*. New York: International Universities Press.

Audi, R. (Ed.) (1995). *The Cambridge Dictionary of Philosophy*. Cambridge: Cambridge University Press.

Auld, F., Hyman, M., & Rudinski, D. (2005). *Resolution of inner conflict: An introduction to psychoanalytic therapy*. Washington, DC: American Psychological Association.

Bacal, H. A. (1987). British object-relations theorists and self psychology: Some critical reflections. *The International Journal of Psychoanalysis*, *68*, 81–98.

Baker, A. J. (1986). *Australian realism*. Cambridge: Cambridge University Press.

Bandura, A. (1999). Social cognitive theory of personality. In D. Cervone & Yuichi Shoda (Eds.), *The coherence of personality: Social-cognitive bases of consistency, variability, and organization* (pp. 185–241). New York: Guilford Press.

Barratt, B. B. (2015a). Critical notes on the neuro-evolutionary archaeology of affective systems. *Psychoanalytic Review*, *102*, 183–208.

Barratt, B. B. (2015b). Rejoinder to Mark Solms's response to 'Critical notes on the neuro-evolutionary archaeology of affective systems'. *Psychoanalytic Review*, *102*, 221–227.

Baumeister, R. F., Dale, K. & Sommer, K. L. (1998). Freudian defence mechanisms and empirical findings in modern social psychology: Reaction formation, projection,

140 References

displacement, undoing, isolation, sublimation, and denial. *Journal of Personality, 66,* 1081–1124.

Bazan, A. & Detandt, S. (2013). On the physiology of jouissance: Interpreting the mesolimbic dopaminergic reward functions from a psychoanalytic perspective. *Frontiers in Human Neuroscience, 7,* 1–13.

Bazan, A. & Snodgrass, M. (2012). On unconscious inhibition: Instantiating repression in the brain. In A. Fotopoulou, D. Pfaff, & M. Conway (Eds.), *From the couch to the lab: Trends in psychodynamic neuroscience* (pp. 307–337). Oxford: Oxford University Press.

Bell, P., Staines, P., & Michell, J. (2001). *Logical Psych.* Sydney: UNSW Press.

Bennett, M. R. & Hacker, P. M. S. (2003). *Philosophical foundations of neuroscience.* Malden, MA: Blackwell Publishing.

Beres, D. (1962). The unconscious fantasy. *Psychoanalytic Quarterly, 31,* 309–328.

Beres, D. (1965). Structure and function in psycho-analysis. *International Journal of Psychoanalysis, 46,* 53–63.

Beres, D. (1971). Ego autonomy and ego pathology. *Psychoanalytic Study of the Child, 26,* 3–24.

Beres, D. (1995). Conflict. In B. E. Moore & B. D. Fine (Eds.), *Psycho-analysis: The major concepts* (pp. 477–484). New Haven: Yale University Press.

Berofsky, B. (Ed.) (1966). *Free will and determinism.* New York: Harper & Row.

Berridge, K. C. (2004). Motivation concepts in behavioral neuroscience. *Physiology & Behavior, 81,* 179–204.

Berridge, K. C. & Winkielman, P. (2003). What is an unconscious emotion? (The case for unconscious 'liking'). *Cognition & Emotion, 17,* 181–211.

Bibring, E. (1969). The development and problems of the theory of the instincts. *International Journal of Psycho-analysis, 50,* 293–308.

Billig, M. (1997). The dialogic unconscious: Psychoanalysis, discursive psychology and the nature of repression. *British Journal of Social Psychology, 36,* 139–159.

Billig, M. (1999). *Freudian repression: Dialogue creating the unconscious.* Cambridge: Cambridge University Press.

Blass, R. B. & Carmeli, Z. (2007). The case against neuropsychoanalysis: On fallacies underlying psychoanalysis' latest scientific trend and its negative impact on psychoanalytic discourse. *International Journal of Psychoanalysis, 88,* 19–40.

Blatt, S. J. & Levy, K. N. (2003). Attachment theory, psychoanalysis, personality development, and psychopathology. *Psychoanalytic Inquiry, 23,* 102–150.

Bleichmar, H. (2004). Making conscious the unconscious in order to modify unconscious processing: Some mechanisms of therapeutic change. *International Journal of Psychoanalysis, 85,* 1379–1400.

Blum, H. P. (2003a). Psychoanalytic controversies: Repression, transference and reconstruction. *International Journal of Psychoanalysis, 84,* 497–503.

Blum, H. P. (2003b). Response to Peter Fonagy. *International Journal of Psychoanalysis, 84,* 509–513.

Blum, H. P. (2010). Panel report: Object relations in clinical psychoanalysis. *International Journal of Psychoanalysis, 91,* 973–976.

Boag, S. (2005). Addressing mental plurality: Justification, objections and logical requirements of strongly partitive accounts of mind. *Theory and Psychology, 15,* 747–767.

Boag, S. (2006a). Freudian repression, the common view, and pathological science. *Review of General Psychology, 10,* 74–86.

Boag, S. (2006b). Freudian dream theory, dream bizarreness, and the disguise-censor controversy. *Neuro-psychoanalysis, 8,* 5–17.

Boag, S. (2006c). Can repression become a conscious process? *Behavioral and Brain Sciences*, *29*, 513–4.

Boag, S. (2007a). 'Real processes' and the explanatory status of repression and inhibition. *Philosophical Psychology*, *20*, 375–392.

Boag, S. (2007b). Realism, self-deception and the logical paradox of repression. *Theory and Psychology*, *17*, 421–447.

Boag, S. (2007c). Pathological science and the myth of recovered memories: Reply to McNally. *Review of General Psychology*, *11*, 361–362.

Boag, S. (2008a). 'Mind as feeling' or affective relations? A contribution to the School of Andersonian Realism. *Theory and Psychology*, *18*, 505–525.

Boag, S. (2008b). Making sense of subliminal perception. In A. M. Columbus (Ed.), *Advances in psychology research* (pp. 117–139). New York: Nova Science Publishers.

Boag, S. (2010a). Repression, suppression, and conscious awareness. *Psychoanalytic Psychology*, *27*, 164–181.

Boag, S. (2010b). Description and explanation within personality psychology research. In R. E. Hicks (Ed.), *Personality and individual differences: Current directions*. Bowen Hills: Australian Academic Press.

Boag, S. (2011a). Explanation in personality research: 'Verbal magic' and the Five-Factor Model. *Philosophical Psychology*, *24*, 223–243.

Boag, S. (2011b). The role of conceptual analysis in personality research. In S. Boag & N. Tiliopoulos (Eds.), *Personality and individual differences: Theory, assessment and application* (pp. 321–330). New York: Nova.

Boag, S. (2012). *Freudian repression, the unconscious, and the dynamics of inhibition*. London: Karnac.

Boag, S. (2014). Ego, drives, and the dynamics of internal objects. *Frontiers in Psychoanalysis and Neuropsychoanalysis, 5*, 1–13.

Boag, S. (2015a). Personality assessment, 'construct validity', and the significance of theory. *Personality & Individual Differences*, 84, 36–44.

Boag, S. (2015b). Repression, defence and the psychology of science. In S. Boag, L. A. W. Brakel, & V. Talvitie (Eds.), *Philosophy, science, and psychoanalysis* (pp. 247–268). London: Karnac.

Boag, S. (2015c). In defence of unconscious mentality. In S. Boag, L. A. W. Brakel, & V. Talvitie (Eds.), *Psychoanalysis and philosophy of mind* (pp. 239–265). London: Karnac.

Bobzien, S. (1998). *Determinism and freedom in Stoic Philosophy*. Oxford: Clarendon Press.

Bodden, M. E., Dodel, R., & Kalbe, E. (2010). Theory of mind in Parkinson's disease and related basal ganglia disorders: A systematic review. *Movement Disorders, 25*, 13–27.

Boesky, D. (1995). Structural theory. In B. E. Moore & B. D. Fine (Eds.), *Psycho-analysis: The major concepts* (pp. 494–507). New Haven: Yale University Press.

Bohleber, W., Jiménez, J. P., Scarfone, D., Varvin, S., & Zysman, S. (2015). Unconscious phantasy and its conceptualisations: An attempt at conceptual integration. *International Journal of Psychoanalysis, 96*, 705–730.

Bonanno, G. A. & Keuler, D. J. (1998). Psychotherapy without repressed memory: A parsimonious alternative based on contemporary memory research. In S. J. Lynn & K. M. McConkey (Eds.), *Truth in memory* (pp. 437–463). New York: Guilford.

Bowers, K. S. (1984). On being unconsciously influenced and informed. In K. S. Bowers & D. Meichenbaum (Eds.), *The unconscious reconsidered* (pp. 228–272). New York: John Wiley & Sons.

Bowlby, J. (1969). *Attachment and loss: Vol. 1: Attachment*. London: Hogarth.

142 References

Bowlby, J. (1973). *Attachment and loss: Vol. 2: Separation*. London: Hogarth.

Bowlby, J. (1980). *Attachment and loss: Vol. 3: Loss*. London: Hogarth.

Bowlby, J. (1982). Attachment and loss: Retrospect and prospect. *American Journal of Orthopsychiatry, 52*, 664–678.

Boysen, G. A. & VanBergen, A. (2013). A review of published research on adult dissociative identity disorder: 2000–2010. *The Journal of Nervous and Mental Disease, 201*, 5–11.

Boysen, G. A. & VanBergen, A. (2014). Simulation of multiple personalities: A review of research comparing diagnosed and simulated dissociative identity disorder. *Clinical Psychology Review, 34*, 14–28.

Brakel, L. A. W. (2009). *Philosophy, psychoanalysis, and the a-rational mind*. Oxford: Oxford University Press.

Brakel, L. A. W. (2010). *Unconscious knowing and other essays in psycho-philosophical analysis*. Oxford: Oxford University Press.

Brakel, L. A. W. (2013). *The ontology of psychology*. New York: Routledge.

Brakel, L. A. W. (2015). Two fundamental problems for philosophical psychoanalysis. In S. Boag, L. A. W. Brakel, & V. Talvitie (Eds.), *Philosophy, science, and psychoanalysis* (pp. 119–143). London: Karnac.

Brenner, C. (1957). The nature and development of the concept of repression in Freud's writings. *Psychoanalytic Study of the Child, 12*, 19–46.

Brenner, C. (1974). On the nature and development of affects: A unified theory. *Psychoanalytic Quarterly, 43*, 532–556.

Brenner, C. (1980). Metapsychology and psychoanalytic theory. *Psychoanalytic Quarterly, 49*, 189–214.

Brenner, C. (1994). The mind as conflict and compromise formation. *Journal of Clinical Psychoanalysis, 3*, 473–488.

Brentano, F. (1874/1973). *Psychology from an empirical standpoint*. (Translated by A. C. Rancurello, D. B. Terrell, & L. L. McAlister). London: Routledge & Kegan Paul.

Breuer, J. & Freud, S. (1895d). *Studies in hysteria (1893–1895). Standard Edition, S. E.* II. London: Hogarth.

Brierley, M. (1942). 'Internal objects' and theory. *International Journal of Psychoanalysis, 23*, 107–112.

Bucci, W. (1997). *Psychoanalysis and cognitive science: A multiple code theory*. New York: Guilford.

Carhart-Harris, R. L. & Friston, K. J. (2010). The default-mode, ego functions, and free energy: A neurobiological account of Freudian ideas. *Brain, 133*, 1265–1283.

Carhart-Harris, R. L. & Friston, K. J. (2012). Free-energy and Freud: An update. In A. Fotopoulou, D. Pfaff & M. Conway (Eds.), *From the couch to the lab: Trends in psychodynamic neuroscience* (pp. 219–229). Oxford: Oxford University Press.

Carver, C. S. (2006). Approach, avoidance, and the self-regulation of affect and action. *Motivation and Emotion, 30*, 105–110.

Cervone, D. (1999). Bottom-up explanation in personality psychology: The case of cross-situational coherence. In D. Cervone & Yuichi Shoda (Eds.), *The coherence of personality: Social-cognitive bases of consistency, variability, and organization* (pp. 303–341). New York: Guilford Press.

Cheshire, N. & Thomä, H. (1991). Metaphor, neologism and 'open texture': Implications for translating Freud's scientific thought. *International Review of Psycho-analysis, 18*, 429–454.

Cisek, P. & Kalaska, J. F. (2010). Neural mechanisms for interacting with a world full of action choices. *Annual Review of Neuroscience, 33*, 269–298.

Colace, C. (2004). Dreaming in addiction: A study on the motivational bases of dreaming processes. *Neuro-Psychoanalysis, 6*, 165–179.

Colace, C. (2010). *Children's dreams: From Freud's observations to modern dream research.* London: Karnac.

Colace, C. (2014). *Drug dreams: Clinical and research implications of dreams about drugs in drug-addicted patients.* London: Karnac Books.

Colace, C. & Boag, S. (2015). Persisting myths surrounding Sigmund Freud's dream theory: A reply to Hobson's critique of the scientific status of psychoanalysis. *Contemporary Psychoanalysis, 51*, 107–125.

Compton, A. (1972). A study of the psychoanalytic theory of anxiety: I. The development of Freud's theory of anxiety. *Journal of the American Psychoanalytic Association, 20*, 3–44.

Compton, A. (1981). On the psychoanalytic theory of instinctual drives: IV. Instinctual drives and the ego-id-superego model. *Psychoanalytic Quarterly, 50*, 363–392.

Crews, F. (1995). *The memory wars: Freud's legacy in dispute.* New York: New York Review.

Dalenberg, C. J., Brand, B. L., Gleaves, D. H., Dorahy, M. J., Loewenstein, R. J., Cardeña, E., … & Spiegel, D. (2012). Evaluation of the evidence for the trauma and fantasy models of dissociation. *Psychological Bulletin, 138*, 550–588.

Dalenberg, C. J., Brand, B. L., Loewenstein, R. J., Gleaves, D. H., Dorahy, M. J., Cardeña, E., … & Spiegel, D. (2014). Reality versus fantasy: Reply to Lynn et al. (2014). *Psychological Bulletin, 140*, 911–920.

Davis, J. T. (2001). Revising psychoanalytic interpretations of the past: An examination of declarative and non-declarative memory processes. *International Journal of Psychoanalysis, 82*, 449–462.

Descartes, R. (1641/1984). Objections and replies. In *The philosophical writings of Descartes, Vol. II.* (Translated by J. Cottingham, R. Stoohoff & D. Murdoch, pp. 66–398). Cambridge: Cambridge University Press.

Descartes, R. (1648/1991). *The philosophical writings of Descartes, Vol. III: Correspondence.* (Translated by J. Cottingham, R. Stoohoff, D. Murdoch & A. Kenny). Cambridge: Cambridge University Press.

De Sousa, R. (1976). Rational homunculi. In A. O. Rorty (Ed.), *The identities of persons* (pp. 217–238). Berkeley: University of California Press.

Diamond, S., Balvin, R. S., & Diamond, F. R. (1963). *Inhibition and choice: A neurobehavioral approach to the problems of plasticity in behaviour.* New York: Harper & Row.

Dreher, A. U. (2005). Conceptual research. In E. S. Person, A. M. Cooper, & G. O. Gabbard (Eds.), *Textbook of psychoanalysis* (pp. 361–372). Washington, DC: American Psychiatric Publishing.

Eagle, M. (2000). Repression: Part II. *Psychoanalytic Review, 87*, 161–187.

Elliot, A. J. (2006). The hierarchical model of approach-avoidance motivation. *Motivation and Emotion, 30*, 111–116.

Epstein, A. W. (1998). Neural aspects of psychodynamic science. *Journal of the American Academy of Psychoanalysis, 26*, 503–512.

Erdelyi, M. H. (1974). A new look at the new look: Perceptual defense and vigilance. *Psychological Review, 81*, 1–25.

Erdelyi, M. H. (1985). *Psychoanalysis: Freud's cognitive psychology.* New York: W. H. Freeman & Co.

Erwin, E. (1996). *A final accounting: Philosophical and empirical issues in Freudian psychology.* Cambridge, MA: MIT Press.

144 References

Erwin, E. (2015). Psychoanalysis and philosophy of science: Basic evidence. In S. Boag, L. A. W. Brakel, & V. Talvitie (Eds.), *Philosophy, science, and psychoanalysis* (pp. 37–58). London: Karnac.

Eslinger, P. J., Dennis, K., Moore, P., Antani, S., Hauck, R., & Grossman, M. (2005). Metacognitive deficits in frontotemporal dementia. *Journal of Neurology, Neurosurgery & Psychiatry, 76*, 1630–1635.

Fairbairn, W. R. D. (1931/1952). Features in the analysis of a patient with a physical genital abnormality. In *Psychoanalytic studies of the personality* (pp. 197–222). London: Tavistock.

Fairbairn, W. R. D. (1943/1952). The repression and the return of bad objects (with special reference to the 'War Neuroses'. In *Psychoanalytic studies of the personality* (pp. 59–81). London: Tavistock.

Fairbairn, W. R. D. (1944/1952). Endopsychic structure considered in terms of object-relationships. In *Psychoanalytic studies of the personality* (pp. 82–136). London: Tavistock.

Fairbairn, W. R. D. (1946/1952). Object-relationships and dynamic structure. In *Psychoanalytic studies of the personality* (pp. 137–151). London: Tavistock.

Fairbairn, W. R. D. (1951/1952). A synopsis of the development of the author's views regarding the structure of personality. In *Psychoanalytic studies of the personality* (pp. 162–179). London: Tavistock.

Fairbairn, W. R. D. (1952). *Psychoanalytic studies of the personality*. London: Tavistock.

Fancher, R. E. (1977). Brentano's psychology from an empirical standpoint and Freud's early metapsychology. *Journal of the History of the Behavioral Sciences, 13*, 207–227.

Feldman, M. (2000). Some views on the manifestation of the death instinct in clinical work. *The International Journal of Psychoanalysis, 81*, 53–65.

Fonagy, P. (1999a). Points of contact and divergence between psychoanalytic and attachment theories: Is psychoanalytic theory truly different. *Psychoanalytic Inquiry, 19*, 448–480.

Fonagy, P. (1999b). Memory and therapeutic action. *International Journal of Psychoanalysis, 80*, 215–233.

Fonagy, P. (2003). Rejoinder to Harold Blum. *The International Journal of Psychoanalysis, 84*, 503–509.

Fonagy, P. & Campbell, C. (2015). Bad blood revisited: Attachment and psychoanalysis, 2015. *British Journal of Psychotherapy, 31*, 229–250.

Fonagy, P. & Target, M. (2000). The place of psychodynamic theory in developmental psychopathology. *Development and Psychopathology, 12*, 407–425.

Fonagy, P. & Target, M. (2007). The rooting of the mind in the body: New links between attachment theory and psychoanalytic thought. *Journal of the American Psychoanalytic Association, 55*, 411–456.

Fotopoulou, A. (2013). Beyond the reward principle: Consciousness as precision seeking. *Neuropsychoanalysis, 15*, 33–38.

Fraley, C. R. & Brumbaugh, C. C. (2007). Adult attachment and preemptive defenses: Converging evidence on the role of defensive exclusion at the level of encoding. *Journal of Personality, 75*, 1033–1050.

Frampton, M. F. (1991). Considerations on the role of Brentano's concept of intentionality in Freud's repudiation of the seduction theory. *International Review of Psycho-analysis, 18*, 27–36.

Frank, A. (1969). The unrememberable and the unforgettable: Passive primal repression. *Psycho-analytic Study of the Child, 24*, 48–77.

Frank, A. & Muslin, H. (1967). The development of Freud's concept of primal repression. *Psycho-analytic Study of the Child, 22*, 55–76.

References   **145**

Frank, G. (1996). Beliefs and their vicissitudes. *Psychoanalytic Psychology*, *13*, 421–431.

Frank, G. (2000). The status of psychoanalytic theory today: There is an elephant there. *Psychoanalytic Psychology*, *17*, 174–179.

Freud, A. (1968). *The ego and the mechanisms of defence*. London: The Hogarth Press.

Freud, S. (1894). The neuro-psychoses of defence. *S. E.*, *3*: 41–61. London: Hogarth.

Freud, S. (1898b) The psychical mechanism of forgetfulness. *S. E.*, *3*: 287–297. London: Hogarth.

Freud, S. (1900a). *The interpretation of dreams. S. E.*, *4–5*. London: Hogarth.

Freud, S. (1901a). *On dreams. S. E.*, *5*: 629–686. London: Hogarth.

Freud, S. (1901b). *The psychopathology of everyday life. S. E.*, *6*. London: Hogarth.

Freud, S. (1905d). Three essays on the theory of sexuality. *S. E.*, *7*: 123–246. London: Hogarth.

Freud, S. (1905e). Fragment of an analysis of a case of hysteria. *S. E.*, *7*: 1–122. London: Hogarth.

Freud, S. (1906c). Psycho-analysis and the establishment of the facts in legal proceedings. *S. E.*, *9*: 97–114. London: Hogarth.

Freud, S. (1907a). Delusions and dreams in Jensen's *Gradiva. S. E.*, *9*: 1–96. London: Hogarth.

Freud, S. (1908a). Hysterical phantasies and their relation to bisexuality. *S. E.*, *9*: 157–166. London: Hogarth.

Freud, S. (1908b). Character and anal erotism. *S. E.*, *9*: 167–175. London: Hogarth.

Freud, S. (1909b). Analysis of a phobia in a five-year old boy. *S. E.*, *10*: 1–150. London: Hogarth.

Freud, S. (1909d). Notes upon a case of obsessional neurosis. *S. E.*, *10*: 151–138. London: Hogarth.

Freud, S. (1910a). Five lectures on psycho-analysis. *S. E.*, *11*: 1–56. London: Hogarth.

Freud, S. (1910i). The psycho-analytic view of the psychogenic disturbance of vision. *S. E.*, *11*: 209–218. London: Hogarth.

Freud, S. (1910k). 'Wild' psycho-analysis. *S. E.*, *11*: 219–228. London: Hogarth.

Freud, S. (1911b). Formulations on the two principles of mental functioning. *S. E.*, *12*: 213–226. London: Hogarth.

Freud, S. (1911c). Psycho-analytic notes on an autobiographical account of a case of paranoia (Dementia paranoides). *S. E.*, *12*: 3–82. London: Hogarth.

Freud, S. (1912b). The dynamics of transference. *S. E.*, *12*: 97–108. London: Hogarth.

Freud, S. (1912d). On the universal tendency to debasement in the sphere of love (Contributions to the psychology of love II). *S. E.*, *11*: 179–190. London: Hogarth.

Freud, S. (1912g). A note on the unconscious in psycho-analysis. *S. E.*, *12*: 256–266. London: Hogarth.

Freud, S. (1912–1913d). *Totem and taboo. S. E.*, *13*. London: Hogarth.

Freud, S. (1913c). On beginning the treatment (Further recommendations on the technique of psycho-analysis I). *S. E.*, *12*: 121–144. London: Hogarth.

Freud, S. (1913j). The claims of psycho-analysis to scientific interest. *S. E.*, *13*: 163–190. London: Hogarth.

Freud, S. (1914a). Fausse reconnaissance ('Déjà Raconté') in psycho-analytic treatment. *S. E.*, *13*: 199–207. London: Hogarth.

Freud, S. (1914c). On narcissism: An introduction. *S. E.*, *14*: 67–102. London: Hogarth.

Freud, S. (1914d). On the history of the psycho-analytic movement. *S. E.*, *14*: 1–66. London: Hogarth.

Freud, S. (1914g). Remembering, repeating and working-through. (Further recommendations on the technique of psycho-analysis II). *S. E.*, *12*: 145–156. London: Hogarth.

146 References

Freud, S. (1915a). Observations on transference-love (Further recommendations on the technique of psycho-analysis III). *S. E.*, *12*: 157–174. London: Hogarth.

Freud, S. (1915c). Instincts and their vicissitudes. *S. E.*, *14*: 109–140. London: Hogarth.

Freud, S. (1915d). Repression. *S. E.*, *14*: 141–158. London: Hogarth.

Freud, S. (1915e). The unconscious. *S. E.*, *14*: 159–215. London: Hogarth.

Freud, S. (1916–1917). *introductory lectures on psycho-analysis. S. E.*, *15–16*. London: Hogarth.

Freud, S. (1917d). A metapsychological supplement to the theory of dreams. *S. E.*, *15*. London: Hogarth.

Freud, S. (1919a). Lines of advance in psycho-analytic therapy. *S. E.*, *17*: 157–168. London: Hogarth.

Freud, S. (1919g). Preface to Reik's *Ritual: Psycho-Analytic Studies. S. E.*, *17*: 257–264. London: Hogarth.

Freud, S. (1920g). *Beyond the pleasure principle. S. E.*, *18*: 1–64. London: Hogarth.

Freud, S. (1923b). *The ego and the id. S. E.*, *19*: 1–66. London: Hogarth.

Freud, S. (1924c). The economic problem of masochism. *S. E.*, *19*: 155–170. London: Hogarth.

Freud, S. (1924f). A short account of psycho-analysis. *S. E.*, *19*: 189–210. London: Hogarth.

Freud, S. (1925d). *An autobiographical study. S. E.*, *20*: 1–74. London: Hogarth.

Freud, S. (1925i). Some additional notes on dream-interpretation as a whole. *S. E.*, *19*: 124–138. London: Hogarth.

Freud, S. (1926d). *inhibitions, symptoms and anxiety. S. E.*, *20*: 75–176. London: Hogarth.

Freud, S. (1926e). The question of lay analysis. *S. E.*, *20*: 1177–1258. London: Hogarth.

Freud, S. (1926f). Psycho-analysis. *S. E.*, *20*: 259–270. London: Hogarth.

Freud, S. (1930b). Civilization and its discontents. *S. E.*, *21*: 57–146. London: Hogarth.

Freud, S. (1932c). My contact with Josef Popper-Lynkeus. *S. E.*, *22*: 217–224. London: Hogarth.

Freud, S. (1933a). *New introductory lectures on psycho-analysis. S. E.*, *22*. London: Hogarth.

Freud, S. (1936a). A disturbance of memory on the acropolis. *S. E.*, *22*: 237–248. London: Hogarth.

Freud, S. (1937c). Analysis terminable and interminable. *S. E.*, *23*: 209–254. London: Hogarth.

Freud, S. (1937d). Constructions in analysis. *S. E.*, *23*: 255–270. London: Hogarth.

Freud, S. (1939a). Moses and monotheism: Three essays. *S. E.*, *23*: 1–138. London: Hogarth.

Freud, S. (1940a[1938]). *An outline of psycho-analysis. S. E.*, *23*: 1–138. London: Hogarth.

Freud, S. (1940b[1938]). Some elementary lessons in psycho-analysis. *S. E.*, *23*: 279–286. London: Hogarth.

Freud, S. (1950[1895]). A project for a scientific psychology. *S. E.*, *1*: 283–397. London: Hogarth.

Friston, K. (2009). The free-energy principle: A rough guide to the brain? *Trends in Cognitive Sciences*, *13*, 293–301.

Friston, K. (2010). The free-energy principle: A unified brain theory? *Nature Reviews Neuroscience*, *11*, 127–138.

Friston, K. (2013). Consciousness and hierarchical inference. *Neuropsychoanalysis*, *15*, 38–42.

Friston, K. J., Daunizeau, J., Kilner, J., & Kiebel, S. J. (2010). Action and behavior: A free-energy formulation. *Biological Cybernetics*, *102*, 227–260.

Friston, K. J., Kilner, J., & Harrison, L. (2006). A free energy principle for the brain. *Journal of Physiology-Paris*, *100*, 70–87.

Fulgencio, L. (2005). Freud's metapsychological speculations. *International Journal of Psychoanalysis*, *86*, 99–123.

References **147**

Fulgencio, L. (2007). Winnicott's rejection of the basic concepts of Freud's metapsychology. *The International Journal of Psychoanalysis, 88,* 443–461.

Gabbard, G. O. & Westen, D. (2003). Rethinking therapeutic action. *International Journal of Psychoanalysis, 84,* 823–841.

Galloway, G. (2000). Direct realism and the analysis of perceptual error. *Theory and Psychology, 10,* 605–613.

Gardner, S. (1993). *Irrationality and the philosophy of psychoanalysis.* Cambridge: Cambridge University Press.

Gay, P. (1988). *Freud: A life for our time.* New York: W. W. Norton.

Gill, M. M. (1963). *Topography and systems in psychoanalytic theory.* New York: International Universities Press.

Gill, M. M. (1976). Metapsychology is not psychology. In M. M. Gill & P. Holzman (Eds.), *Psychology vs metapsychology: Psycho-analytic essays in memory of George Klein. Psychological issues.* Monograph 36, Vol. 9 (pp. 71–105). New York: International Universities Press.

Gill. M. M & Holzman. P. (Eds.)(1976). *Psychology vs metapsychology: Psycho-analytic essays in memory of George Klein. Psychological issues.* Monograph 36, Vol. 9. New York: International Universities Press.

Gillett, E. (1988). The brain and the unconscious. *Psychoanalysis and Contemporary Thought, 11,* 563–578.

Gillett, E. (1990). The problem of unconscious affect: Signal anxiety versus the double-prediction theory. *Psychoanalysis and Contemporary Thought, 13,* 551–600.

Goertzen, J. R. (2008). On the possibility of unification: The reality and nature of the crisis in psychology. *Theory & Psychology, 18,* 829–852.

Goertzen, J. R. (2010). Dialectical pluralism: A theoretical conceptualization of pluralism in psychology. *New Ideas in Psychology, 28,* 201–209.

Gouws, A. (2000). Will the real Freud please stand up? The distribution of power between the unconscious and the preconscious according to the Traumdeutung. *International Journal of Psychotherapy, 5,* 227–239.

Green, A. (2005). The illusion of *common ground* and mythical pluralism. *International Journal of Psychoanalysis, 86,* 627–632.

Green, C. D. (2015). Why psychology isn't unified, and probably never will be. *Review of General Psychology, 19,* 207–214.

Greenberg, J. R. & Mitchell, S. A. (1983). *Object relations in psychoanalytic theory.* Cambridge, MA: Harvard University Press.

Greenwald, A. G. (1992). New Look 3: Unconscious cognition reclaimed. *American Psychologist, 47,* 766–779.

Groenewegen, H. J. (2003). The basal ganglia and motor control. *Neural Plasticity, 10,* 107–120.

Grossman, W. I. (1982). The self as fantasy: Fantasy as theory. *Journal of the American Psychoana-lytic Association, 30,* 919–937.

Grossman, W. I. & Simon, B. (1969). Anthropomorphism: Motive, meaning, and causality in psychoanalytic theory. *Psychoanalytic Study of the Child, 24,* 78–111.

Grünbaum, A. (1983). Logical foundations of psychoanalytic theory. *Erkenntnis, 19,* 109–152.

Grünbaum, A. (2015). Critique of psychoanalysis. In S. Boag, L. A. W. Brakel, & V. Talvitie (Eds.), *Philosophy, science, and psychoanalysis* (pp. 1–36). London: Karnac.

Gullestad, S. E. (2003). The Adult Attachment Interview and psychoanalytic outcome studies. *International Journal of Psychoanalysis, 84,* 651–668.

Hartman-Maeir, A., Soroker, N., Oman, S. D., & Katz, N. (2003). Awareness of disabilities in stroke rehabilitation: A clinical trial. *Disability & Rehabilitation, 25,* 35–44.

148 References

Hartmann, H. (1950). Comments on the psychoanalytic theory of the ego. *Psychoanalytic Study of the Child, 5,* 74–96.

Hartmann, H. (1958). *Ego psychology and the problem of adaptation.* New York: International Universities Press.

Hartmann, H., Kris, E., & Loewenstein, R. M. (1949). Notes on the theory of aggression. *Psychoanalytic Study of the Child, 3,* 9–36.

Hatzimoysis, A. (2007). The case against unconscious emotions. *Analysis, 67,* 292–299.

Hibberd, F. J. (2014). The metaphysical basis of a process psychology. *Journal of Theoretical and Philosophical Psychology, 34,* 161–186.

Hilgard, E. R. (1980). The trilogy of mind: Cognition, affection, and conation. *Journal of the History of the Behavioral Sciences, 16,* 107–117.

Hoffman, T. (2004). Revival of the death instinct: A view from contemporary biology. *Neuropsychoanalysis, 6,* 63–75.

Holmes, J. (2000). Attachment theory and psychoanalysis: A rapprochement. *British Journal of Psychotherapy, 17,* 157–172.

Holt, R. R. (1976). Drive or wish? A reconsideration of the psycho-analytic theory of motivation. In M. M. Gill & P. Holzman (Eds.), *Psychology vs metapsychology: Psycho-analytic essays in memory of George Klein. Psychological issues.* Monograph 36, Vol. 9 (pp. 158–197). New York: International Universities Press.

Holt, R. R. (1981). The death and transfiguration of metapsychology. *International Review of Psycho-Analysis, 8,* 129–143.

Holt, R. R. (1982). The manifest and latent meanings of metapsychology. *The Annual of Psychoanalysis, 10,* 233–255.

Holt, R. R. (2002). Metapsychology. In E. Erwin (Ed.), *The Freud encyclopedia: Theory, therapy and culture* (pp. 337–341). New York: Routledge.

Hopkins, J. (1995). Reply: Irrationality, interpretation and division. In C. Macdonald and G. Macdonald (Eds.), *Philosophy of psychology: Debates on psychological explanation,* Vol. I (pp. 461–484). Oxford: Blackwell.

Hopkins, J. (2012). Psychoanalysis, representation and neuroscience: The Freudian unconscious and the Bayesian brain. In A. Fotopoulou, D. Pfaff, & M. Conway (Eds.), *From the couch to the lab: Trends in psychodynamic neuroscience* (pp. 230–265). Oxford: Oxford University Press.

Hopkins, J. (2013). Conflict creates an unconscious id. *Neuropsychoanalysis, 15,* 45–48.

Hopkins, J. (2015). The significance of consilience: Psychoanalysis, attachment, neuroscience, and evolution. In S. Boag, L. A. W. Brakel, & V. Talvitie (Eds.), *Psychoanalysis and philosophy of mind* (pp. 47–136). London: Karnac.

Horowitz, M. H. (1977). The quantitative line of approach in psycho-analysis: A clinical assessment of its current status. *Journal of the American Psycho-analytic Association, 25,* 559–579.

Howe, M. J. A. (1990). Does intelligence exist? *The Psychologist, 3,* 490–493.

Hyer, L. A., Woods, M. G., & Boudewyns, P. A. (1991). PTSD and alexithymia: Importance of emotional clarification in treatment. *Psychotherapy: Theory, Research, Practice, Training, 28,* 129–139.

Immergluck, L. (1964). Determinism-freedom in contemporary psychology: An ancient problem revisited. *American Psychologist, 19,* 270–281.

Jacobson, E. (1953). The affects and their pleasure–unpleasure qualities in relation to psychic discharge processes. In R. M. Loewenstein (Ed.), *Drives, affects, behaviour* (pp. 38–66). New York: International Universities Press.

James, W. (1884/1965). The dilemma of determinism. In P. Edwards & A. Pap. (Eds.), *A modern introduction to philosophy* (pp. 25–37). New York: Free Press.

References **149**

James, W. (1890/1950). *The principles of psychology* (volume I). New York: H. Holt and Company.

Johnson, A. (1998). Repression: A reexamination of the concept as applied to folktales. *Ethos, 26*, 295–313.

Jones, B. P. (1993). Repression: The evolution of a psycho-analytic concept from the 1890's to the 1990's. *Journal of the American Psycho-analytic Association, 41*, 63–95.

Jones, E. (1953). *Sigmund Freud: Life and work, Vol. 1.* London: Hogarth.

Jones, E. (1955). *Sigmund Freud: Life and work, Vol. 2.* London: Hogarth.

Kandel, E. R. (1999). Biology and the future of psychoanalysis: A new intellectual framework for psychiatry revisited. *The American Journal of Psychiatry, 156*, 505–524.

Kane, R. (Ed.) (2002). *The Oxford handbook of free will.* Oxford: Oxford University Press.

Kaplan-Solms, K. & Solms, M. (2000). *Clinical studies in neuro-psychoanalysis: Introduction to a depth psychology.* London: Karnac.

Karlsson, G. (2010). *Psychoanalysis in a new light.* Cambridge: Cambridge University Press.

Kernberg, O. (2001). Object relations, affects, and drives: Toward a new synthesis. *Psychoanalytic Inquiry, 21*, 604–619.

Kernberg, O. (2009). The concept of the death drive: A clinical perspective. *The International Journal of Psychoanalysis, 90*, 1009–1023.

Kihlstrom, J. F. (1987). The cognitive unconscious. *Science, 237*, 1445–1452.

Kinston, W. & Cohen, J. (1988). Primal repression and other states of mind. *Scandinavian Psychoanalytic Review, 11*, 81–105.

Kirschner, S. R. (2006). Psychology and pluralism: Toward the psychological studies. *Journal of Theoretical and Philosophical Psychology, 26*, 1–17.

Klein, G. S. (1976). Freud's two theories of sexuality. In M. M. Gill & P. Holzman (Eds.), *Psychology vs metapsychology: Psycho-analytic essays in memory of George Klein. Psychological issues.* Monograph 36, Vol. 9 (pp. 14–70). New York: International Universities Press.

Kluft, R. P. (2000). The psychoanalytic psychotherapy of dissociative identity disorder in the context of trauma therapy. *Psychoanalytic Inquiry, 20*, 259–286.

Kravitz, A. V., Freeze, B. S., Parker, P. R., Kay, K., Thwin, M. T., Deisseroth, K., & Kreitzer, A. C. (2010). Regulation of parkinsonian motor behaviours by optogenetic control of basal ganglia circuitry. *Nature, 466*, 622–626.

Kroger, R. O. & Wood, L. A. (1993). Reification, 'faking,' and the Big Five. *American Psychologist, 48*, 1297–1298.

Kubie, L. S. (1947). The fallacious use of quantitative concepts in dynamic psychology. *Psychoanalytic Quarterly, 16*, 507–518.

Lacewing, M. (2007). Do unconscious emotions involve unconscious feelings? *Philosophical Psychology, 20*, 81–104.

Laplanche, J. & Pontalis, J.-B. (1973). *The language of psychoanalysis.* London: Karnac.

Lettieri, R. (2005). The ego revisited. *Psychoanalytic Psychology, 22*, 370–381.

Linke, D. B. (1998). Discharge, reflex, free energy and encoding. In G. Guttman & I. Scholz-Strasser (Eds.), *Freud and the neurosciences: From brain research to the unconscious* (pp. 103–108). Vienna: Österreichischen Akademie der Wissenschaften.

Liotti, M. & Panksepp, J. (2004). Imaging human emotions and affective feelings: Implications for biological psychiatry. In J. Panksepp (Ed.), *Textbook of biological psychiatry* (pp. 33–74). Hoboken, NJ: Wiley-Liss.

Locke, J. (1690/1947). *An essay concerning human understanding.* London: J. M. Dent & Sons.

Loftus, E. F. (1993). The reality of repressed memories. *American Psychologist, 48*, 518–537.

Lynn, S. J., Lilienfeld, S. O., Merckelbach, H., Giesbrecht, T., McNally, R. J., Loftus, E. F., ... & Malaktaris, A. (2014). The trauma model of dissociation: Inconvenient truths and stubborn fictions. Comment on Dalenberg et al. (2012). *Psychological Bulletin, 140*, 896–910.

150 References

Machado, A. & Silva, F. J. (2007). Toward a richer view of the scientific method: The role of conceptual analysis. *American Psychologist, 62,* 671–681.

MacIntyre, A. C. (1958). *The unconscious: A conceptual analysis.* London: Routledge & Kegan Paul.

Mackay, N. (1996). The place of motivation in psychoanalysis. *Modern Psychoanalysis, 21,* 3–17.

Mackay, N. (2002). Desire, symbol, enactment, and some puzzles about the concepts of phantasy and substitute satisfaction. *Modern Psychoanalysis, 27,* 3–11.

Mackay, N. (2006). Commentary on Freudian dream theory, dream bizarreness, and the disguise-censor controversy. *Neuropsychoanalysis, 8,* 40–42.

Mackay, N. & Petocz, A. (Eds.) (2011). *Realism and psychology: Collected essays.* Leiden: Brill.

Mackie, J. L. (1974). *The cement of the universe: A study of causation.* Oxford: Oxford University Press.

Macmillan, M. (1991). *Freud evaluated: The completed arc.* North-Holland: Elsevier Science Publishers.

Macmurray, J. (1961). *Persons in relation.* New York: Harper & Brothers.

Macmurray, J. (1969). *The self as agent.* London: Faber and Faber.

Madison, P. (1956). Freud's repression concept: A survey and attempted clarification. *International Journal of Psycho-analysis, 37,* 75–81.

Madison, P. (1961). *Freud's concept of repression and defense: Its theoretical and observational language.* Minneapolis: University of Minnesota Press.

Mancia, M. (2006). Implicit memory and early unrepressed unconscious: Their role in the therapeutic process (How the neurosciences can contribute to psychoanalysis). *International Journal of Psychoanalysis, 87,* 83–103.

Marsh, T. & Boag, S. (2013). Evolutionary and differential psychology: Conceptual conflicts and the path to integration. *Frontiers in Psychology, 4,* 1–15.

Martin, J., Sugarman, J., & Thompson, J. (2003). *Psychology and the question of agency.* Albany: SUNY Press.

Martindale, C. (1975). The grammar of altered states of consciousness: A semiotic reinterpretation of aspects of psychoanalytic theory. *Psychoanalysis and Contemporary Science, 4,* 331–354.

Maslow, A. H. (1943). A theory of human motivation. *Psychological Review, 50,* 370–396.

Masson, J. M. (Ed.) (1985). *The complete letters of Sigmund Freud and Wilhelm Fliess, 1887–1904.* Cambridge: Belknap Press.

Matte-Blanco, I. (1975). *The unconscious as infinite sets: An essay in bi-logic.* London: Duckworth.

Maze, J. R. (1954). Do intervening variables intervene? *Psychological Review, 61,* 226–234.

Maze, J. R. (1983). *The meaning of behaviour.* London: Allen & Unwin.

Maze, J. R. (1987). The composition of the ego in a deterministic psychology. In W. J. Baker, M. E. Hyland, H. Van Rappard & A. W. Staats (Eds.), *Current issues in theoretical psychology* (pp. 189–199). North Holland: Elsevier Science Publishers.

Maze, J. R. (1993). The complementarity of object-relations and instinct theory. *International Journal of Psycho-analysis, 74,* 459–70.

Maze, J. R. & Henry, R. M. (1996). Problems in the concept of repression and proposals for their resolution. *International Journal of Psycho-analysis, 77,* 1085–1100.

McCarley, R. W. (1998). Dreams: Disguise of forbidden wishes or transparent reflections of a distinct brain state? In R. M. Bilder & F. F. LeFever (Eds.), *Neuroscience of the mind on the centennial of Freud's Project for a Scientific Psychology* (pp. 116–133). New York: New York Academy of Sciences.

McDougall, W. (1923). *An outline of psychology.* London: Methuen & Co.

References 151

McIntosh, D. (1986). The ego and the self in the thought of Sigmund Freud. *International Journal of Psycho-analysis, 67*, 429–448.

McMullen, T. (1982). A critique of humanistic psychology. *Australian Journal of Psychology, 34*, 221–229.

McMullen, T. (1996). Psychology and realism. In C. R. Latimer & J. Michell (Eds.), *At once scientific and philosophic: A festschrift for John Philip Sutcliffe* (pp. 59–66). Brisbane: Boombana.

Meadow, P. W. (1989). Object relations in a drive theory model. *Modern Psychoanalysis, 14*, 57–74.

Meissner, W. W. (2003). Mind, brain, and self in psychoanalysis: II. Freud and the mind-body relation. *Psychoanalysis and Contemporary Thought, 26*, 321–344.

Meissner, W. W. (2007). Therapeutic alliance: Theme and variations. *Psychoanalytic Psychology, 24*, 231–254.

Mele, A. (1987). Recent work on self-deception. *American Philosophical Quarterly, 24*, 1–17.

Mele, A. R. (2001). *Self-deception unmasked*. Princeton, NJ: Princeton University Press.

Michell, J. (1988). Maze's direct realism and the character of cognition. *Australian Journal of Psychology, 40*, 227–249.

Michell, J. (2000). Normal science, pathological science and psychometrics. *Theory and Psychology, 10*, 639–667.

Michell, J. (2011). Observing mental processes. A new look at new realism. *The psychology and philosophy of E. B. Holt,* (pp. 5–32). New Brunswick: Transaction Publishers.

Mikulincer, M. & Shaver, P. R. (2003). The attachment behavioral system in adulthood: Activation, psychodynamics, and interpersonal processes. In M. P. Zanna (Ed.), *Advances in experimental social psychology,* Vol. 35 (pp. 53–152). New York: Academic Press.

Mikulincer, M. & Shaver, P. R. (2008). Commentary on 'Is there a drive to love?' *Neuropsychoanalysis, 10*, 154–165.

Mink, J. W. (1996). The basal ganglia: Focused selection and inhibition of competing motor programs. *Progress in Neurobiology, 50*, 381–425.

Mitchell, S. A. (1988). *Relational concepts in psychoanalysis*. Cambridge, MA: Harvard University Press.

Morgan, C. L. (1894). *An introduction to comparative psychology*. London: W. Scott Ltd.

Nagel, E. (1959). Methodological issues in psychoanalytic theory. In S. Hook (Ed.), *Psychoanalysis, scientific method and philosophy* (pp. 38–56). New York: New York University Press.

Nesse, R. M. (1990). The evolutionary functions of repression and the ego defenses. *Journal of the American Academy of Psychoanalysis, 18*, 260–285.

Neu, J. (1988). Divided minds: Sartre's 'bad faith' critique of Freud. *Review of Metaphysics, 42*, 79–101.

Newbery, G. (2011). Drive theory reconsidered (again!). In N. Mackay & A. Petocz (Eds.), *Realism and psychology: Collected essays* (pp. 839–871). Leiden: Brill.

Northoff, G. (2012). What is the unconscious? A novel taxonomy of psychoanalytic, psychological, neuroscientific, and philosophical concepts. In A. Fotopoulou, D. Pfaff & M. Conway (Eds.), *From the couch to the lab: Trends in psychodynamic neuroscience* (pp. 266–281). Oxford: Oxford University Press.

Novick, K. K. & Novick, J. (2002). Reclaiming the land. *Psychoanalytic Psychology, 19*, 348–377.

Ogden, T. H. (1983). The concept of internal object relations. *International Journal of Psycho-analysis, 64*, 227–241.

Ogden, T. H. (1993). *The matrix of the mind: Object relations and the psychoanalytic dialogue.* London: Karnac.

152 References

Ogden, T. H. (2011). Reading Susan Isaacs: Towards a radically revised theory of thinking. *International Journal of Psychoanalysis, 92,* 925–942.

Öhman, A. (2005). The role of the amygdala in human fear: Automatic detection of threat. *Psychoneuroendocrinology, 30,* 953–958.

Öhman, A. (2009). Human fear conditioning and the amygdala. In P. J. Whalen & E. A. Phelps (Eds.), *The human amygdala* (pp. 118–154). New York: Guilford Press.

Öhman, A., Carlsson, K., Lundqvist, D., & Ingvar, M. (2007). On the unconscious subcortical origin of human fear. *Physiology & Behaviour, 92,* 180–185.

Oppenheim, L. (2012). The lexicographer's nightmare. In A. Fotopoulou, D. Pfaff & M. Conway (Eds.), *From the couch to the lab: Trends in psychodynamic neuroscience* (pp. 282–292). Oxford: Oxford University Press.

Ornston, D. (2002). Cathexis. In E. Erwin (Ed.), *The Freud Encyclopedia: Theory, therapy and culture* (pp. 69–72). New York: Routledge.

Panksepp. J. (1999). Emotions as viewed by psychoanalysis and neuroscience: An exercise in consilience. *Neuro-psychoanalysis, 1,* 15–38.

Panksepp. J. (2001). The long-term psychobiological consequences of infant emotions: Prescriptions for the twenty-first century. *Infant Mental Health Journal, 22,* 132–173.

Panksepp. J. (2003). At the interface of the affective, behavioural, and cognitive neurosciences: Decoding the emotional feelings of the brain. *Brain & Cognition, 52,* 4–14.

Panksepp, J. & Biven, L. (2012). *The archaeology of mind: Neuroevolutionary origins of human emotions.* New York: WW Norton & Company.

Panksepp, J. & Moskal, J. (2008). Dopamine and SEEKING: Subcortical 'reward' systems and appetitive urges. In A. J. Elliot (Ed.), *Handbook of approach and avoidance motivation* (pp. 67–87). New York: Psychology Press.

Panksepp, J. & Solms, M. (2012). What is neuropsychoanalysis? Clinically relevant studies of the minded brain. *Trends in Cognitive Sciences, 16,* 6–8.

Pasnau, R. (1997). *Theories of cognition in the later middle ages.* Cambridge: Cambridge University Press.

Passmore, J. (1961). *Philosophical reasoning.* London: Gerald Duckworth & Co.

Passmore, J. A. (1935). The nature of intelligence. *Australasian Journal of Psychology and Philosophy, 13,* 279–289.

Pataki, T. (2014a). *Wishfulfilment in philosophy and psychoanalysis: The tyranny of desire.* London: Routledge.

Pataki, T. (2014b). Fairbairn and partitive conceptions of mind. In D. Scharff & G. Clarke (Eds.), *Fairbairn and the object relations tradition* (pp. 417–430). London: Karnac.

Pataki, T. (2015). Wish-fulfilment revisited. In S. Boag, L. A. W. Brakel, & V. Talvitie (Eds.), *Psychoanalysis and philosophy of mind* (pp. 1–46). London: Karnac.

Pears, D. (1984). *Motivated irrationality.* Oxford: Clarendon Press.

Pears, D. (1986). The goals and strategies of self-deception. In J. Elster (Ed.), *The multiple self* (pp. 59–77). Cambridge: Cambridge University Press.

Petocz, A. (1999). *Freud, Psychoanalysis, and Symbolism.* Cambridge: Cambridge University Press.

Petocz, A. (2006). Commentary on 'Freudian dream theory, dream bizarreness, and the disguise-censor controversy'. *Neuropsychoanalysis, 8,* 48–53.

Petocz, A. (2015). The scientific status of psychoanalysis revisited. In S. Boag, L. A. W. Brakel, & V. Talvitie (Eds.), *Philosophy, science, and psychoanalysis* (pp. 145–192). London: Karnac.

Petocz, A. & Mackay, N. (2013). Unifying psychology through situational realism. *Review of General Psychology, 17,* 216–223.

Petocz, A. & Newbery, G. (2010). On conceptual analysis as the primary qualitative approach to statistics education research in psychology. *Statistics Education Research Journal, 9*, 123–145.

Pfaff, D. W. (1999). *Drive: Neurobiological and molecular mechanisms of sexual motivation*. Cambridge, MA: MIT Press.

Pfaff, D. W. & Fisher, H. E. (2012). Generalized brain arousal mechanisms and other biological, environmental, and psychological mechanisms that contribute to libido. In A. Fotopoulou, D. Pfaff & M. Conway (Eds.), *From the couch to the lab: Trends in psychodynamic neuroscience* (pp. 64–84). Oxford: Oxford University Press.

Phelps, E. A. & LeDoux, J. E. (2005). Contributions of the amygdala to emotion processing: From animal models to human behavior. *Neuron, 48*, 175–187.

Piper, A. & Merskey, H. (2004a). The persistence of folly: A critical examination of dissociative identity disorder. Part I. The excesses of an improbable concept. *Canadian Journal of Psychiatry, 49*, 592–600.

Piper, A. & Merskey, H. (2004b). The persistence of folly: Critical examination of dissociative identity disorder. Part II. The defence and decline of multiple personality or dissociative identity disorder. *Canadian Journal of Psychiatry, 49*, 678–683.

Popper, K. (1959). *The logic of scientific discovery* (originally published in 1959). New York: Harper & Row.

Pugh, G. (2002). Freud's 'problem': Cognitive neuroscience and psychoanalysis working together on memory. *International Journal of Psychoanalysis, 83*, 1375–1394.

Pulver, S. E. (1971). Can affects be unconscious? *International Journal of Psycho-analysis, 52*, 347–354.

Pulver, S. E. (1974). Unconscious versus potential affects. *Psycho-analytic Quarterly, 43*, 77–84.

Pulver, S. E. (2003). On the astonishing clinical irrelevance of neuroscience. *Journal of the American Psychoanalytic Association, 51*, 755–772.

Ramachandran, V. S. (1994). Phantom limbs, neglect syndromes, repressed memories, and Freudian psychology. *International Review of Neurobiology, 37*, 291–333.

Ramachandran, V. S. (1996). The evolutionary biology of self-deception, laughter, dreaming and depression: Some clues from anosognosia. *Medical Hypotheses, 47*, 347–362.

Rangell, L. (1988). The future of psychoanalysis: The scientific crossroads. *The Psychoanalytic Quarterly, 57*, 313–340.

Rangell, L. (1995). Affects. In B. E. Moore & B. D. Fine (Eds.), *Psycho-analysis: The major concepts* (pp. 381–391). New Haven: Yale University Press.

Rangell, L. (2000). Psychoanalysis at the millennium: A unitary theory. *Psychoanalytic Psychology, 17*, 451–466.

Rankin, K. P., Baldwin, E., Pace-Savitsky, C., Kramer, J. H., & Miller, B. L. (2004). Self-awareness and personality change in dementia. *Journal of Neurology, Neurosurgery & Psychiatry, 76*, 632–639.

Rapaport, D. (1951). Toward a theory of thinking. In D. Rapaport (Ed.), *Organization and pathology of thought: Selected sources* (pp. 689–730). New York: Columbia University Press.

Rapaport, D. & Gill, M. M. (1959). The points of views and assumptions of metapsychology. *International Journal of Psycho-analysis, 40*, 153–162.

Redgrave, P., Prescott, T. J. & Gurney, K. (1999). The basal ganglia: A vertebrate solution to the selection problem? *Neuroscience, 89*, 1000–1023.

Redgrave, P., Rodriguez, M., Smith, Y., Rodriguez-Oroz, M. C., Lehericy, S., Bergman, H., … & Obeso, J. A. (2010). Goal-directed and habitual control in the basal ganglia: Implications for Parkinson's disease. *Nature Reviews Neuroscience, 11*, 760–772.

154 References

Reinders, A. S., Willemsen, A. T., Vos, H. P., den Boer, J. A., & Nijenhuis, E. R. (2012). Fact or factitious? A psychobiological study of authentic and simulated dissociative identity states. *PloS ONE*, 7(6), e39279.

Ricoeur, P. (1977). The question of proof in Freud's psychoanalytic writings. *Journal of the American Psychoanalytic Association*, 25, 835–871.

Ritvo, S. & Solnit, A. J. (1995). Instinct theory. In B. E. Moore & B. D. Fine (Eds.), *Psychoanalysis: The major concepts* (pp. 327–333). New Haven: Yale University Press.

Rofé, Y. (2008). Does repression exist? Memory, pathogenic, unconscious and clinical evidence. *Review of General Psychology*, 12, 63–85.

Rosenblatt, A. D. (1985). The role of affect in cognitive psychology and psychoanalysis. *Psychoanalytic Psychology*, 2, 85–97.

Rosenblatt, A. D. & Thickstun, J. T. (1977). Energy, information, and motivation: A revision of psycho-analytic theory. *Journal of the American Psycho-analytic Association*, 25, 537–558.

Rychlak, J. E. (2000). Agency: An overview. In A. E. Kazdin (Ed.), *Encyclopedia of psychology* (pp. 102–104). Washington, DC: American Psychological Association.

Salmon, E., Perani, D., Herholz, K., Marique, P., Kalbe, E., Holthoff, V., Delbeuck, X., Beuthien-Baumann, B., Pelati, O., Lespagnarde, S., Collette, F., & Garraux, G. (2006). Neural correlates of anosognosia for cognitive impairment in Alzheimer's disease. *Human Brain Mapping*, 27, 588–597.

Sandler, J. (1985). Towards a reconsideration of the psycho-analytic theory of motivation. *Bulletin of the Anna Freud Centre*, 8, 223–244.

Sandler, J. (1990). On internal object relations. *Journal of the American Psychoanalytic Association*, 38, 859–880.

Sandler, J. & Joffe, W. G. (1969). Towards a basic psychoanalytic model. *International Journal of Psycho-analysis*, 50, 79–90.

Sandler, J. & Sandler, A.-M. (1983). The 'second censorship', the 'three box model' and some technical implications. *International Journal of Psycho-analysis*, 64, 413–425.

Sandler, J. & Sandler, A.-M. (1994). The past unconscious and the present unconscious: A contribution to a technical frame of reference. *Psychoanalytic Study of the Child*, 49, 278–292.

Sandler, J., Dreher, A. U., & Drews, S. (1991). An approach to conceptual research in psychoanalysis illustrated by a consideration of psychic trauma. *International Review of Psychoanalysis*, 18, 133–141.

Sappington, A. A. (1990). Recent psychological approaches to the free will versus determinism debate. *Psychological Bulletin*, 108, 19–29.

Sarkissian, H., Chatterjee, A., De Brigard, F., Knobe, J., Nichols, S., & Sirker, S. (2010). Is belief in free will a cultural universal? *Mind & Language*, 25, 346–358.

Sartre, J-.P. (1956). *Being and nothingness*. (Translated by H. E. Barnes). New York: Philosophical Library.

Schafer, R. (1990). The search for common ground. *International Journal of Psychoanalysis*, 71, 49–52.

Schlumpf, Y. R., Nijenhuis, E. R., Chalavi, S., Weder, E. V., Zimmermann, E., Luechinger, R., … & Jäncke, L. (2013). Dissociative part-dependent biopsychosocial reactions to backward masked angry and neutral faces: An fMRI study of dissociative identity disorder. *NeuroImage: Clinical*, 3, 54–64.

Schmidt-Hellerau, C. (2012). Drive and structure: Reconsidering drive theory within a formalized conception of mental processes. In A. Fotopoulou, D. Pfaff & M. Conway (Eds.),

References 155

From the couch to the lab: Trends in psychodynamic neuroscience (pp. 109–129). Oxford: Oxford University Press.

Schore, A. N. (2002). Dysregulation of the right brain: A fundamental mechanism of traumatic attachment and the psychopathogenesis of posttraumatic stress disorder. *Australian and New Zealand Journal of Psychiatry, 36*, 9–30.

Schore, A. N. (2009). Relational trauma and the developing right brain: An interface of psychoanalytic self psychology and neuroscience. *Self and Systems, 1159*, 189–203.

Schwartz, A. (1987). Drives, affects, behavior—and learning: Approaches to a psychobiology of emotion and to an integration of psychoanalytic and neurobiologic thought. *Journal of the American Psychoanalytic Association, 35*, 467–506.

Searle, J. R. (1992). *The rediscovery of the mind.* Cambridge: MIT Press.

Searle, J. R. (1995). Consciousness, explanatory inversion and cognitive science. In C. Macdonald and G. Macdonald (Eds.), *Philosophy of psychology: Debates on psychological explanation,* Vol. I (pp. 331–355). Oxford: Blackwell.

Searle, J. R. (2004). *Mind: A brief introduction.* Oxford: Oxford University Press.

Segal, H. (1993). On the clinical usefulness of the concept of death instinct. *International Journal of Psycho-Analysis, 74*, 55–61.

Sewards, T. V. & Sewards, M. A. (2002). The medial pain system: Neural representations of the motivational aspects of pain. *Brain Research Bulletin, 59*, 163–180.

Sewards, T. V. & Sewards, M. A. (2003). Representations of motivational drives in mesial cortex, medial thalamus, hypothalamus and midbrain. *Brain Research Bulletin, 61*, 25–40.

Shane, M. G. & Shane, M. (2001). The attachment motivational system as a guide to an effective therapeutic process. *Psychoanalytic Inquiry, 21*, 675–687.

Shaver, P. R. & Mikulincer, M. (2002). Attachment-related psychodynamics. *Attachment & Human Development, 4*, 133–161.

Shaver, P. R. & Mikulincer, M. (2005). Attachment theory and research: Resurrection of the psychodynamic approach to personality. *Journal of Research in Personality, 39*, 22–45.

Shill, M. A. (2004). Signal anxiety, defense, and the pleasure principle. *Psychoanalytic Psychology, 21*, 116–133.

Sjöbäck, H. (1973). *The psychoanalytic theory of defensive processes: A critical survey.* Lund: CWK Gleer Up.

Skinner, B. F. (1953). *Science and behaviour.* New York: The Free Press.

Slap, J. W. & Saykin, A. J. (1984). On the nature and the organisation of the repressed. *Psychoanalytic Inquiry, 4*, 107–124.

Slap, J. W. & Slap-Shelton, L. (1994). The schema model: A proposed replacement paradigm for psychoanalysis. *Psychoanalytic Review, 81*, 677–693.

Slavin, M. O. (1985). The origins of psychic conflict and the adaptive function of repression: An evolutionary biological view. *Psychoanalysis and Contemporary Thought, 8*, 407–440.

Slavin, M. O. (1990). The dual meaning of repression and the adaptive design of the human psyche. *Journal of the American Academy of Psychoanalysis, 18*, 307–341.

Slavin, M. O. & Grief, D. (1995). The evolved function of repression and the adaptive design of the human psyche. In H. R. Conte & R. Plutchik (Eds.), *Ego defenses: Theory and measurement* (pp. 139–175). New York: John Wiley & Sons.

Solms, M. (2003). Do unconscious phantasies really exist? In R. Steiner (Ed.), *Unconscious phantasy* (pp. 89–105). London: Karnac.

Solms, M. (2013). The conscious id. *Neuropsychoanalysis, 15*, 5–19.

Solms, M. (2014). A neuropsychoanalytical approach to the hard problem of consciousness. *Journal of Integrative Neuroscience, 13*, 173–185.

156 References

Solms, M. (2015). Reply to Barratt. *Psychoanalytic Review, 102,* 209–219.

Solms, M. & Panksepp, J. (2012). The 'id' knows more than the 'ego' admits: Neuropsycho-analytic and primal consciousness perspectives on the interface between affective and cognitive neuroscience. *Brain Science, 2,* 147–175.

Solms, M. & Turnbull, O. (2002). *The brain and the inner world: An introduction to the neuroscience of subjective experience.* New York: Other Press.

Solms, M. & Turnbull, O. H. (2011). What is neuropsychoanalysis? *Neuropsychoanalysis, 13,* 133–145.

Solms, M. & Zellner, M. R. (2012a). Freudian drive theory today. In A. Fotopoulou, D. Pfaff & M. Conway (Eds.), *From the couch to the lab: Trends in psychodynamic neuroscience* (pp. 49–63). Oxford: Oxford University Press.

Solms, M. & Zellner, M. R. (2012b). Freudian affect theory today. In A. Fotopoulou, D. Pfaff & M. Conway (Eds.), *From the couch to the lab: Trends in psychodynamic neuroscience* (pp. 133–144). Oxford: Oxford University Press.

Sperry, R. W. (1969). Hemisphere deconnection and unity in conscious awareness. *American Psychologist, 23,* 723–733.

Sperry, R. W. (1982). Some effects of disconnecting the cerebral hemispheres. *Science, 217,* 1223–1226.

Spruiell, V. (1988). The indivisibility of Freudian object relations and drive theories. *Psycho-analytic Quarterly, 57,* 597–625.

Stephenson-Jones, M., Samuelsson, E., Ericsson, J., Robertson, B., & Grillner, S. (2011), Evolutionary conservation of the basal ganglia as a common vertebrate mechanism for action selection. *Current Biology, 21,* 1081–1091.

Sternberg, R. J. & Grigorenko, E. L. (2001). Unified psychology. *American Psychologist, 56,* 1069–1079.

Stolar, D. & Fromm, E. (1974). Activity and passivity of the ego in relation to the superego. *International Review of Psychoanalysis, 1,* 297–311.

Stolorow, R. D. & Atwood, G. E. (2013). The tragic and the metaphysical in philosophy and psychoanalysis. *The Psychoanalytic Review, 100,* 405–421.

Symington, N. (1993). *Narcissism: A new theory.* London: Karnac.

Talvitie, V. (2009). *Freudian unconscious and cognitive neuroscience: From unconscious fantasies to neural algorithms.* London: Karnac.

Talvitie, V. (2012). *The foundations of psychoanalytic theories: Project for a scientific enough psychoa-nalysis.* London: Karnac.

Talvitie, V. (2015). Beyond the philosophy of the (unconscious) mind: The Freudian cornerstone as scientific theory, a cult, and a way of talking. In S. Boag, L. A. W. Brakel, & V. Talvitie (Eds.), *Psychoanalysis and philosophy of mind: Unconscious mentality in the twenty-first century* (163–192). London: Karnac.

Talvitie, V. & Ihanus, J. (2002). The repressed and implicit knowledge. *International Journal of Psychoanalysis, 83,* 1311–1323.

Talvitie, V. & Ihanus, J. (2003a). On the nature of repressed contents—A working-through of John Searle's critique. *Neuro-psychoanalysis, 5,* 133–142.

Talvitie, V. & Ihanus, J. (2003b). Response to commentaries. *Neuro-psychoanalysis, 5,* 153–158.

Talvitie, V. & Ihanus, J. (2005). Biting the bullet: The nature of unconscious fantasy. *Theory & Psychology, 15,* 659–678.

Talvitie, V. & Ihanus, J. (2006). The psychic apparatus, metapsychology, and neuroscience: Toward biological (neuro)psychoanalysis. *Neuro-psychoanalysis, 8,* 85–98.

Talvitie, V. & Ihanus, J. (2010). On the relation between neural and psychological mechanisms: Neuropsychoanalysis and the 'new mechanists'. *The Scandinavian Psychoanalytic Review*, *33*, 130–141.

Talvitie, V. & Ihanus, J. (2011). On neuropsychoanalytic metaphysics. *International Journal of Psychoanalysis*, *92*, 1583–1601.

Talvitie, V. & Tiitinen, H. (2006). From the repression of contents to the rules of the (narrative) self: A present-day cognitive view of the 'Freudian phenomenon' of repressed contents. *Psychology and Psychotherapy: Theory, Research and Practice*, *79*, 165–181.

Tauber, A. I. (2010). *Freud, the reluctant philosopher.* Princeton, NJ: Princeton University Press.

Thalberg, I. (1977). *Perception, emotion and action.* Oxford: Basil Blackwell.

Thalberg, I. (1982). Freud's anatomies of the self. In R. Wollheim & J. Hopkins (Eds.), *Philosophical essays on Freud* (pp. 241–263). Cambridge: Cambridge University Press.

Thompson, N. S. (1987). The misappropriation of teleonomy. In P. P. G. Bateson & P. H. Klopfer (Eds.), *Perspectives in ethology* (pp. 259–274). New York: Plenum.

Tonneau, F. (2004). Consciousness outside the head. *Behavior and Philosophy*, *32*, 97–123.

Turnbull, O. H. & Solms, M. (2007). Awareness, desire, and false beliefs: Freud in the light of modern neuropsychology. *Cortex*, *43*, 1083–1090.

Turnbull, O. H., Fotopoulou, A., & Solms, M. (2014). Anosognosia as motivated unawareness: The 'defence' hypothesis revisited. *Cortex*, *61*, 18–29.

Turnbull, O. H., Jones, K., & Reed-Screen, J. (2002). Implicit awareness of deficit in anosognosia? An emotion-based account of denial of deficit. *Neuropsychoanalysis*, *4*, 69–87.

Uleman, J. S. (2005). Introduction: Becoming aware of the new unconscious. In R. R. Hassin, J. S. Uleman, & J. A. Bargh (Eds.), *The new unconscious* (pp. 3–15). Oxford: Oxford University Press.

Vallar, G. & Ronchi, R. (2006). Anosognosia for motor and sensory deficits after unilateral brain damage: A review. *Restorative Neurology & Neuroscience*, *24*, 247–257.

van Inwagen, P. & Zimmerman, D. W. (2008). Introduction: What is metaphysics? In P. van Inwagen & D. W. Zimmerman, *Metaphysics: The big questions* (pp. 1–14). Malden, MA: Blackwell.

Waelder, R. (1960). *Basic theory of psychoanalysis.* New York: International Universities Press.

Wallerstein, R. S. (1977). Psychic energy reconsidered: Introduction. *Journal of the American Psycho-analytic Association*, *25*, 529–535.

Wallerstein, R. S. (2002). The trajectory of psychoanalysis: A prognostication. *International Journal of Psychoanalysis*, *83*, 1247–1267.

Wallerstein, R. S. (2005a). Will psychoanalytic pluralism be an enduring state of our discipline? *International Journal of Psychoanalysis*, *86*, 623–626.

Wallerstein, R. S. (2005b). Dialogue or illusion? How do we go from here? Response to André Green. *International Journal of Psychoanalysis*, *86*, 633–638.

Wallerstein, R. S. (2006). The relevance of Freud's psychoanalysis in the 21st century: Its science and its research. *International Journal of Psychoanalysis*, *90*, 109–133.

Wallerstein, R. S. (2009). What kind of research in psychoanalytic science? *International Journal of Psychoanalysis, 90*, 109–133.

Watt, D. F. (2008). Commentary on 'Is There a Drive to Love?' *Neuropsychoanalysis*, *10*, 173–178.

Watt, D. F. (2012). Theoretical challenges in the conceptualization of motivation in neuroscience: Implications for the bridging of neuroscience and psychoanalysis. In A. Fotopoulou, D. Pfaff & M. Conway (Eds.), *From the couch to the lab: Trends in psychodynamic neuroscience* (pp. 85–108). Oxford: Oxford University Press.

158 References

Wegner, D. M. (2005). Who is the controller of controlled processes? In R. R. Hassin, J. S. Uleman, & J. A. Bargh (Eds.), *The new unconscious* (pp. 19–36). Oxford: Oxford University Press.

Wegner, D. M. & Wheatley, T. (1999). Apparent mental causation: Sources of the experience of will. *American Psychologist, 54*, 480–492.

Weinberger, J. & Westen, D. (2001). Science and psychodynamics: From arguments about Freud to data. *Psychological Inquiry, 12*, 129–166.

Weiskrantz, L. (1986). *Blindsight: A case study and implications.* Oxford: Oxford University Press.

Weiskrantz, L., Warrington, E. K., Sanders, M. D., & Marshall, J. (1974). Visual capacity in the hemianopic field following a restricted occipital ablation. *Brain, 97*, 709–728.

Westen, D. (1997). Towards a clinically and empirically sound theory of motivation. *International Journal of Psycho-analysis, 78*, 521–548.

Westen, D. (1999). The scientific status of unconscious processes: Is Freud really dead? *Journal of the American Psychoanalytic Association, 47*, 1061–1105.

Westen, D. & Gabbard, G. O. (2002). Developments in cognitive neuroscience: I. Conflict, compromise, and connectionism. *Journal of the American Psychoanalytic Association, 50*, 53–98.

White, P. A. (1990). Ideas about causation in philosophy and psychology. *Psychological Bulletin, 108*, 3–18.

White, R. W. (1963). Ego and reality in psychoanalytic theory. In *Psychological Issues*, Vol. 3, Monograph 11. New York: International Universities Press.

Wiedeman, G. H. (1972). Comments on the structural theory of personality. *International Journal of Psycho-analysis, 53*, 307–313.

Willick, M. S. (1995). Defence. In B. E. Moore & B. D. Fine (Eds.), *Psycho-analysis: The major concepts* (pp. 485–493). New Haven: Yale University Press.

Wise, R. A. (2004). Drive, incentive, and reinforcement: The antecedents and consequences of motivation. In R. Dienstbier, R. A. Bevins & M. T. Bardo (Eds.), *Motivational factors in the etiology of drug abuse: Volume 50 of the Nebraska Symposium on Motivation* (pp. 159–195). Lincoln, NE: University of Nebraska Press.

Wollheim, R. (1991). *Freud.* London: Fontana Press.

Wright, J. S. & Panksepp, J. (2012). An evolutionary framework to understand foraging, wanting, and desire: The neuropsychology of the SEEKING system. *Neuropsychoanalysis, 14*, 5–39.

Yankelovich, D. (1973). The idea of human nature. *Social Research, 40*, 407–428.

Yovell, Y. (2008a). Is there a drive to love? *Neuropsychoanalysis, 10*, 117–144.

Yovell, Y. (2008b). Response to commentaries. *Neuropsychoanalysis, 10*, 183–188.

Yovell, Y., Solms, M., & Fotopoulou, A. (2015). The case for neuropsychoanalysis: Why a dialogue with neuroscience is necessary but not sufficient for psychoanalysis. *The International Journal of Psychoanalysis.* PAGES.

Zepf, S. (2001). Incentives for a reconsideration of the debate on metapsychology. *International Journal of Psychoanalysis, 82*, 463–482.

Zepf, S. (2010). Libido and psychic energy—Freud's concepts reconsidered. *International Forum of Psychoanalysis, 19*, 3–14.

Zepf, S. (2011). The relations between language, consciousness, the preconscious, and the unconscious: Freud's approach conceptually updated. *The Scandinavian Psychoanalytic Review, 34*, 50–61.

Zepf, S. (2012). Repression and substitutive formation: The relationship between Freud's concepts reconsidered. *Psychoanalytic Review, 99*, 397–420.

INDEX

aboutness of mental acts 88, 90
activation-deactivation mechanism of behaviour 48–49
affects: and cognition and motivation responses to drives 57–59; defining 59–63; and drives 60–61; unconscious 96–97
agency, human 107–8; and determinism 31–33
aggression: and conflict 84; as a primary drive 55; reactive 55; and sexuality 66
alexithymia 97
Alzheimer's dementia 99
Anderson, John 21
anosognosia 99, 100
anticathexis and repression 78–81
anticipation 58–59
a-rational mentality 103
Aristotle 33–34
Arlow, J. A. 9
attachment theory 4, 7–8, 46–49; and the ego 118; and object relations 124, 130; and repression 76–78
Auld, F. 66

Barratt, B. B. 26, 46
basal ganglia 83
Bazan, A. 69
behaviour: desires explaining 43–44; explaining 41–43; instinct theory of 53–54
beliefs 41–43
Bell, P. 22

Bennett, M. R. 13
Beres, D. 23, 24–25, 108, 109
Berridge, K. C. 63
Besetzung 89
Bibring, E. 53
Biven, L. 27, 57, 60
Blass, R. B. 11
blindness to evidence 73
blindsight 99
blocked excitation 39
Blum, H. P. 13, 66
body: in relation to psychological activities and the brain 29–30; in relation to the mind 18, 26–29
body-as-object 113
body-as-subject 113, 115
body-ego 120
Bohleber, W. 2, 3, 104
Bonanno, G. A. 74
Bowers, K. S. 99
Bowlby, J. 7, 10, 13, 34, 44, 46–49, 52, 61–62, 63, 76–78, 118, 124, 125, 130
brain: and metapsychology 10–12; minimizing free energy 40, 42; processes causing repression 81–84; and psychological activities 29–30; in relation to mind 26–29; states of 91; and unconscious awareness 99–100
BrainMind 27
Brakel, L. A. 26, 203
Brenner, C. 4, 5, 29, 80, 109
Brentano, F. 60, 88–94
Brentano's thesis of Intentionality 88–94

160 Index

Campbell, C. 2, 3, 7, 66
Carhart-Harris, R. L. 40, 103, 111
Carmeli, Z. 11
Cartesian rational faculty 111–12
cathexis of the id 110
causal antecedents 34–36
causal field 31
causality 30–31
censoring agency and repression 71–72,
  74–76, 78
Cheshire, N. 25
circularity 24, 25–26
clinical theory and metapsychology 10, 18
cognition: and behaviour 48; embodied and
  motivation 114–15; and motivation and
  affect 58–59; as a relation 89–90
cognitive-perceptual account of motivation
  42–43
'coming to know' activities 28–29
commitment to determinism 21
common-sense model of behaviour 41–42
conation 41
conceptual analysis 22–26
conceptual research 12–14
confirmation bias 73–74
conflict 69; and aggression 84; with the
  ego and drives 115–16; and motivation
  63, 69–70; protagonists of 69–70; and
  repression and the id 117–20
conscious id 112–14, 131
conscious mentality 88
consciousness: nature of 88–90; primary
  95; secondary reflective 95; unconscious
  90–94
consummatory actions 52
counter-cathexes 78
cupboard-love theory of object relations 124

death drive 55
defence: in attachment theory 76–78; and
  repression 65–85
defensive exclusion 76–77
Descartes, R. 92
desires 41–43; nature of 43–44
determinism 137; and agency 31–33; and
  teleology 33–36
deterministic psychology 51–52
dispositional unconscious 91
dissociative identity disorder (DID) 133–4
Dreher, A. U. 10, 12
drive: concept of 44–46; relation with
  object 60
drive-discharge theory 7, 38, 46, 47,
  50–51, 136

drives 136–7; and affects 60–61; aggression as
  55; being controlled by cognitive processes
  110–11; as biological engines 51–53;
  composing of the ego 115–17; conflicting
  drives as protagonists of repression 69–70;
  death 55; from economic viewpoint
  38–40; as forces 46; homeostatic 51, 56;
  of the id 110; identifying 53–54; and
  motivation 129; and multiple personality
  131–2; and object relations 122–4, 129–30;
  as psychobiological systems 114; and
  repression 65, 68, 70–71, 82; secondary and
  tertiary 55–56; separate from the ego 110
drive sources 49–50
drive theory and neuropsychoanalysis
  55–58
dual-agent monism 27–29
dual-aspect monism 95
dynamic structures in Fairbairn's theory
  125–6
dynamic unconscious 97–99

Eagle, M. 98
economic viewpoint of nervous energies
  38–40
ego: and attachment theory 118; autonomy
  of 110–11; Central 127; constituted by
  drives 115–17; as a dynamic structure
  126; and Freud's structural theory of id,
  ego and superego 107–9; and identity
  120–1; known 120; motivation of 112,
  114–15; and multiple personality 131–3;
  multiplicity of ego structures 127–9;
  unconsciousness of 113
ego-drives 115–17
ego-structures and multiple personality 132
embodied cognition and motivation
  114–15
emotional systems 56
empiricism 21
energy being discharged by drives 38–39
Erdelyi, M. H. 77
executive agent role of the ego 110
external body 120, 131–2

failure of awareness caused by
  repression 67
Fairbairn, W. R. D. 122, 124–32
fallacy of circular explanation 25–26
fallacy of constitutive relations 24–25
fallacy of misplaced concreteness 24
feedback 52, 63; of affects 61; and
  behaviour 48
fixed action patterns 48

Index

Fliess, Wilhelm 5
flight from pain 68
Fonagy, P. 1, 2, 3, 7, 13, 66, 87, 124
Fotopoulou, A. 42
foundational drives. *See* drives
Frank, A. 3
free energy being minimized 40, 42
free-energy principle 103
free will 32–33
Freud, Sigmund 3, 135–8; and anosognosia 100; avoiding unpleasure 35; becoming conscious of mental acts 94–95; body-ego 120; concept of anticathexes 78–81; death drive 55; defining affects 59–60; and determinism 31; drive-discharge-force account 50–51; drive-discharge model 44–4; ego-drives account 115–17; and multiple personality 132–3; nature of conflicting forces 69–70; and neuroscience 2, 11; and object relations 122–4; *Pcs.* processes 71, 101–2, 104; pleasure principle 116; psychoanalytic theory 17; realist philosophy 21; reality principle 116; repression and the id 117–20; role of human agency 107–8; specific view of metapsychology 6–8; structural theory of id, ego and superego 107–12; theory of personality 38–40; theory of repression 65–66; theory of the unconscious 87–88; topographic theory 109; *Ucs.* processes 101; unconscious affects 96; unpleasant principle 68, 73; use of *Besetzung* term 89; use of metaphors 25–26; use of metapsychology term 5–6
Friston, K. J. 40, 42, 103, 111
frontier-force concept of drive 50–51
frustration and unpleasure 61–62
Fulgencio, L. 9, 17, 18, 46, 51

Gardner, S. 74
Gay, P. 8
Gill, M. M. 6, 9, 17
gratification and pleasure 61–62
Greenberg, J. R. 125
Grossman, W. I. 26

Hacker, P. M. S. 13
Hatzimoysis, A. 97
Henry, R. M. 67
Hibberd, F. J. 21, 25
Holt, R. R. 8, 10, 18, 19, 22, 44, 46, 53
homeostatic drives 51, 56
Hopkins, J. 51, 82, 117

horse-and-rider analogy for id and ego 109–12, 125–6
human agency, role of 107–8
Hyman, M. 66
hysterical amnesia 69

id: conscious 112–14; as a dynamic structure 126; and Freud's structural theory of id, ego and superego 107–9; and multiple personality 131–3; and repression and conflict 117–20
identity and the ego 120–1
ignoring, motivated 100
Ihanus, J. 11, 12, 14, 18, 20–21, 26, 27, 35, 67
Immergluck, L. 32
indeterminism 31–32
instinctive behaviour 47–48
instincts 51, 117, 126; conflicting 70
instinct theory for behaviour 53–54
Intentionality, Brentano's thesis of 88–94
internal body 113, 120, 131–2
internalised authority 124
internal objects and ego-structures 127–9
irrationality 101–2

James, William 33

Kant, Immanuelle 17
Kaplan-Solms, K. 100
Karlsson, G. 28
Kernberg, O. 55
Keuler, D. J. 74
Klein, Melanie 122, 136
Kluft, R. P. 134
knowing and knowing that one knows 92–95; and neuroclinical phenomena 99–100
known ego 120
Korsakoff's syndrome 99

Laplanche, J. 5, 8, 116
libidinal drives 70, 116–20
life and death drive 46
Loftus, E. F. 98
logic of relations 22–26

Machado, A. 12
Mackay, N. 10, 34, 44, 51, 61, 137
Mackie, J. L. 22
Macmillan, M. 6, 10, 23, 35, 67, 80, 81, 82, 85
Macmurray, J. 24
Madison, P. 69
main system of the mind 75–76
Martin, J. 32

162 Index

Maslow, A. H. 53
Maze 57
Maze, J. R. 14, 22, 29, 34, 41, 44, 51–52, 67, 110, 112, 114–15, 118, 130, 131
McDougall, W. 53
McIntosh, D. 40
McMullen, T. 31
meaningfulness 61
Mele, A. 73
mental acts: becoming conscious of 94–96; primary and secondary processes 101–3; in relation to object of mental act 88–92
mental economics 6, 7
mental energy 38–40
mentality, systemic account of 101–4
metaphors, use of 25–26
metaphysics 8; evaluating standpoints 20–21; of metapsychology 17–36; of neuropsychoanalysis 26–29; of psychoanalysis 36; realist 21–22
metapsychology: and the brain 10–12; and clinical theory 18; as defined by Freud 5–6; division between psychoanalysis 8–9; as foundation for psychoanalysis 4–5, 14–15; Freud's specific view of 6–8; metaphysics of 17–36; of multiple personality 130–4; of object relations 122–38; and philosophy 8–10; pluralism in 135–6; of the self 107–21
Michell, J. 22
mind: as the brain's activities 29; conflict with conscious id 117; lower and higher cognitive processes 111; main and protective systems 75–76; in relation to the body 18, 26–29
MindBrain 27
Mink, J. W. 82
Mitchell, S. A. 125
motivated ignoring 100; and repression 68–69
motivation 41–3; and cognition and affect 58–59; cognitive-perceptual accounts of 42–43; common-sense model 41–42; and drives 129; of the ego 112, 114–15; and embodied cognition 114–15; and object relations 124; sources of 109–10
motivational conflict 69–70
multiple personality 130–4

neural processes causing repression 81–84
neuropsychoanalysis 11–12; and attachment theory 61–63; and drive theory 55–58; metaphysics of 26–29; and motivational sources 83, 111

neuroscience: and metapsychology 11; and psychoanalysis 2, 11–12, 26
new unconscious 87
Nirvana principle 39
Novick, J. 4
Novick, K. K. 4

object relational approaches 4, 7
object relations 122–38; and drives 129–30; and Fairbairn's theory 125–6; Freudian theory of 122–4
objects: dynamic internal 126–9; in relation with drive 60
Occam's razor 20–21
Oedipus complex 123–4
Ogden, T. H. 124, 126–9, 131
orienting stimuli 48–49

pacification 51
Panksepp, J. 12, 13, 27, 56, 57, 60, 62, 83, 99, 111, 113
Panksepp's taxonomy of basic emotions 56
particularity 18
Pataki, Tamas 30, 45, 129
Pcs. processes 71, 101–2, 104
Pears, David 75–76, 78
person, development of 107
personality: biological foundations of 38–64; development of 107; Freud's theory 38–40; identifying with dynamic internal objects 126–9; metapsychology of multiple personality 130–4; structural theory of 108–9
personation 129
Petocz, A. 89, 104, 115
phantasying 9, 103, 106, 127–9
philosophy and metapsychology 8–10
pleasure and gratification 61–62
pleasure principle 35, 109, 116
Pontalis, J.-B. 5, 8, 116
primary consciousness 95
primary/secondary processes in mental acts 101–5
principal system and repression 77–78
Project (Freud) 11
protective system of the mind 75–76
proximity seeking behaviour 54
psychical energy 39–40
psychoanalysis: conceptual and theoretical research 12–14; fragmentation of 1–2; metaphysics of 36; metapsychology and its foundations 4–5, 14–15; and neuroscience 2, 11–12, 26; pluralism

of 1–3, 7, 13, 19; theoretical foundation 3–4; unity in 2–4
psychoanalytic metapsychology 6
psychoanalytic theory, foundations of 17
psychobiological systems and drives 50–51
psychological processes in relation to the brain and body 28–30
psychology of the unconscious 5
psychoneuroses and repression 65

Rangell, L. 1, 2, 3, 136
Rapaport, D. 6, 9, 17
reaction-formation 80
reactive aggression 55
realism 21
realist metaphysics 21–22
reality, unknowable 18
reality principle 102, 109, 116
Redgrave, P. 85
reflexive awareness 95
reification 24
relationship and innate need for 7
relations to one another 21–22
repressed wishes 65
repression 97; and anticathexis 78–81; in attachment theory 76–78; causing failure of awareness 67; and censorship 71–72; and conflict and the id 117–20; conflicting theories of 66–67; and the ego 116; Freud's theory 65–66; and motivated ignoring 68–69; neural mechanism underlying 81–84; protagonists of 69–70; and resistance 98–99; and self-deception 72–76
Rudzinski, D. 66

satiation 51
Searle, J. R. 87, 90–91, 93
secondary drive theory 124
secondary reflective consciousness 95
SEEKING emotional system 56–57, 83
selection problem 83
selective exclusion 76
selective inattention 74
self: as agent 24; metapsychology of 107–21; sense of 121
self-deception: and Pears' theory 75–76; and repression 72–76
self-preservative drives 70, 116, 118, 120
sense of self 121
sexuality and aggression 66
Silva, F. J. 12
Simon, B. 26

simple awareness 95
Snodgrass, M. 69
soft determinism 32
Solms, M. 12, 18, 26, 28, 40, 45, 46, 55, 56, 57, 59, 60, 62, 67, 90, 95, 99, 100, 111, 113, 115, 117
split-brain procedures 99
Spruiell, V. 122
Staines, P. 22
substitute investment of anticathexis 79–81
Sugarman, J. 32
superego 123–4; and Freud's structural theory of id, ego and superego 107–9; and multiple personality 131–3; theory 71, 75
Symington, N. 59, 131
syndromes of unawareness 99

Talvitie, V. 11, 12, 14, 18, 20–21, 26, 27, 35, 67, 91, 98
Target, M. 1, 13, 87
teleology and determinism 33–36
telos 33–35
tension of object-seeking tendencies 125, 129–30
terminating stimuli 48–49
theoretical research 12–14
theory dualism with facts 18
thesis of Intentionality 88–94
Thomä, H. 25
Thompson, J. 32
topographics 6
topographic theory of Sigmund Freud 109
transcendental agency 75
Triebe 38
Turnbull, O. 12, 20, 27, 28, 45, 100
turning away 68

Ucs. processes 71, 101–2, 104
unconscious 18, 87–105; dynamic 97–99
unconscious affects 96–97
unconscious awareness 99–100
unconscious beliefs 91
unconscious consciousness 90–94
unconscious mentality 88, 90–94, 101–2
unconscious threat evaluation 72, 77, 81
universality 18
unknowable reality 18
unpleasant principle of Freud's 68, 73
unpleasure and frustration 61–62
unpleasure-pleasure principle 35

Vorstellungen 89

164 Index

Waelder, R. 11, 35
Wallerstein, R. S. 2, 3
Watt, D. F. 54, 56, 58, 83, 114
Weltbild 10
Westen, D. 51
White, R. W. 112
Winnicot, Donald 122
Wise, R. A. 35
wishes 44; being repressed 72
wish-fulfilment 51

wishful thinking 73
Wollheim, R. 41
Wright, J. S. 13, 83, 111

Yovell, Y. 46, 54

Zellner, M. R. 40, 46, 55, 57, 59, 60, 62, 111
Zepf, S. 4, 9, 29, 35, 60, 62, 66, 68, 69, 80–81